DISEASES OF MEDICINAL PLANT

DISEASES OF MEDICINAL PLANT

By

Dr. Sumia Fatima

M.Sc., Ph.D, F.S.Sc., F.S.L.Sc.
Professor and Head
Dept. of Botany
Dr. Rafiq Zakaria College for Women
Jublee Park, Aurangabad - 431 001
Maharashtra (India)

&

Dr. Milind Jadhav

M.Sc., Ph.D.
Associate Professor and Head
Dept. of Botany
Sir Sayyed College of Arts, Science and Commerce
Aurangabad - 431 001
Maharashtra (India)

DPH

DISCOVERY PUBLISHING HOUSE PVT. LTD.
NEW DELHI-110 002

Published by:

Namit Wasan

DISCOVERY PUBLISHING HOUSE PVT. LTD.

4383/4B, Ansari Road, Darya Ganj
New Delhi-110 002 (India)
Phone : +91-11-23279245, 43596064-65
Fax : +91-11-23253475
E-mail : discoverypublishinghouse@gmail.com
namitwasan9@gmail.com
sales@discoverypublishinggroup.com
web : www.discoverypublishinggroup.com

First Edition: **2016**

ISBN: 978-93-5056-807-1

Diseases of Medicinal Plant

Printed at:
Infinity Imaging Systems
Delhi

Foreword

Today we have a great command on commercial success in the control of various human diseases by the use of medicinal plant products. Such an intensely interesting success is attributed primarily due to the effective drugs that occur in plants that act against human diseases .Extensive research on the use of medicinal plants against different types of human diseases is going on in different parts of the world. Awareness about medicinal plants among population has been increased due to no side effect of plant medicine on the environment and consumer. It seems quite safe non- hazardous, easily available and apparently cheap.

I am very happy to "Foreword" this book because no more emphasis has been given on the health of medicinal plants. Hence this book will be an interesting data for the researchers, students and plant pathologist because no more data is available about diseases of medicinal plants of India.

Dr. Gangawane L.V.
Prof. Emeritus
Soil-microbiologist and Plant Pathologist
Dr. Babasaheb Ambedkar Marathwada University
Aurangabad (MH) (India)

Preface

In the recent years awareness among people about use of medicinal plants has been increased. Recently farming of medicinal plants has also been started at various plants in India but there is no more information is available on diseases of medicinal plants in the form of book. Researchers in India and abroad worked on various diseases of medicinal plants, but the publications have restricted only up to the research journals. Hence, to produce a book of such an interesting matter of diseases of medicinal plants. The data about use of medicinal plants is available from all parts of the world. But scanty information is available about the health of medicinal plants. So to elaborate and spread the knowledge of such neglected but interesting information of diseases of medicinal plants the book is constructed. Various viral bacterial and fungal diseases of plants because greater loss of health of medicinal plants takes place due to fungal pathogens. Hence only the diseases of medicinal plants caused by fungi have been noted. Still today there is no information is available about the management of diseases of medicinal plants.

This is a book not only for the Botanists, but also useful for the Agriculturist, Pharmacologist, Researchers and students of Plant pathology. The pathology of medicinal plants has not yet been studied more. This book will definitely create awareness about the study and management of diseases of medicinal plants.

Sumia Fatima

Milind Jadhav

Acknowledgement

The authors are grateful to Professor Emeritus Dr. L.V. Gangawne, Plant pathologist and soil microbiologist, Dr. Babasaheb Ambedkar Marathwada University, and Aurangabad. (M.S.) India for everlasting encouragement and identification of fungal pathogens of medicinal plants. I would particularly like to thanks late Dr. V.N. Nike for preparing such an interesting flora of this region entitled "Flora of Marathwada" which has helped me to study all basic characteristics of each and every medicinal plant included in the text. I am also grateful to Prof. D.S.Mukadam, former H.O.D. of Botany, Dr. Babasaheb Ambedkar Marathwada University, and Aurangabad, (M.S.) India for help, encouragement and support for successful completion of the book.

I would specially like to thank Dr. Mohd. Umar Principal of Aurangabad College for Women, Aurangabad for his help and support all the time and providing facilities of Research laboratory and different types of scientific journals of plant pathology in the Department of this institute.

It is difficult to find words to thank Prof. L.V. Gangawane a world known pathologist and soil microbiologist of India and ex- Professor of Dr. Babasaheb Ambedkar Marathwada University, Aurangabad (M.S.) India, for writing the "Foreword" of the book by sparing his valuable time. Last but not the list, I would like to thank Dr. Zafar Javeed, who encouraged and helped me by spending their valuable time to put up to my idiosyncrasies during the preparation of the book.

Sumia Fatima

Milind Jadhav

Contents

CHAPTER 1

Introduction

Plant medicine offers an attractive option. We have few commercial successes to point to in the use of plant medicine for the control of human disease. In comparison to plant medicines many of the allopathic medicines are expensive which cannot be bearable by poorer. Now a day, awareness about plant medicine has been increased. It has been surprising that several of the diseases of human beings can be effectively controlled by the use of plant medicine. Indeed, use of plant medicine does appear to be more effective in the control of anemia, leprosy, dropsy, rheumatism, tooth disease and skin diseases etc. Recently there has been an explosion of research in the world; a number of plant medicines have been patented for various diseases of man and animals and some are approaching commercialization. There is need of huge research on medicinal plants of India. Substantial control may be obtainable through the management of naturally occurring plant medicines.

Today we have a great commercial success to point to in the control of human diseases by the use of medicinal plants. Plants contain different types of alkaloids which show great promises in the control of various diseases caused due to viral, bacterial, biochemical &physiological disorders of human health. Such a great success is attributable primarily due to effective inpatients in the plants against disease. Such a positive experiences have encouraged research from exploring use of medicinal plants as an alternative to allopathic medicines. The unlimited range of effectiveness of medicinal plants against human diseases, encouraged the researchers to find out new plant medicines against the carcinogenic diseases like aids, cancer, TB, anemia skin diseases and so on.

A variety of medicines have been prepared from different types of plants and today many of the plant medicines are available in the market.

The use of medicinal plants has become popular in the world market only because of its no side effects. Indian soil and climate is highly favorable for richest flora of medicinal plants. In Marathwada region 260 medicinal plants have been observed which are listed in the table of medicinal plants and their use."

The use of medicinal plants offers one of the most effective means of controlling the disease without any adverse effect on the environment and the consumer. The only advantage which seems quite safe, non hazardous, easy availability and apparently cheap. An ideal plant medicine would be one which is as effective as allopathic means of control and that too at low concentration, genetically stubble, economical and safe or in other words lacks toxicity to consumers.

Any plant medicine may undergo commercialization if it possesses most of the attributes and producers and consumers are satisfied that plant medicines is likely to replace the potent allopathic medicines used in disease control. Further the metabolic principle produced by the plant medicine should be toxic to the casual agent of human diseases and it should not be hazardous to consumer in any way. Finally, a sufficient potential market for plant medicine is needed to justify is development. Researchers can address this by selecting medicinal plants against particular diseases and by selecting medicinal plants which have a wide range of activity on a variety of human diseases.

In the villages and tribal areas of India; still the tribal are dependent on plant medicines. Tribes are using hundreds of plants as medicine since generation to generation but still most of the plants have not been studied scientifically for their use.

Naik, (1987) observed a variety of medicinal plants in Marathwada region of India. We use allopathic medicines which cure disease within a short period, but know little about what happens due to its residual effect on body.

Once the plant medicine is identified as effective means must be found for integrating its application into present disease control procedures. Formulations have to be developed which can be stored and applied. Even if, plant medicines are proven effective and safe as alternatives to Allelopathic medicines; they still must gain public acceptance. Will the patient accept the application of plant medicine for cure of disease? A large number of plants have been reported in Aayurvedic literature dating back to 250 BC to possess medicinal properties. Greeks and Romans used the Juices of Walnut shells against infection by fungal disease of skin. Scartezzini and Speroni, (2000) presented "Review on some Plants of Indian Traditional Medicine with Antioxidant Activity". Ven Murthy, (2010) worked on "Scientific Basis for the use of Indian Aayurvedic Medicinal Plants in the Treatment of Neurodegenerative Disorders: Ashwagandha". Cooley, *et. al*, (2009) reported "Naturopathic Care for Anxiety is possible by the use of plants.

If developed and represented plant medicines on scientific base, it would seem that plant medicines will be accepted as alternative to Allopathic medicines for control of all types of disease of human beings and animals. The plants medicines are eco-friendly .These medicines pose no threat to man or the environment. The medicinal plant can be selected which have a high assurance that they will not post a threat to man or animals. Even with such assurance, it will still be necessary to develop toxicology data before these plants can be registered for use (Mukherjee, 2003).

In general, most researchers hope that their research will find application in practice or product. However, at the inception of research programmers this is generally not a primary consideration. According to Gupta, *et.al*, (2011) pants acting on colon cancer".

Once the medicinal plants show promise, it is important that is to be properly identified. If the identified plants has closely related species, which show up in literature concerns over its safety will probably prohibit its commercialization .If the identified medicinal plant has been previously reported as medicinal plant, it will not be patentable. Commercial companies of medicinal plant products license and develop primarily patented medicinal plant in order to protect their investment in developing plant.

It is important that chosen medicinal plants should be genetically stable and non-fastidious in their nutrient requirements. In order for it to be economically feasible to grow large quantities of medicinal plants, it must grow well on any type of soil. Finally, a sufficient potential market for medicinal plant products is needed to justify its development. In India cultivation of medicinal plants has been recently started in large scale.

Researchers can address the medicinal plants by selecting its effectiveness and activity and site of action on the pathogens of serious human disease. Until recently Allelopathic medicines have been considered relatively fast theater compared Homeopathic, Aayurvedic, plant medicines.

There are reports indicate that there is acrogenic risk from medicines comes from Allelopathic branch. The allelopathic medicines cure disease within a short period it leaves side effects. A critical need exists for alternatives for allelopathic medicines for control of human diseases. Fortunately control of human diseases by plant medicine offers a viable option. The development of these plant medicines is already at advanced stages of commercialization in foreign countries.

India exports several tons of medicinal plants to foreign countries every year. In India especially in Maharashtra and Marathwada we also need to learn more about cultivation, are and harvesting practices of medicinal plants in our environment and soil .Through a better understanding we can achieve the aim and our target of growing and production of medicinal plants on commercial basis. Such efforts will partially helps to the rapid progress towards the commercialization of medicinal plants of India. Pandit, et. al, (2013) studied "Effects of *Withania somnifera* on the growth and virulence properties of *Streptococcus mutans* and *Streptococcus sobrinus* at sub-MIC levels".

The medicinal plants suffer from different types of fungal, bacterial, viral and nematodal diseases. The plant pathogens affect the growth and development .It is also responsible for physiological and biochemical alteration of plant. Of the medicinal plants suffer from diseases, which affect the quality and usefulness of plant to mankind. Therefore the study of diseases of medicinal plants is very important to save the quality of drug and active ingredients of a particular medicinal plant. The plant medicine prepared from diseased plant must not pusses those qualities and effects as the medicine prepared from healthy plants.

The chapters of this book are the survey report of various diseases of medicinal plants of India. Especially this work has prepared to create awareness about the diseases of medicinal plants among medicinal plant growers, researchers, students of plant pathology of the region.

CHAPTER 2

Diseases of Medicinal Plants

1. DISEASES OF HOG-WEED

English name : Hog weed

Botanical name : *Boerhavia diffusa*

Family : Nyctaginaceae

Indian name : Punarnava

There are about 50 species of hog weed (*Boerhavia diffusa* Linn.) distributed all over the word. There are only eight species of *Boerhavia* found as a wild plant spread all over the open land in India. It is commonly called as spreading hogweed. Boerhavia grows extensively along the railway tracks and open dry land in India.

It is branched creeping perennial herb with a stout root-stock and many erect and spreading branches. It grows 1-2 meters in length leaves simple, broad, somewhat rough, thick & brittle. Flowers pink or red in colour. Fruits oval, dull green or brown. It is a weed plant grows on open land. It grows abundantly along railway tracks during rainy season. It is eaten as vegetable.

Medical Use

This plant is commonly used medicine from time immemorial. It is laxative & produces cooling sensation. Roots are medicinally important, which is beneficial for several common ailments. The plant is effective in the treatment of dropsy. The herb in used in the treatment of as cites, (Joseph Jose and Rayalakshmi, 2005). The drug is useful in strengthening the stomach and promoting its action. Hag weed promotes the removal of catarrhal matter and phlegm from the bronchial tubes. There for it is beneficial in the treatment of Asthma. It is also beneficial in the treatment of fevers. It is useful in treatment of diseases of Kidney, heart, gonorrhea, etc. It is also valuable in edema, anemia, cough, pleurisy, nervous weakens, constipation, paralysis and skin diseases.

This is a weed is very common along the railway tracks. Recently it has been cultivated as a leafy vegetable as well as a medicinal plant in some states of India. The white flowered variety is especially used in the preparations of various medicines in homeopathy, Aayurveda and naturopathy systems. It is a small spreading herb with no erect system of branches. It has a perennial rhizome. It occurs extensively during rainy season but it occurs throughout the year even in presence of little amount of water especially near gutter lines, bathrooms of railway stations etc.

There are number of fungal parasites causing serious diseases of various parts of hogweed plant. Some of the diseases are described here. The leaf spot diseases of hogweed caused by various fungi reported by plant pathologist from deferent parts of India are as follow:

CERCOSPORA LEAF SPOT OF HOG-WEED

Thirumalachr, *et.al.*, (1966) reported the leaf spot disease of hog weed (*Boerhavia diffusa* Linn.) caused by *Cercospora boerhavicola* from Bihar India. The symptoms on the leaves consist of numerous irregular spots of various sizes. The spots are more distinct on the upper surface of the leaf. Initially the pale green areas appear on the upper surface of the leaf which gradually turn yellowish and then becomes brown. Within a short period the discoloration of leaf spread and the affected leaves dry up. The intercellular mycelium accumulates under the leaf epidermis which later produces conidiophores. The conidiophores are slender, club shaped structures that are brown in colour. The conidia are elongated, 1-8 septa with tapering ends.

Pavgi & Singh (1964a) from Varanasi reported leaf blight of hogweed (*Boerhavia diffusa*). It was a widespread disease, caused by *Cercospora diffusa* that consists of elongated spots on the leaf. Initially a pin- sized chlorotic spots with a necrotic centre with a diffused border are formed on the infected leaf. The mature spots turn dark brown with greenish yellow hollow around it. In severe cases spots are also formed on the petioles. The mycelium grows and spared in the intercellular spaces of leaf tissue under the leaf epidermis. The fertile mycelial mats accumulate under the epidermis which produces dark coloured unbranched clusters of conidiophores. The conidiophores bear hyaline septate conidia. The clusters of conidia come out through the stomata. The infected plant debris acts as primary inoculums for the next season. The younger leaves get infected first which are found more susceptible. The spots mature simultaneously as the leaf mature.

Rao, (1967) from Hyderabad AP (India) reported spots of *Cercospora furfurella* on hogweed (*Boerhavia diffuse)* leaf. He observed the first symptoms appear as small chocklet coloured areas on the affected leaf that increase gradually and forms a dark brown coloured spot with necrotic center. Such a spots are also developed on the petioles which are elongated in shape. The clusters of unbranched conidiophores get exposed through the necrotic centre of the spot. Several hyaline multiseptate conidia are produced on the conidiophores. The conidia are broader at the basal region and narrower towards the upper region. The broader region is attached to the conidiophores. The conidium measure about 2.4-3.4 × 20-254 µm. The pathogenic fungus survives on the affected plant debris. Sporulation of this pathogenic fungus is greatest during high relative humidity (>90%) and temperatures less than 15 °C.

Disease Cycle

The air borne spores of Cercospora acts as primary inoculum. The spores fell off on the leaves and the germs tube of spore enters the leaf through stomata. The fungal spores remain viable in soil for longer duration and attack the host plant. The fallen infected leaves also act as source of inoculum. There is great influence of environmental factors on disease development.

Collateral Host

There are no reports of alternate host of *Cercospora furfurella.*

The Causal Organism

The leaf spot disease of hogweed is caused by *Cercospora furfurella* Ell and Martin. Spots on the leaves stem and pods are dark brown, roughly spherical which are randomly distributed. The centre of the spot showing growth of fungus which is grey coloured. There is reddish brown coloured area present around each spot. Transverse section of infected leaf showing clusters of conidiophores emerging through the burst open epidermis. The mycelium consist of inter and intracellular septate hyphae, the conidiophores are thin, unbranched, and septate. The conidiophores develop in a cluster from the fertile mycelial mat. The conidia are hyaline appear singly at the tip of the conidiophores. The conidia are septate and narrow towards both the ends.

Disease management:

1. Field sanitation reduces soil borne inoculums.
2. Spraying of crop with systemic fungicides like Mancozeb (2gm/ltr.) reduces disease intensity.

3. Seed treatment with Carbendazim (2g/kg of seeds) helps to manage disease.
4. Use resistant varieties for sowing purpose.
5. Crop rotation helps to reduce disease intensity in the field.

COLLETOTRICHUM LEAF SPOT OF BOERHAVIA

Trujillo, *et.al*, (2001) studied leaf spot disease of hogweed (*Boerhavia diffusa*) caused by *Colletotrichum boerhaaviae* at Varanasi UP India. The disease causes spotting on leaves. The disease appear late in the growing season. The disease extends slowly at first but spreading occurs quickly during wet moist weather. The spots on the leaves usually appear above the vein in the form of pale water soaked areas. Later on the spot get dried and turn reddish brown in colour, with a yellowish coloured margin around it. As the time proceeds many spots coalesce to form large blighted patches on the leaves which is responsible for the death & defoliation of leaves. There are small pink coloured acervuli are seen on the upper surface of the affected leaf. In severe cases the leaf stalks & stems get affected showing elongated ash coloured lesions which consists of a mycelium as well as acervuli. The acervuli originate from the mycelial mat which is accumulated under the sub-epidermal stomatal region of the affected leaf. The spores are produced in the short conidiophores which are one celled. The conidia are oval with a slightly pointed region at one end. Numerous spores (conidia) together appear as a reddish pink mass. The groups of conidiophores are found intermixed with many unbranched setae. The setae are the sterile hyphae which may have 2-3 septa. The setae are hyaline to brown in colour with thick walls. It has found that high humidity between 90 to 95% & the temperature at 24°C favors the development. & spread of the disease extensively.

Pandotra and Ganguly, (1964) observed die back of hogweed (*Boerhavia diffusa*) due to *Colletotrichum capsici*. The mature plants during flower production get attacked by this fungus causing considerable damage to the health of the host plant. The pathogen attack firstly at the growing regions of the branches. The effected tops start withering from top to bottom. Affected tops turn brown & dry up.

The infected host show dark brown coloured spots with grayish burst open center on leaves. The pathogen produces numerous acervuli on the affected regions. The mycelium is septate with inter and inter cellular hyphal threads. The fertile hyphal mats under the affected leaf epidermis produce dark brown coloured acervuli on the affected area. The conidiophores are unbranched which produce single conidium at its tip. The conidiophores are intermixed with setae. The setae are unbranched multiseptate structures. Each conidium is unicellular with slightly curved ends. There is a distinct oil globule present in each conidium which is approximately situated at the centre of the spore. The conidia measure about 12-20 × 2.3 µm in size. It has believed that the fungus scurvies in soil on the infected plant debris and the pathogen has a broad spectrum of host range which acts as a source of inoculums for infection of next seasons healthy plants.

Pawgi and Singh, (1965a) reported one more leaf spot disease of hogweed (*Boerhavia diffuse*) due to the infection of *Colletotrichum* species from Andhra Pradesh India. He observed the spots that are found initially on the juvenile foliage as a brown papery lesions which become dark and dotted with black asexual spore producing structures called as pycnidia. During the moist weather the lesions get surrounded by a halo of white fluffy mycelium.

WHITE RUST DISEASE OF BOERHAVIA

White rust disease of hogweed (*Boerhavia diffusa*) occurs on the leaf and stem. It is a very common and wide spread disease of hogweed found everywhere in India where the plants are cultivated as a medicinal plant or grown as a weed. The disease appears just after the rainy seasons. In India the disease was noted by Mumtaz Baig and Sumia Fatima (2015).

Symptoms

The main symptoms first appear as an off whitish pustules on the leaves, stem and rarely on the flowing parts of the plant. The pustules are most commonly seen on the lower surface of the leaf. The infected leaves become rough in appearance, by the time carling of leaves inwardly seen in the severely affected of the leaves. The leaves of all the age group show equal response towards the disease. The size of new leaf of infected plant show reduced size. The plant remains stunted. Heavy defoliation of affected leaf reduces greatly the number of leaves on the plant. The rust pustules formed on stem resemble the pustules of leaf. During cool moist environment, the disease appears as more destructive. Like other host plants of the respective pathogen plants of *Boerhavia* shows hypertrophy of affected stem & leaves (Joseph Jose and Rayalakshmi, 2005). The prolonged period of cool weather with slightly warmer days favors the disease extensively. During warm dry environment, the disease rarely occurs. The younger plants are more susceptible than the older plants. Rapid spread of the disease occurs during rainy season mostly on younger plants. The affected plants easily get recognized from the distance because of shining white blisters on the infected leaf and stem. Swelling of the infected stem (hypertrophy) takes place which is very common but the petiole does not show hypertropism at any stage of disease development.

The pustules are small oval slightly raised structures that are emerging through the broken epidermis. The pustules are of variable size. During severe cases, numerous pustules coalesce to from large affected regions of the irregular shape, or a blotch; The leaf tissue at the affected region get killed. The roots of affected plant show slow & stunted growth.

The Causal Organism

The white rust disease of hogweed (*Boerhavia diffusa*) is caused by *Albugo platensis* (Speg.) Swingle (Balasubhramanaiun, 1967). It is among the oomycetes fungi. The mycelium is aseptate, branched hyaline to light brown and intercellular. The pathogen produces haustoria for absorption of food from host cell that are spherical in shape. The pustules contain large number of sporangiophore. The sporangiophore produces sporangia in the form of chain. Each sporangium is globular to lemon shaped structure with a beak like structure at its tip. The sporangia are mostly disseminated by rainwater, air currents, or any other mechanical agency to a long distance. The sporangia germinate on the host leaf in presence of temperature near about 20-22°C on the moist host surface. The sporangium consists of motile spores called zoospores. The zoospores are biflagellate, unicellular uninucleate bean shaped structure. The zoospores release their flagella before germination. The zoospores germinate and produce a young thread of promycelium that enters the leaf through the natural openings like stomata & lenticels. The disease becomes naked within 8-20 days after infection (Abhijit Ranware, *et.al*, 2010).

The oospores are dark brown spherical structures formed extensively on the hypertrophied dead tissue of the respective host. The plant debris even consists of numerous oospores. Trujillo, *et.al*, (2001). The oospores are thick walked spores which are highly resistant to adverse environmental conditions. The oospores persist in soil on the plant debris as well as on the affected host plants and collateral hosts. The germination and infection by zoospores and oospores is greatly influenced by the environmental factors like temperature and humidity. The temperature favorable for the germination of zoospores is 21°C.

Source of Inoculum

The medicinal plant hogweed (*Boerhavia diffusa*) is a perennial weed that occurs throughout the season as a weed plant in our country. It grow mostly on the waste land and on open crop field soils. The repeated recycling of the pathogen during the same season helps to increase the intensity of the inoculums. The affected living plants or plant debris also acts as a source of inoculums.

Disease management

1. Collect all the infected leaves from plant as well as from the ground and burn it carefully. This process may help to reduce disease intensity for some extent.
2. Good air circulation among vegetation reduces disease intensity.
3. Remove collateral host of the pathogen to avoid primary inoculums to next season's plant.

LEPTOSPHAERULINA LEAF SPOT OF BOERHAVIA

The leaf spot of *Boerhavia* caused by *Leptosphaerulina argentinensis* is a very common and more destructive disease. Bilgrami, (1963), reported greatest losses of Boerhavia due to leaf spot of *Leptosphaerulina argentinensis* Speg. from Andhra Pradesh India.

Symptoms

The symptoms of pathogenic fungus *Leptosphaerulina argentinensis* are observed only on the leaves. The immature and mature, both the type of leaves was found equally susceptible to the infection. Initially very small spherical dot like spots appear on the leaf surface. The spots increase gradually attaining a size of ½ centimeter in diameter. Every spot encircled by a chlorotic zone. The center of the spot turn light brown in colour and the peripheral region of the spot becomes dark brown in colour.

The leaves present close to the soil surface shows first symptoms of the disease. Later on the disease gradually proceeds to other uninfected leaves. The *Boerhavia* is a creeping plant hence most of the leaves are very close to the soil surface. The infection causes loss of premature leaves, hence reduces the growth and development of the host plant. The vigorousness of the plant is greatly affected by the disease. The spots increase in size. Many spots coalesce to form large patches of dead tissue on the leaf. The moist cool environment favors the disease development. The spores produced in affected plant part carried away by wind insect or by any other mechanical agencies.

The Causal Organism

The disease is caused by a pathogenic fungus *Leptosphaerulina argentinensis.*

Disease Cycle

The pathogenic fungus remains in soil in the form of conidia on infected plant debris. It is a facultative parasite which grows on dead organic matter in soil, in absence of specific host plant. The conidia disseminated by wind remain in environment for longer duration even under unfavorable environment. The air and soil borne conidia occur on infected plant material in soil acts as source of inoculums.

Disease management

1. Collect all the fallen plant debris from soil because the fungus survive on the infected leaves sand burn carefully to reduce disease intensity.
2. No chemical methods suggested for the control of *Leptosphaerulina argentinensis* from any part of the country.

DISEASES REPORTED ON HOG-WEED (*Boerhavia diffusa Linn.*)

Sl. No.	Disease	Pathogen
1.	Leaf spot	*Cercospora boerhaavicola*
2.	Leaf spot	*C. diffusa*
3.	Leaf spot	*C.furfurella.*
4.	Leaf spot	*Colletotrichum boerhaaviae*
5.	Leaf spot	*C. capsici*
6.	Leaf spot	*Leptoshaerulina argentinensis*
7.	Leaf and stem rust	*Albugo platensis*

2. DISEASES OF SENNA

English name : Indian senna
Botanical name : *Cassia angustifoslia*
Family : Caesalpinaceae
Indian name : Bhumari

The Cassia (*Cassia angustifolia*) is a small perennial erect under shrub which is cultivated at various parts of India for its medicinal properties. It grows best in red lomi semi-irrigated soil. The plants are grown by the use of seeds. The leaves and fruits are laxative and purgative. The leaves are compound with 5 to 8 pairs of leaflets. Leaflets oval, the inflorescence is Recemose type. Flowers yellow in terminal clusters, fruit a legume, seeds flat, obovate.

Medicinal Use

All the parts of tree have medicinal properties the fruits pulp is well known laxative which is used in treatment of constipation. The pulp is mild, pleasant & safe purgative. It should not be used alone. In combination with other drug it is safe. The root is useful in common cold. In case of running nose, smoke from the burning root can be in haled. The root extract reduces fever. The pulp of cassia useful in loss of sense of taste due to excessive use of *Opium poppy*. Leaves are useful in reliving irritation of the skin, swellings & pains. The juice or paste of leaf useful for dressing for ringworm & inflammation of the hands or feet, cause by exposure to cold. The plant is useful in constipation, loss of appetite, liver complaints, spleen enlargements, dyspepsia, typhoid, jaundice, anemia, leprosy. Its flowers are consumed as vegetables.

DAMPING OFF OF CASSIA SEEDLING

It is one of the important diseases of senna (*Cassia angustifolia* Linn.) that causes heavy destruction of the seedlings hence it is of a major importance. The damping off is a serious disease in the cultivated fields of North West India. The disease spread takes place very fast in the water-logged areas of the field (Rangaswami, *et.al*, 1968).

Symptoms

Initially the stem of the seedling just above the soil surface shows water soaked blackish spot that gradually increase around the collar region of the seedling; Simultaneously the cotyledons of seedling turn yellowish. The infection starts extending upwardly from the collar region causing drying & death of the seedling (Rangaswami and Sheshadri, 1970). The infected dried seedlings when split open that shows dark powdery mass (sclerotia) of the fungus. The infected collar region of seedling consists of numerous dark brown coloured fruiting bodies like structures which are called as pycnidia.

The Causal Organism

The disease is caused by a soil borne fungus which is identified as *Macrophomina phaseolina* (Tassi) Goid. The mycelium is branched, septate, intercellular which later becomes intracellular. The mature mycelia produce short unbranched conidiophores which are hyaline, cylindrical that measure about 5-12 × 5-6 µm in size. The conidia are unicellular, ovoid or ellipsoid or roundish in shapes which are hyaline that measure about 15-30 × 5-10 µm in size. The infected region consists of numerous black coloured sclerotia. The sclerotia are hard 100 µm in diameter with smooth wall. There are numerous pycnidia found on the affected region of the seedling. The Pycnidia are dark brown, solitary, immersed, about 100-200 µm in diameter. The wall of pycnidium made up of interwoven hyphae. The pycnidia open at the upper end. The opening is called as mouth or ostiole.

Disease management:

1. Collection and destruction of infected entire seedling can reduce disease intensity for same extent.
2. Treatment (2.5 g/kg) reduced disease.
3. The pathogen is a soil borne fungus hence drenching of field soil with Bavistin (0.1%). Brassicol (0.2%) controlled the disease.
4. Select pathogen free soil for growing seedlings.

LEAF BLIGHT OF CASSIA

The leaf blight of senna (*Cassia angustifolia* Linn.) occurs in different part of India. It is a most serious, highly destructive disease of senna commonly found during rainy season. Leaf blight is a wide spread disease in almost all cassia growing regions of the world. The disease is prevalent in heavy monsoon areas. The disease is of a great importance in several countries and has been reported to cause numerous losses.

Symptoms

After infection to the plant, the symptoms occur as tiny, dark brown spots on the surface of leaflet of the host plants; especially at the tips and marginal region. The spots increase in size as the disease develops and spread within the host tissue. The spots are roughly circular with necked marks of concentric zones on the surface of the spot. Later on the spots extend and the chlorotic streaks are formed which run from the spot to the remaining part of lamina. The entire leaf turns yellow and then starts drying. The entire leaf blade dry up and fell off. The premature leaf fall is very common. The older leaves were found to be more susceptible for the attack of the pathogen. Rao, (1963a) reported that the Alternaria blight of senna (*Cassia angustifolia* Linn.) is a disease of major importance that affects the quality and quantity of the produce.

The Causal Organism

The disease causing pathogenic fungus is *Alternaria alternata* (fr.) Keissler. The mycelium is highly branched septate, olivacious brown in colour. The conidiophores are isolated in small groups which are simple or branched, septate with numerous conidial scars. The conidial chains are distinct. The conidia are ovoid with 3-8 transverse septa. The conidia measure about 2-63 × 9-18 µm in size. The conidium is multicellular hence produce many germ tubes during germination.

Disease Cycle

The pathogenic fungus is soil borne. The mycelium of the fungus remain in dry infected leaves in dormant conditions for more than twelve months. The fungus produces numerous conidia which remain viable for more than 17 months.

The mycelium and conidia which survive on plant debris that acts as primary source of inoculum. The climate and soil factors exert a considerable influence on the development and spread of the disease. High humidity favors disease development.

Disease management:

1. Spraying of Diathane M-45 (0.15%) at an interval of 15 days for two months has been suggested for the control of Alternaria blight disease.

COLLETOTRICHUM LEAF SPOT OF CASSIA

Gupta, *et.al*, (1972) observed a new leaf spot disease of senna (*Cassia angustifolia* Linn.) from Lucknow (India). It is also one of the destructive diseases hence considered as a major disease of senna in senna cultivating areas.

Symptoms

The symptoms consist of numerous small spots on the leaf surface. The spots are dark brown in colour. By the time the spots enlarge to form large necrotic patches on the leaf. The affected leaves droop off at any stage of its maturity due to spread of the infection. The acervuli are abundantly produced by the fungus which are scattered all over the infected patches of leaves, stem and other parts of respective host plant. The acervuli are visible on the infected regions leaf (Gupta, *et.al*, 1972). The host tissue around the patches formed due to infection gets discolored. In severe cases, the affected plants remain stunted and without leaves, hence that affects the productivity of the plant.

The Causal Organism

The causal organism is *Colletotrichum gloesporioides* (Penz) sacc. (Perfect stage: *Glomerella cingulata* (Stonem) Spauld. Gupta, *et.al*, (1972) explained the pathogenic fungus in the following way. The mycelium consists of branched septate hyphae which are grayish to light brown in colour. The mycelium produces light brown coloured groups of conidiophores on which the conidia are produced. The conidia are cylindrical slightly ellipsoid with blunt apex and truncate base. Each conidium is two celled structure that measure about 9-2 × 4-6 μm in size. There are abundance of acervuli develop on the affected regions of the leaves. The acervuli are globular elongated or irregular in shape. The perithecia are also observed on the severely affected region of host, mostly on the affected dried leaves & twigs. The perithecia are globose, dark brown to black in colour that measure about 85-300 μm in diameter. The perithecial wall consists of numerous interwoven hyphae. Each perithecium has an opening called as an ostiole which is slightly raised. Inside the perithecia at the basal region a group of club shaped asci & paraphysis (sterile hyphae) are situated. The ascus consists of eight ascospores. The ascospores are oval to cylindrical, unicellular uninucleate hyaline structures which are light in weight.

Disease Cycle

The pathogenic fungus is thought to survive in soil on infected plant debris, which causes primary infection during next season. The fungus produces numerous conidia which are blown away by wind. The wind bore conidia also acts as primary or secondary inoculum. The infectious hyphae also remain viable in the infected tissue for longer duration. The seeds of the infected plants also carry infectious fungal threads.

Disease management:

1. The seeds should be treated with recommended fungicides to avoid disease free plant.
2. The Mancozeb (0.25%) spraying at 15 day intervals can reduce disease intensity.

DISEASES REPORTED ON SENNA (*Cassia angustifolia*)

Sl.No.	Disease	Pathogen
1.	Leaf spot	*Aecidium cassiae*
2.	Leaf spot	*Alternaria alternata*
3.	Leaf spot	*Alternaria cassia*
4.	Leaf spot	*Cercospora cassiocarpa*
5.	Leaf spot	*Cercospora nigricans*
6.	Leaf spot	*Cercospora occidentalis*
7.	Leaf spot	*Cercospora sphaeroidea*
8.	Leaf spot	*Choenophora cucurbitarum*
9.	Leaf spot	*Cochiliobolus nodulosus*
10.	Leaf spot	*Colletotrichum lindemuthianum*
11.	Leaf spot	*Curvularia lunata*
12.	Leaf spot	*Drechslera rostrata*
13.	Leaf rust	*Endophyllum cassiae*
14.	Wood rot	*Fomes senex*
15.	Wood rot	*Ganoderma applanatum*
16.	Die back	*Hypoxylon archeri*
17.	Sooty mould	*Meliola aethiops*
18.	Root rot	*Pellicularia rolfsii*
19.	Tar spot	*Phyllachora cassicola*
20.	Leaf spot	*Phyllosticta cassianea*
21.	Stem and root rot	*Polyporus gilvus*
22.	Leaf spot	*Septoria cassicola*
23.	Root gall	*Synchytrium cassiae*

3. DISEASES OF MINT

English name : Mint

Botanical name : *Mentha longifolia*

Family : Lamiaceae

Local name : Pudina

Mint (*Mentha longifolia* Linn. Huds.) is a vigorously growing perennial plant which grows extensively on wet land. It has leafy stolons, stems erect with ascending branches, roots numerous in clusters, Sessile leaves, lanceolate, long, sharply serrate, dark green, aromatic; grow in wet places, cultivated for its aromatic leaves. Mints are aromatic, almost exclusively perennial, erect, branched stems, the leaves are arranged in opposite pairs, which are oblong to lanceolate in shape, often downy and with a serrate margin. The flowers are white and with a serrated margin. The flowers are white to purple and produced in false whorls called verticelaster. The corolla is two lipped. The fruit is a nut let with four seeds.

Medicinal Use

The plant is useful in preparation of Aayurvedic and several traditional medicines. The leaves are eaten against cold and cough. The mint oil is found effect against asthma. The mint leaves are used as salad throughout the world. The plant possesses antibacterial and antifungal properties.

STOLEN ROT DISEASE OF MINT

The stolen rot is a common disease of mint (*Mentha longifolia* Linn. Huds) and causes considerable loss. It occurs throughout the world wherever mint is grown.

Symptoms

The pathogen infects the root hairs and extends to the cortical region of the stolen. In severe cases the intercellular mycelium becomes intracellular. The fungus produces numerous sclerotic bodies within the host cells that plug the vessels and destruct the host tissue. At the initial stage of infection the plant shows spots of dead tissue on the stolen and other branches of mint plant. Heavily infected plants die before maturely due to black rooting of the stolen. This reduces plant growth & yield.

The Causal Organism

The stolen rot disease of mint (*Mentha longifolia* Linn. Huds) is caused by *Macrophomina phaseolina*. It is a soil borne fungus characterized by the production of both pycnidia & sclerotia in the host tissue. The pycnidiospores are ellipsoid to obovoid. The sclerotia are formed by the aggregation of many hyphal cells hence the sclerotia are multicellular bodies that are black in colour and are variable in size and shape. The mycelium is branched, septate, intercellular which later becomes intracellular. The mature mycelia produce short unbranched conidiophores which are hyaline, cylindrical that measure about 5-12 × 5-6 µm in size. The conidia are unicellular, ovoid or ellipsoid or roundish in shapes which are hyaline that measure about 15-30 × 5-10 µm in size (Zimowska, 2004b).

The infected region consists of numerous black coloured sclerotia. The sclerotia are hard 100 µm in diameter with smooth wall. There are numerous pycnidia found on the affected region of the seedling. The Pycnidia are dark brown, solitary, immersed, about 100-200 µm in diameter. The wall of pycnidium made up of interwoven hyphae. T he pycnidia open at the upper end. The opening is called as mouth or ostiole.

There are more than 500 cultivated and wild plant species are the hosts for the pathogen *Macrophomina phaseolina.*

STEM ROT DISEASE OF MINT

The stem rots of mint which occurs in India and other countries of the world. It is usually of major importance and appears to be restricted to mint. It is a very wide spread disease which commonly assumes economic importance in India.

Symptoms

It is a pathogen of broad spectrum of host range; it causes root rot disease of a variety of plants. It is a soil borne pathogen infects the root system of plant and reaches the stolon. Initially the affected region turns brownish and later becomes dark brown in colour. Distinct patches of brown colour appear at the affected stolon of mint. In severe cases of disease development the rotted stolons shows strands of mycelium and sclerotia of fungus.

The Causal Organism

There are reports of stem rot of mint due to infection of *Rhizoctonia bataticola* (Taub) Butler. The mycelium is septate, branched and intracellular. It produces both micro and macroconidia. The hyphae are 1.5-2.5 µm thick. The fungus produces sclerotia of about 100 mm in diameter which are irregular in shape and black in colour. The microconidia measure about 4.8 - 14.4 × 2.2 - 4.8 µm and macroconidia 21.0-53.0 × 2.4-5.6 µm in size. The optimum temperature for development of mycelium is 24 °C.

The Disease Cycle

According to the Kalra (2004) the sclerotia are produced in affected root and stem region which survive in soil on infected plant debris for longer duration. The sclerotia are very resistant spores that can tolerate to adverse environmental factors. The pathogenic fungus grows on number of plants hence there is a great possibility of availability of host plant.

Mint is a perennial plant hence affected stolen acts as inoculum for healthy ones. In favorable environment the soil borne sclerotia germinates and the young hyphae enters the host plant through the root hairs or any mechanical injuries. Ever after the death of the infected plant the mycelium produce sclerotia in the affected host tissue that continue until the host cells get completely degradation. The mycelium along with sclerotia from the residue of the affected plant acts as primary inoculum for new branches or new plants.

Disease management:

1. The pathogen is soil borne hence it is very difficult to avoid contact of soil with plant and soil sterilization is a expensive process hence change of field is one of the remedy should be used to reduce disease intensity to a great extent.
2. Shastri, (1969) suggested polarization of soil in which the crop field is ploughed and the soil is exposed to sunlight of summer season.
3. Mundkur, (1952) recommended addition of organic amendments for control the of *M. phaseoli.*
4. Crop rotation is good to reduce disease intensity.

POWDERY MILDEW DISEASE OF MINT

The powdery mildews are probably the most common, conspicuous and extensively occurring disease especially during the rainy season in India. It is an easily recognizable disease of plants because of its typical talcum powder like patches on the leaf stem and inflorescence of the host plant. Except root system all the parts of the host get affected. The powdery mildew pathogen had a broadest range of host spectrum. The powdery mildew of mint causes quantitative and qualitative loss of plant. The disease causes 100% loss of affected plant because there is no market value for such affected plants. Hence the disease is responsible for great economic losses.

Symptoms

Initially the powdery mildew is most commonly observed on the upper surface of the mint leaves. During severe cases of disease development the powdery patches extend at the underside of the leaves, young shoots, sterns, and buds except root system of the host plant. The powdery mildew is characterized by the appearance of small white to grayish coloured spot on the leaf surface. The spots increase very fast during humid weather. During advanced stage of the disease development, many spots coalesce to form large patches of mycelial growth with irregular margin.

The large patches of mycelium on the host tissue shows small dark brown to black coloured dot like fruiting body which are called as cleistothecia which are produced at the end of the favorable season. The severely affected leaves show inward curling of leaves. The young shoots gradually dry up. The disease directly affects the process of photosynthesis by occupying the leaf area. The growth of the plant reduced to a great extent. Drying of young shoot and defoliation are the common symptoms. It has been observed that the plants grown at the shady places were found to be more severely affected.

The Causal Organism

The disease is caused by *Erysiphe cinchoracearum* DC. The mycelium is branched that grows only on the surface of leaf the tissues but never invading the tissues themselves. The pathogenic fungus obtains food from the host plant by sending food sucking organs (haustoria) in the epidermal cells of host tissue.

The pathogen produces infinity of conidia on the affected plant parts. The conidiophores are short; septate that produces chains of conidia at its tip. The conidia are oval, hyaline, unicellular and light in weight (Bylka, 2003).

The conidia are easily carried away to a long distances even in presence of normal air currents. The pathogen produces closed fruiting bodies which are called as cleistothecia. The cleistothecium consists of a series of asci inside. The ascus is a club shaped body that filled by haploid ascospores. The ascospores are oval, unicellular uninucleate structures which are formed by the meiotic division of diploid nucleus.

Disease Cycle

The fungus causing powdery mildew diseases of plants is an obligate parasite, hence cannot be grown artificially in the laboratories on any media. There are two possibilities of spread of pathogen. The cleistothecia are the resistant fruiting bodies can survive in soil on plant debris for long period that acts as inoculums. Secondly the pathogen grows on number of collateral hosts hence the contaminated air is responsible for new infection to the plants. The important is that mint is a perennial crop hence remains green & growing for throughout the year of the proper care in taken. The infected plants in the field acts as an important inoculum.

The pathogen responsible for powdery mildew disease of mint has a broad spectrum of hosts. The pathogen causes powdery mildew of cucurbits, cucumber, sugar beets, strawberries, cloves, many ornamentals, Rose, grapes, many forest trees, numbers of weeds, apple, oak and cereals.

Disease management:

1. Removal and distraction of infected leaves at very initial stage of infection could control disease to a great extent.
2. Use resistant variety for plantation purpose.
3. There are some reports of spraying of systemic fungicides such as Tridemorph on affected leaves to control powdery mildews in general.
4. Removal and burning of plant residue cold control the disease.
5. Collect all the waste weeds around the field and destroy.

ALTERNARIA BLIGHT OF MINT

The blight disease o mint (*Mentha avensis* Linn) caused by *Alternaria* is one of the most common and destructive in mint growing areas. It is primarily a leaf blight disease occurs in the field but it continue after harvest of mint crop and causes rot of affected leaves.

Symptoms

The first symptom of *Alternaria* occur in the form of small round brown coloured spot on the oldest leaves of host plants which are closer to the soil surface. The spot vary in size i.e. from 1 mm to ½ an inch in diameter. The temperature between 22-27 °C and high humidity favors the disease development. The gradual increase of spot shows concentric ring pattern. The ring pattern on the spots is an evidence of growth and spore production by the fungal pathogen. The spots are encircled by narrow yellow zones. The enlarged spots become irregular and cover major portion of the leaf. The symptoms gradually proceed from lower leaves to upper ones. In severe cases most of the leaves show large blighted areas and the main stem also gets affected.

The Causal Organism

The blight disease of mint caused by the fungal pathogen *Alternaria tennuis*. The mycelium is highly branched that consists of septate hyphae. The mycelium is woolly in appearance, whitish to grayish, olivacious or brownish in colour, hyphae hyaline, septate. Conidiophores simple or branched, erect, septate, olivacious, conidia olive brown to dark brown, usually 3-5 transverse septa and with longitudinal septa in the second and third cells, very variable in size and shape, obclavate with short beaks and borne in long chains, 20-50 × 10-16 µm (Fokkema, 1993).

Disease Cycle

The pathogen complete its several disease cycles during the same season so that extensive damage of the crop takes place. The severely affected leaves fell off on the ground that acts as primary inoculum. The pathogen persists in soil on the affected plant debris which acts as primary source of infection during the next season. In presence of favorable environment the dormant spores germinate by producing a promycelium which enters the leaf through the natural openings and the leaf get infected. The spores germinate by producing one, two or more than two germ tubes which enters the host leaf through stomata. The pathogen is mostly transferred to a new locality along with the harvested mint leaves. The wind also responsible to carry some spores from heavily affected leaves hence the wind also acts as a source of inoculum. The air spora when comes in contact with the host leaf that causes blight disease in presence of favorable environmental conditions.

Disease management:

1. Avoid repeated sowing of the same crop in the same field.
2. Collect the affected leaves in early stage of disease development and destroy.
3. Avoid wetting of foliage.
4. Avoid crowding of mint plants in the field.
5. Destroy all the possible alternate hosts grown around the crop field.

DISEASES REPORTED ON MINT (*Mentha longifolia*)

Sl. No.	Disease	Pathogen
1.	Rust	*Aecidium lophanthi*
2.	Leaf spot	*Alternaria alternata*
3.	Leaf spot	*Cercospora menthicola*
4.	Stem blight	*Corynespora cassicola*
5.	Powdery mildew	*Erysiphe cinchoracearum*
6.	Leaf rust	*Puccinia menthae*
7.	Stolon rot	*Rhizoctonia bataticola*
8.	Stem and root rot	*Sclerotium rolfsii*

4. DISEASES OF PERIWINKL

English name : Periwinkle

Botanical name : *Catharanthus roseus*

Family : Apocynaceae

Indian name : Sadabahar

The periwinkle (*Catharanthus roseus* (Linn).G. Don) is a cosmopolitan plant which occurs throughout the world. These are perennial herbs with decussate arrangement of leaves. Leaves elliptical, petiolate. Flowers are usually solitary in the leaf axils, pentamerous, fruit follicle type of fruit. Seeds numerous, black, 1-2 mm in size.

Medicinal Use

The plant part is used in various types of traditional medicines which is used to treat a variety of diseases. In the recent years it is reported to use against leukemia, cancer, high blood pressure. The rural medicine practiceners using periwinkle leaves against blood sugar balancing. The leaf paste is applied over cracks to stop bleeding. Various types of ointments are prepared from the plant parts. It is poisonous in high doses. Without prescription of registered doctors it is harmful to take medicine prepared by periwinkle.

A Twig of Periwinkle

STEM ROT DISEASE OF PERIWINKLE

The Rhizoctonia is a fungal pathogen of a variety of economically important plant; occur in a variety of soil on dead organic matter of host plant. Sahni, (1964) reported stem rot disease of periwinkle *Catharanthus roseus* (Linn.) G. Don.

Symptoms

The initial symptoms were seen as yellowish green water soaked lesions especially near the collar region of the plant. The infected plant shows decay of cortical tissue of collar region hence the plant bend downwards. The decay around the color region of plant increase gradually in all direction hence the slimy wet rot becomes distinct. The affected plant ultimately turns pale yellow to brown. In this way death of the affected plant takes place. The infected dried stems that collapse which remain in soil that act as the inoculum for the next season's crop.

Sundaraman, (1922 b,) observed burning of tips of plant that gradually spread downwards causing drying of entire branch along with leaves, auxiliary buds and twigs. Withering of growing tips and defoliation of young leaves occur. The leaves just above the soil surface are more susceptible for the disease hence the lower leaves get infected first. The infected leaf possesses water soaked areas along the midrib especially near the leaf base and then spread towards the tip of the leaf. The affected region of leaf gets decayed and dry up within short period. The dried leaf turns blackish in colour. The heavily infected plants possess numerous brown to black coloured sclerotia on the affected regions. Sometimes the spots shows dark and light coloured concentric rings. The disease was very common during the rainy season. Formation of necrotic patches on the leaves and defoliation are the common symptoms during disease cycle. Balasubramoniam and Bhama, (1977) observed dark brown coloured concentric rings on the necrotic spot of the disease. Numerous lesions coalesce to form large blighted spots.

The Causal Organism

The causal organism of leaf spot of disease of periwinkle is *Rhizoctonia solani* (Taub.) Butl. The mycelium consists hyphae that are fairly thick. The pathogen produces abundance of spores. Each spore may be 100mm in diameter. The entire root system gets rotted during severe infection. The sclerotia are dark brown which are irregular in shape that occurs on heavily affected regions. It consists of highly branched mycelium. Mycelium consists of septate hyphae. The mycelium may be inter or intercellular.

It is a saprophytic fungus. The infected plant parts or the soil of previous crop acts as the inoculum.

Disease Cycle

The mycelium of the pathogen produce numerous sclerotia which are dark black in colour, The Rhizoctonia is a soil borne fungus which survives on dead organic matter. It has broad spectrum of hosts on which pathogen survive. The sclerotia produced on affected region which remain in soil acts as an inoculums.

Disease management:

The disease is one of the most difficult to control in the field. Crop rotation is also a not much supportive method because the sclerotia persist in soil for year after year. Flooding of crop field during summer reduces the incidence of sclerotia. There is need of resistant varieties against the disease.

1. Remove and discard the rotted stolons during plantation.
2. Pretreatment of stolons with 250 ppm solution of Captan is recommended.
3. Pruning of the diseased twigs 7-8 cm below the infection site followed by spray of Bordeaux mixture (5:5: 50) or 0.3% Copper oxychloride is recommended against the disease.

ALTERNARIA BLIGHT OF PERIWINKLE

The blight disease of periwinkle caused by *Alternaria* species that spread extensively during the rainy season, Mohanti and Das, (1958), observed blight of periwinkle in Lucknow. Initially the small dotted chlorotic spots appear on the surface of the leaf. The spots become more distinct on the lower surface of the leaf. The spots increase gradually showing discolored spots which consists of ring pattern. The rings represent the growth and sporulation of the pathogen. The rings are distinct on the fully developed spots. By the time the spots turns brown. Many such spots coalesce to form a large necrotic patch of irregular margin. Such a large blighted regions on leaf directly reduces the photosynthetic area. In severe cases of the disease, drying of leaves and defoliation are common. The affected plants remain stunted and delicate.

The Causal Organism

The leaf blight disease is caused by *Alternaria alternata* (Fr.) Keissler. The young colony of Alternaria on PDA possesses fluffy margins and off white center. The mycelium is septate, highly branched, grayish black in colour. The conidia are 1-6 septate which measure about 13.1-46.2 × 7.2 - 10.1 µm. The conidia are beaked. The size of beak range from 3.0 x10.0µm.

Disease Cycle

The Alternaria alternata is a facultative parasite. The fungus survives in soil on infected plant debris. The conidia overwinter to initiate primary infection. They germinate in presence of little moisture. Each conidium produces two to many germ tubes which enters the leaf through stomata or by direct penetration. The pathogen is very common in the air and in soil where it survives on plant debris. The optimum temperature for the fungus growth is 28°C but it can make significant progress at low temperature.

Disease management:

1. Field sanitation: collect all types of plant debris from the field and burn away from the field before sowing.
2. The crop rotation reduces disease intensity caused by *Alternaria* sp.

FOOT ROT DISEASE OF PERIWINKLE

Umbala and Ramarao, (1972) reported foot rot disease of periwinkle in west Bengal orchards. The infected pants possess rotted bark at the collar region of the plant. In advanced stages of disease development the affected region shows white cottony mycelial mats that can easily be removed by the needle. The plants of all the age group are found susceptible for the disease. The yellowing and drying of leaf tips are the common symptoms.

Defoliation during disease development takes place. The affected young plants bend at the collar region and get dried. The mature plants show heavy defoliation and drying of all the branches.

The Causal Organism

The foot rot disease of periwinkle is caused by *Sclerotium rolfsii* Sacc. The fungus consists of silky white sparsely septate hyphae. The hyphae are hyaline, thin walled, structures. The broader hyphae show clamp connections which are absent in thin hyphae. The number of nuclei in each hyphal compartment is one, two or many. The fungal hyphae produce sclerotial initials. The sclerotia are brown cinnamon coloured which measure about 3-4 µm in diameter, hard in touch, but at maturity turn dark brown.

Disease Cycle

The fungus survive in soil on infected plant debris. It has a broad range of hosts. The fungus is a saprophyte survive on a variety of crop debris. The fungus also produces numerous brown coloured sclerotia that are left in soil for longer duration. The sclerotia acts as primary inoculum. In favorable environmental condition, sclerotia germinate and cause infections.

The fungus overwinters in soil on plant debris and can survive as saprophyte. The fungus produces numerous sclerotia of cinnamon colour which survive in soil as inoculums. In favorable the sclerotia germinate and cause infections to proper host plant. High temperature and humidity favor the disease development. The fungal threads and sclerotia get disseminated by wind currents, rain splashes, irrigation water and by any other mechanical agency during work in the field.

Disease Management

The management of Sclerotium rolfsii is difficult and depends partly on cultural practices of management; sowing of plants in healthy soil and by providing proper interval of irrigation the disease can be minimized or restricted by vigorousness of plant. Deep ploughing helps to dug out inoculums deep into the soil that helps to avoid disease in the field. Pruning of infected branches and their prompt destruction prevents the spread of the disease.

CERCOSPORA LEAF SPOT OF PERIWINKLE

Groenewald, *et.al*, (2006) reported marginal leaf spot disease of periwinkle. Due to infection the small spots of 1mm diameter develop on leaf which consists of dead tissue. Mostly these appear along the leaf margins. The leaves of all the age group were found to be infected by the pathogen. The spots increase gradually which turn brown in colour.

The pathogenic fungus causes yellowing of leaf. Heavy defoliation occurs during the severe cases. Yellowing of the affected premature leaves was found to be faster than the affected mature leaves.

The Causal Organism

The Corynespora spots of periwinkle caused by *Corynespora cassicola* (Berk & Curt) Wei. The mycelium is highly branched, septate, intercellular, and grayish brown in colour. It absorbs food material with the help of haustoria. The conidiophores are erect which arise from the fertile hyphae. The conidiophores are simple unbranched straight light brown in colour. The conidiophores measure about 108-8.45 µm in length and 3-10 µm in thickness. The conidiophores bear conidia of variable shape. The conidia may be obclavate cylindrical, elongated, slightly curved or straight. The conidia are hyaline or light yellow in colour or olivacious brown in colour. The conidia are 4-198 µm long and 9-20 µm thick at one end and 4-8 µm wide at the end. The conidiophores emerge through the epidermal layer of the infected plant part (Abou-Zeid *et.al*, 2008).

Disease Cycle

The pathogen overwinters on infected plant part. During favorable environment the pathogen becomes active and infects the host plant. The soil and infected plant debris acts as source of inoculum.

Disease management:

1. Remove all types of plant debris from the field before sowing.
2. Field sanitation helps to reduce disease intensity.
3. Remove carefully the infected plants from the field and dug it away from the field.

DAMPING OFF DISEASE OF SEEDLINGS OF PERIWINKLE

The damping off of seedling have been reported in the field of Periwinkle. The pathogen present in soil causes seedling blight of periwinkle. This is a disease of considerable importance. It is one of the most devastating seedling diseases caused by pathogen and responsible for significant loss of emerging seedlings.

Symptoms

This is one of the serious diseases of nursery. The disease cause damping off of pre and post emerging young seedlings. The infected seedling turns yellowish because of interaction of pathogen with the host tissue. Gradually the infected seedling dry up & collapse.

The Causal Organism

The damping off of seedling of Periwinkle is caused by *Phytopthora nicotianae* var. *parasitica*. It is a soil borne pathogen mycelium consists of coenocytic branched hyphae, which are hyaline to pale yellow in colour.

It produces oospores after sexual reproduction. Oospores are sexual spores that are smooth, spherical of about 25 µm in diameter. The fertile hyphae produce numerous lemon or pear shaped sporangia. Each sporangium is having a beak like structure at its tip which is termed as papilla. Sporangia are hyaline, straw coloured, measure about 25 µm in diameter. The sporangia consist of fill of zoospores which are biflagellate & 7-11 µm in size. The pathogen also produces thick walled resistant chlamydospores which are resistant to drought.

Disease Cycle

The pathogen is soil borne and seed borne in nature. It survives in soil on infected plant debris. The fungus overwinters in the form of sexual spores or oospores. The oospores are spherical, thick walled spores which are resistant to adverse environmental conditions. High humidity and moderate temperature is highly favorable for disease occurrence. The seeds of infected plants act as carrier of inoculums.

Disease management:

1. Spraying of Bordeaux mixture was of some value.
2. The seeds used for sowing purpose should be selected from healthy plants.
3. Sanitation and rotation of crop are necessary.
4. Removal of plant debris after the crop is desirable.

ROOT ROT DISEASE OF PERIWINKLE

The affected plants show yellowing of leaves and gradual drying of branches. The infected plants do not collapse immediately. The affected plants when uprooted, severe rotting of roots was observed. Nagata and Aragaki, (1989) Observed disintegration of cortical region of the plant. In advanced stage of disease, complete collar region of the plant get disintegrated and plants get collapsed. The affected plant parts fell off on the soil surface which acts as primary inoculums for newly sown crop.

The Causal Organism

The rot disease of Periwinkle is caused by *Pythium aphanidermatum.* (Eds) Fitz. The pathogen isolated from infected plant part PDA (potato Dextrose Ager) medium was well developed, cottony white, with hyphal diameter of 7.4µm. No zoosporangia seen on the PDA medium. Nagata and Aragaki. (1989) observed small zoosporangia in liquid culture media. The zoosporangia were small bud like structures arised from the main sporangial elements. The zoosporangia are lemon shaped structures that consists of many zoospores of 8-9 µm. diameter. Numerous oogonia were observed at the terminal ends of lateral hyphae in laboratory culture. The oogonia were smooth walled 18-30 µm in diameter. The antheridia were developed on the hyphal branches adjacent to the oogonium. The position of antheridium was terminal or intercalary. The antheridia were somewhat elongated, broadly clavate cells of the size 9-10 × 8-13 µm.

Disease Cycle

The fungus Pythium is a natural inhabitant of soil. It is a root infecting weak parasite. The pathogen produces numerous oospores that overwinters and remain alive in soil for longer duration. Soil moisture is important for its growth and development. The zoospores spread along with irrigated water and are responsible for secondary infection. The fungus produce oospores and chlamydospores persist for many years.

Disease management:

1. A complete control of disease is difficult because the *Pythium* survive on a variety of plant residue in soil.
2. Soil fumigation with Chloropicrin and Methyl bromide is recommended against diseases caused by Pythium sp.
3. Low concentration of Dexon is applied.
4. Crop rotation is another method of reducing inoculums potential, in soil.
5. Seed treatment with Trichoderma harzianum used to manage damping off disease.
6. Some cultured practices recommended such as thin sowing of seeds found successful.

DISEASES REPORTED ON PERIWINKLE (*Catharanthus roseus*)

Sl. No.	Disease	Pathogen
1.	Leaf spot	*Alternaria longipes*
2.	Anthracnose	*Colletotrichum capsici*
3.	Leaf spot	*C. gloesporioides*
4.	Powdery mildew	*Laveillula taurica*
5.	Root rot	*Macrophomina phaseolina*
6.	Leaf spot	*Myrothecium roridum*
7.	Shoot blight	*Ophiobolus catharanthicola*
8.	Root rot	Phytopthora colocasiae
9.	Stem rot	Rhizoctonia solani

5. DISEASES OF HOLY BASIL

English name : Holy basil

Botanical name : *Ocimum sanctum*

Family : Labiatae

Indian name : Tulsi

The holy basil (*Ocimum sanctum* Linn.) is a branched, erect aromatic herb of about 70-75 in height which is covered with hairy trichomes. The leaves are egg shaped, Smooth, 2.5cm in length, green or violet in colour. Flowers small purple or reddish arranged on slender spikes. Fruits small with reddish seeds.

Holy Basil

It is a small, erect, stout, erect aromatic herb. Entire plant may have trichomes (hairs). Leaves tender, egg shaped, and smooth petiolate with reticulate venations. The flowers reddish or purplish occur in compact cluster in verticelaster type of inflorescence or slender spikes. The taste of leaf is bitter and pungent. The plant is grown in India as a medicinal plant. It is the native of India and spread all over the world. The leaves contain essential oil which is antiseptic, antimicrobial & medicinally valuable.

Medicinal Uses

The leaves are nerve tonic and memory enhancer. The leaves strengthen the stomach. The seeds are highly nourishing. Seeds also increased the volume of urine. Leaves help to get relief from fever. Sore throat can be relieved by gargling with basil leaf boiled water. The basil leaves are regarded as an anti stress agent. The leaves are useful in treatment of respiratory disorder. Basil leaves strengthen the kidnies. In case of kidney stones, the juice of basil & honey is given to the patient for six months. Basil leaves are effective against cardiac diseases and weakness. It reduces the level of blood cholesterol. The leaves effective against fever, cough, cold, vomiting and diarrhea in children. The paste of leaf effective against mouth ulcer. The basil leaf paste in effective against ringworm and various skin diseases. The leaves beneficial in teeth disorders. Dry powder of leaf used as toothpaste. It is mixed with mustard oil and applied to teeth. It is an excellent remedy to maintain dental health. The decoction of leaves can give against headache.

The leaves eaten as nerve tonic & to sharpen memory. A fruit possesses soothing effect on the skin. Leave eaten to cure many types of fevers, malaria & Dengue. Boiled leave extract used in case of sore throat, this plant is useful in respiratory disorders, asthma, cough, Influenza, cold, kidney stones, heart disorders, stress, children ailments, mouth infections, insect bites, skin disorders, Eye disorders, Teeth disorders & headaches etc.

DOWNEY MILDEW OF HOLY-BASIL

The downy mildew of *Ocimum* has been known in Asian countries for a number of years.The disease is not of major importance, large brown lesions are developed on the leaves, and the lower surface of affected region of leaf shows violet to white coloured growth of fungus. In severe cases of disease development the entire leaf may die and fell off. Downey mildew is a damaging disease causing drying and heavy defoliation of leaves.

Symptoms

At the initial stage the leaves of infected plant becomes slightly chlorotic, especially near the central vein of the leaf. The leaves show a typical grayish growth of fungus within 4-5 days of infection. The growth occurs on the lower surface of the corresponding spots. Later on the chlorotic patches turn necrotic hence a large blighted patches are seen on the affected leaf. The moderate air temperature & high humidity stimulates the disease development. Garibaldi, *et.al,* (2004) observed that during the poor circulation of air the lower leaves were severely get affected by the disease.

The Causal Organism:

The downey mildew of *Oscimum* (*Ocimum sanctum* Linn.) is caused by *Pernospora* species. Garibaldi, *et.al,* (2004) explained the causal agent of downey mildew of basil in the following way. The conidiophores are branched. The branching is two to seven times. The length of conidiophores is about 50 to 500 um (average 350 µm). Each conidiophore ended with sterigmata which is bearing a single conidium. The conidia measure 15 to 25 × 20 to 35 µm (average 22 × 28 µm). The conidium is unicellular elliptical structure those appear grayish in hues masses. The pathogen was identified as a Pernospora species.

Disease management:

1. Many control experiments with inorganic and organic fungicides show a reduction in the amount of disease.
2. Eradication of highly infected plants as a source of inoculum is important in some sections.
3. Use disease free seeds for sowing purpose.

ALTERNARIA LEAF SPOT OF HOLY-BASIL

It is a most widespread disease which is found and most destructive on the mature plants. The leaf spot of basil in one of the important disease occurs mostly in tropical regions of the world. The disease affects the leaves, twig and stem and can result into heavy loss under favorable weather conditions.

Symptoms

Initially one or two small, spots are formed on the leaf which are spherical or irregular in outline. Keep observation reveled rings, each ring pattern indicate growth and reproduction of the pathogen inside the host tissue. Initially the spots are yellowish but later become dark black coloured with a yellow zone around it. The infection spread by insect visitors or by other mechanical agency.

The seedlings also get infected at a very initial stage of its development due to soil borne spores of the pathogen. The affected cotyledons get shriveled and dry up. The partially affected seedlings develop in to a weak plant with delicate stems and branches which breaks off easily. The infection spread gradually all over the plant that produces rough dark coloured, sunken concentric spots on the stems. The affected leaves dry and fell off. All the species of basil found to be susceptible for the disease. The warm moist weather favors the infection.

The Causal Organism

The disease is caused by *Alternaria alternata* (Fr.) Keisserle. The colony of *Alternaria alternata* on PDA medium produces fluffy growth with whitish center. The fungus consists of highly branched septate hyphae which turn grayish black at maturity. The conidia consist of 1-6 septa. The conidia measure about 13-46.2 × 7.2-10.1 µm. The conidia may have beak and basal region is bulbous broad. The size of beak range from 3.0-10.0µm. The spore also consists of some longitudinal septa.

Discasc Cycle

Infected plant debris acts as inoculum because the pathogens survive on dead organic matter for years. The seeds of affected plant also carry the spores on seed surface. Soil and air also play very important, role as it carries Alternaria spores. This fungus is having a broad spectrum of collateral hosts.

Disease management:

1. Plant debris after harvest should be collected and burned.
2. Avoid crowded plantation.
3. No resistant varieties available

COLLETOTRICHUM LEAF SPOT OF HOLY-BASIL

The leaf spot of Ocimum caused by *Colletotrichum* is a very destructive disease and if the infection takes place in the early stages of plant growth then the plants suffer very badly. It is an important disease particularly during high humidity and moderate temperature.

Symptoms

The disease appeared on the leaves as circular to angular spots of 1-6 mm in diameter. The spots are purplish in colour. Gradually the spots increase in diameter. Eventually multiple spots on a single leaf will merge leading to an extensive destruction of leaf tissue. The infection becomes severe during warm environment, (Thakur, 1973 b). Heavy defoliation during severity of disease is common. The mature spots on the leaf consist of black dot like fruiting bodies that are called as acervuli.

The Causal Organism

The anthracnose disease of holy basil is caused by *Colletotrichum gloesporioides* (Renz) sacc. (Perfect stage: *Glomerella cingulata* (Stonem) spauld). The pathogenic organism is *Colletotrichum gloesporioides.* The mycelium is branched consists of sparsely branched hyphae which turn dark in colour at maturity. There are numerous acervuli are scattered on the affected region of the leaf. The conidiophores are short, simple hyaline structures which occur in compact groups. The conidiophores bear a single conidium at its tip. There are the straight vertical hyphae present between the conidiophores which are called as setae. The conidia are oblong with blunt ends and measure about 12-16mm in size.

The highly infected region of the host shows numerous acervuli which are globose with an ostiole protruding out of the ruptured epidermis. The acervulus consists of a series of club shaped asci. Each ascus is filled by spindle shaped haploid ascospores.

The fungus produces conidiophores of variable length. The conidiophores are 1-4 celled, unbranched, brown in colour and slightly broad at the base and tapering towards the apex. The conidia produced at the apex of the conidiophores. The conidia are ellipsoidal with rounded apex and narrow truncate base which are hyaline uninucleate aseptate structures (Papas and Elena, 1997).

The pathogen produces numerous spores which are blown in air, which acts as source of inoculum. The infected twigs and leaves fell off on the ground which acts as source of inoculum. The pathogen has broad spectrum of host range. The rotted fruits are sorted and thrown away during storage periods which contaminate air. The air spora is an important source of inoculum.

Disease Cycle

Spread of the disease occurs through the contaminated seeds. The insect visitors also carry on the acervuli to healthy leaf. The infected plants residue retains the pathogen for long duration that also acts as an important source of inoculum. Soil is also an important source of this pathogen as its fruiting bodies survive in soil for long time.

Disease management:

1. The external seed borne pathogenic microflora can be washed off when the seeds dipped off in hot water (45ºC) for 10 minutes.
2. The seeds should be selected for sowing purpose from disease free plant.
3. There are no resistant varieties are available against the Colletotrichum leaf spot disease of Oscimum.
4. Spraying of any copper fungicide can restrict the growth of pathogenic flora.
5. There should be proper distance between the mango trees to avoid anthracnose disease is essential.
6. Collect the infected leaves and fruits and dug it more than one foot deep in the soil.
7. Sattar (1946) found spraying of Bordeaux mixture against Anthracnose disease of mango.

WILT DISEASE OF HOLY-BASIL

The pathogen has a wide geographic distribution in warm temperate humid tropical & subtropical regions. It survives as a saprophyte in the soil in absence of proper host plant.

Symptoms

The pathogen is a soil borne fungus that enters the host plant though the wounds or root scars or injuries caused by insect bites. Initially the affected plant becomes yellowish. The leaves lose their turgidity and hang down. As the disease advances the collar region of the plant just above the soil surface turn black in colour. The tissue from this region get replaced by hues growth of the pathogenic fungus and sometimes a whitish cottony growth of fungus may be observed around the collar region of the plant. The internal tissue of the plant becomes red due to pigments secreted by the intracellular fungal pathogen. The roots turn from dark brown to black.

A watery fluid comes out from the infected roots because of degradation of cortex tissue by the pathogen. In case of older plants, the affected root hairs get easily separated from the main root system. All the root hairs turn dark brown in colour. The leaves dry and fell off before maturity. Drying and defoliation causes death of the entire plant. Such an affected plants looks like brooms.

The Causal Organism

The wilt disease of holy basil is caused by the fungal pathogen *Fusarium oxysporum* f.sp. *udum* (Butter) Snyder and Hansen.

The mycelium of *Fusarium oxysporum* is highly branched that consists of septate hyphae that are hyaline. It is a soil borne facultative parasite. When the infective quantity of inoculum comes in contact with root system of the host starts the infection. After entry into the host, the pathogen may be intercellular but later on it becomes intracellular. It shows extensive growth in the vascular tissues. The colour of fungal colony on PDA (Potato Dextrose Agar) medium appear whitish cottony. The sexual stage of the fungus is unknown. It reproduces by producing numerous conidia. In presence of enough nutrition and favorable environmental conditions, many of the hyphal threads act as conidiophores. The conidiophores cut off conidia at its tip. The *Fusarium oxysporum* produces two types of conidia. The small sized conidia termed as microconidia and the large sized conidia termed as microconidia. The microconidia are small elliptical or slightly curved, unicellular with one or two septa, thin walled that measure about 5-15 × 2-4mm in size. The macroconidia are curved, thin walled 3-4 septate, which measure15-50 × 3-5mm Avasthi, et. al, (2013). During unfavorable environmental conditions, the fungal hyphae produce thick walled, round spores, one in each compartment of hyphal thread. These spores are termed as chlamydospores. The chlamydospores are thick walled spores that survive for several years on dead organic matter or plant residue in the soil.

Inoculum

The pathogen is a facultative parasite that means it is a parasite when the host is not available in the field it survive as a saprophyte on any type of organic matter available in field soil for year after year and in the presence of proper host plant it causes disease. Such parasites are termed as facultative parasite. The soil is the source of inoculum. The infected root system (plant residue) remains in the harvested field that acts the as the inoculum. The seeds of infected plant carry the mycoflora, in such cases seed is the source of primary inoculum. The pathogen is a soil borne fungus. This is a facultative parasite that remains in soil on plant residue for several years, and in presence of host that infect the root system of pigeon pea and causes wilt disease. Mc Rae, (1917) reported 8-20 years of survival of this pathogen in soil. Hence, it is highly difficult to manage disease by crop rotation method.

First of all the fungus infect root hairs from which that gradually migrate to the large vessels. The symptoms of wilt appear when infection in more than 50%. The intensity of disease is more in the field where the previous crop was the same host. After harvest of the crop, the root stalks remain in the field which acts as a source of inoculum for the next year's crop. The seed also carry the spores or hyphal thread as an inoculum.

Disease cycle:

The fungal pathogen Fusarium responsible for this disease is soil born in nature. It is a saprophytic fungus which can survive in soil on a variety of crop residue. The fungus produces numerous intercalary thick walled spores which are called as chlamydospores. The chlamydospores are drought resistant spores which perennates in soil for longer duration that acts as primary inoculums. The Fusarium produces abundant conidia as an asexual spore which can cause infection. The pathogen enters the host through wounds or root hairs.

Disease management:

1. The pathogen is a borne fungus that survives as a saprophyte on affected plant residue. It has a wide spectrum of host range hence crop rotation helps to avoid disease intensity for same extent.
2. Remove the entire effected plants carefully and collect all fallen leaves and burn it carefully that helps to reduce disease intensity for some extent.
3. The seeds should be disease free which are used for sowing purpose.
4. No resistant varieties of Ocimum species available to fight against *Fusarium.*

CERCOSPORA LEAF SPOT OF HOLY-BASIL

The disease is common on Oscimum plant in all the parts of tropical and subtropical region of India. It is the most devastating foliar pathogen of Oscimum. There are reports of different species of Cercospora causing leaf spot disease of Oscimum plants from different parts of India. Agrios, (2005) reported leaf spot of Oscimum due to *Cercospora conescens* from Jammu & Kashmir. Munjal, *et.al,* (1959) observed leaf spot of Oscimum due to infection of *Cercospora ocimicola.*

Symptoms

The symptoms of the disease consist of more or less circular lesions on the upper surface of the leaf. Initially the spots are in the form of small yellowish round dots on the leaf. Gradually the yellow dots increase in size and produces a large dried spots which are up to 0.4-1 cm in diameter.

Each spot become brownish due to death of the cells. The spot mostly show a ring of chlorotic zone around it. The centre of the spot may be darker colored than the peripheral region of the spot. In case of mature lesions the centre of the spot turns to grayish in colour. The grey colour of the center of the spot is the indication of Sporulation of the internal mycelium. In severe cases the elongated lesions are seen on the petioles. The affected leaves become yellow, weak, and get dried. The dried leaves fell off on the ground carrying inoculum of the pathogen for next season. It has found that the spots were many and more distinct on the mature leaves.

The Causal Organism

The responsible pathogen for the leaf spot disease of Oscimum (*Oscimum sanctum*) is *Cercospora ocimicola* Petrak & Cif. The mycelium consists of profusely branched septate hyphae. The hyphae grow between the host cells. During development of the pathogen in the host tissue the hyphal threads gets deposited just below the host epidermis which is called as mycelial mat. The mycelial mats at the mature stage produce groups of coloured conidiophores. Sometimes the growing conidiophores responsible to rupture the epidermal layer of the host. The clusters of the conidiophores emerge through the stomata. The conidiophores produce hyaline elongated multiseptate conidia. The conidia are variable in shape that varies from 54-167 um in length. The conidia germinate immediately at 22 ^{0}C temperatures. The conidia are carried away from the affected region of the spot by the rain water flash, wind or by the other mechanical agency to a long distance. Misra, et. al, (1969) the infection to the new host takes place through the air borne conidia.

Source of Inoculum

The air around the infected field consists of numerous conidia. The conidia present in the air come in contact with the host leaf. The conidium germinate on the leaf surface in the presence of small amount of moisture and the germ tube enters the host tissue as a result produce spots on the leaf. The infected plant debris also acts as a source of inoculum. There are reports from different parts of India that the seeds carry the dormant mycelium. The internally or externally seed borne conidia causes disease when the contaminated seeds used for the sowing purpose. The disease also reported from Bangalore Karnataka.

Disease management:

1. The pathogen survive on infected plant debris & seed, hence field sanitation is beneficial.
2. The crop rotation is recommended to reduce disease intensity.

3. Use of disease free seeds for sowing purpose reduces disease in the field.
4. The fungicides like Mancozeb& Copper oxychloride are recommended against Cercospora leaf spot.

DISEASES REPORTED ON HOLY-BASIL (*Ocimum sanctum* L).

Sl. No.	Disease	Pathogen
1.	Leaf rust	*Aecidium ocimi*
2.	Leaf blight	*Alternaria alternata*
3.	Leaf spot	*Cercospora ocimicola*
4.	Leaf spot	*Corynespora cassicola*
5.	Powdery mildew	*Erysiphe biocillata*
6.	Powdery mildew	*Oidium ocimi*
7.	Leaf spot	*Phyllosticta ocimicola*
8.	Leaf rust	*Puccinia thomasiana*
9.	Root rot	*Rhizoctonia bataticola*
10.	Charcoal rot	*Rhizoctonia solani*

6. THE DISEASES OF MARGOSA

English name : Margosa
Botanical name : *Azadiracta indica*
Family : Meliaceae
Indian name : Neem

The margosa or neem (*Azadiracta indica* A. Juss.) is large tree very common in India. It is evergreen with 1 to 10/5 meters in height. The leaves are divided into numerous leaflets. Flowers small, white in armillary bunches and about 1.2 – 1.8 cm large green or yellow fruits with a seed inside. It is large evergreen tree with many branches, woody stems & tap root system. Stem solid, cylindrical, glabrous. Leaves pinnately compound, alternate, estipulate, leaflets oblique based, serrate margin, venation reticulate unicostate, Inflorescence axillary cymose panicle. Flower pedicellate, bracteolate, complete, bisexual & hypogynous. Calyx with 5 sepals & corolla with 5 petals. Stamens 10, monodelphous, Ovary tricarpellary, superior, placed on disc, with 1-2 ovules in each locule on axil placenta. Fruit one seeded drupe, exalbuminous.

Medicinal Use

It is considered as an air purifier and a preventive against material fever and cholera. The leaves are useful in relieving flatulence, promoting the removal of catarrhal matter and phlegm, from the bronchial tubes. Bark is used as bitter tonic & a stimulant. The gum has soothing effect as the skin and mucous membranes. It is very effective in piles, & chronic material fevers, leprosy, skin disorders. It step hair calling &helps re-growth of faller hairs. It is used in treatment of right blindness, eye pain. Steam lamentation with neem decoction provides immediate comfort in case of earache. Cleaning of teeth regularly with a neem twig prevents gum diseases. It firms up loose teeth, relieves toothache, evacuates the bad odour and protects the mouth from various infections. Neem leaf extract also helps to cure pimples & acne.

Margosa (Neem)

WOOD ROT DISEASE OF MARGOSA (NEEM)

Wood rot disease of neem (*Azadiracta indica*) is caused due to the growth of the fungus called as *Fomes senex*. The wood rot disease is a very common rot disease found in India. There are reports of wood rot of neem from different parts of India (Anonymous, 1917).

Symptoms

The wood rot is a most destructive to young trees of up to 10 years old. The infected trees trunk internally turns reddish brown due to interaction of the hyphal threads of the pathogen with the host tissue. The affected plants die within one or two year during severe cases of disease development. The older trees also get affected. The fungus spared within the host tissue causing gradual rotting of heart wood until the trunk becomes hollow. The fruiting bodies or sporophores are not seen on the external region of the wood of the infected living plant. The infection occurs under the soil surface invading the root system especially at the site of root tips which found deeper in the soil. The infected root system get killed and broken easily. The pathogen enters the root through the injured region on the root or invades the soft tissue present at the root tip region. The pathogen gradually trnaslocated in upward direction that reaches inside the tree trunk through the xylem tissue. The affected root system gets completely destroyed (Alam, 1993). There are very thin mycelial pads get accumulated under the bark of the infected root. The roots of the older trees shows rotted centre. In the stumps, decay of the heart wood is very common. In severe cases the wood is decayed till it becomes like a honeycombed in appearance. Small cavities are formed which are broken easily. The sapwood remains solid and functioning.

The Pathogen

The wood rot disease of neem (*Azadiracta indica)* is caused by *Foams senex* nees & Mont. The mycelium consists of highly branched septate hyphae. The fruiting bodies or sporophores develop on the dead region of the tree trunk. The fruiting bodies are bracket shaped structures with great variation in size and shape. The dorsal surface of the fruiting body is brownish with whitish shade and the ventral surface is porous that appear light pink in colour. The fruiting bodies consist of pores. The wall of each pore is made up of fertile layer of fungal hyphae. The fertile hyphae bear a series of basidia. Each basidium produces four basidiospores. The basidiospores are hyaline, oval structures. The sporophores remain intact on an affected stump for year after years. The disease development is favored at the temperature of about 23°C. (Anonymous, 1950).

Mechanism of Infection

The pathogen is a soil borne. The soil born fungal hyphae of the pathogen comes in contact with the broken region of the host roots and enters in the host plant. That is trnaslocated to the inner hard wood through medullary rays. The infectious hyphae also enter the tracheids through the pores. By the time the tissue of the heart wood get enveloped by the dark, thick walled hyphal mat from all the sides. Later on the affected heart wood turns black, pitted in appearance in section. The affected wood becomes light in weight. Sometimes the black persistent spots appear on the affected wood.

Disease management:

1. Apply Bordeaux mixture on affected region.
2. Remove fruiting bodies of fungus from affected region of tree & destroy carefully to avoid intensity of inoculums of pathogen.

CERCOSPORA LEAF-SPOT OF MARGOSA (NEEM)

The disease is very common in all parts of the tropical and subtropical region of India. There are reports of Cercospora leaf spot disease of neem from different parts of India which is caused by different species. Tilak and Rao (1966 b) observed *Cercospora leucosticta* responsible for leaf spot of disease of neem (Azadiracta indica) at Poona Maharashtra. Griwal, et al (1974) reported leaf spot of neem due to C. *leucostictaat* Gualior. Rao (1969) isolated *C. meliae* from leaf spots of neem from Andhra Pradesh.

Symptoms

Symptoms on the leaves consists of numerous brown spots of various sizes especially son the upper surface of the leaf. Initially the spots are light green in colour that gradually turns yellow to brown. The spots are restricted on leaflets only. The affected leaves dry up. The affected leaflets fell off due to excessive spotting. The centre of the spot turns grayish due to profuse growth of the pathogenic fungal hyphae.

The Causal Organism

The pathogen responsible for the leaf spot disease of neem is *Cercospora leucosticta* (Uppal, *et.al.* 1936). The mycelium is septate, hightly branched and olivacious in colour. The intercellular mycelium at the centre of the spot gives rise to small erect conidiophores. The conidiophores are club shaped structures. The conidiophores bear conidia which are born singly or in a row of two or three. The conidia are septate. The clusters of conidiophores along with conidia come out through the broken epidermal region of the host at the center of spot. The conidia are dispersed by insect visitors, wind, and rain splash and by other mechanical means.

Disease Cycle

The fungus overwinters on the infected plant debris in the form of mycelium or conidia. The hyphal threads also carried on seed coat. The infected seeds result in diseased seedlings. In the favorable environment, overwintering mycelium in plant residue starts producing conidia which are easily disseminated by air currents or irrigation water or rain splashes or insect visitors. The disease mostly appears in the month of November - December but severe disease development takes place in the month of March-April. High humidity is an essential factor for hues sporulation. Moderate temperature is highly favorable for disease development.

Source of Inoculum

The wind born conidia reach the host easily and cause disease. The soil also acts as an important source of inoculum that consists of infected plant debris.

Disease management:

1 No control measures suggested.

DISEASES REPORTED ON MARGOSA (*Azadiracta indica*)

Sl. No.	Disease	Pathogen
1.	Powdery mildew	*Acrosporium sp.*
2.	Leaf spot	*Cercospora leucosticta*
3.	Wood rot	*Fomes senex*
4.	Powdery mildew	*Oidium azadirachtae*
5.	Wood rot	*Pellicularia salmonicolor*
6.	Wood rot	*Polyporus gilvus*

7. DISEASES OF ISABGULA

English name : Isabgula
Botanical name : *Plantago ovata*
Family : Plantaginaceae
Indian name : Isabgol

The Ishabgula (*Plantago ovata* Linn.) plant is almost a stem-less small herb which is covered with dense and soft hairy growth. It has very narrow leaves, Flowers minute in oval or cylindrical spikes. The upper half of its fruits open like a lid and its seeds are boat shaped.

It is a small herb, appear stem less. It is covered with dense & soft trichomes which are hairy, shining. The leaves are very narrow. Flowers are very small which are arranged in cylindrical spikes. The upper half part of its fruits green like a lid and the seeds are boat shaped. It is the native of India. It is extensively used as medicines since ancient times.

Medicinal Uses

The seeds are laxative seeds act as a diuretic and have soothing effect on the skin. The husk of seed is called as isaphula, obtained by crushing the seeds. The husk is taken with water against constipation. The seeds are particularly useful in chronic constipation characterized by spasms. Seeds are popular remedy for several kinds of chronic dysentery and diarrhea. It is beneficial in treating abdominal pain. The husk should be soaked in milk & given to the patient twice a day. Seeds are one of the most effective remedies for piles. Seeds oil prevents arteriosclerosis. It reduces serum cholesterol in rabbits. It is helpful in the treatment of gonorrhea because of soothing properties. A paste of seed prepared in vinegar is useful against rheumatism. The husk protects the lining mucosa and helps in the healing of ulcers.

The seeds are cooling & mildly laxative. They act as a diuretic & also have a soothing effect or the skin & mucous membrane. It in the best medicine for the treatment of constipation. The seeds are popular for several types of chronic dysentery & diarrhea. Ispaghula is useful in treating frequent griping in the belly caused by stomach ulcers. The seeds are most effective remedies for piles. The oil of seeds prevents arteriosclerosis. Ispaghula is very useful in the treatment of gonorrhea. The seeds oil with vinegar in useful for the treatment of rheumatism and gout.

LEAF BLIGHT DISEASE OF ISABGULA

The leaf blight disease of Ishabgula (*Plantago ovata*) was reported a very destructive disease in Plantago growing areas. The symptoms appear on the leaves. The older leaves are more susceptible for the attack of the respective pathogen. The older and matured leaves get severely affected. Initially very small faded green yellowish spots appear on the leaf surface and gradually the spots increase in size. Mostly the spots are circular in out line. The spots consist of brown dead tissue at the centre. The growth rings of the fungus can be seen within the spot. Many necrotic spot coalesce to form a large patch on the leaf. In severe cases maximum area of the leaf get covered by large necrotic patches of irregular margin. The infection was favored by high temperature and humidity. The affected leaves shrivel and dry up. Drying of plants and blackening of seeds occur (Roy, 1974).

The Causal Organism

The blight disease of Ishabgula is caused by *Alternaria alternata* (Fr.) Keissler. The mycelium is highly branched, septate, olivacious brown in colour. It bears conidiophores in groups or randomly produced from the fertile mycelial mat. The unbranched septate hyphae act as conidiophores. The conidiophores may have many conidial scars. The conidia are produced in the form of chain. The conidia are ovoid in shapes which are having 3-8 transverse and 2-4 vertical septa. The conidia are 2.62 × 9.18 μm in size. The conidia possess broad base and a short narrow beak measuring 2.5 × 2.5μm. Goal and Patel (1967) observed the conidial germination takes place either from terminal or intercalary cells. The multicellular conidia of Alternaria remain in soil along with the infected host debris. The contaminated soil and seeds of infected plant acts as primary inoculum of the pathogen.

Disease Cycle

The spread of the disease occurs through the seed and soil. Air borne spores of *Alternaria alternata* isolated by Tilak, *et.al*, (1970). The fungal hyphae survive on seed surface as well as inside the seed. The fungus produces conidia that are blown away by wind. The wind borne spore also causes infection in presence of contact of proper host leaf. The pathogen also survives for longer duration in soil on infected plant debris. The spores are transferred from one place to pathogen overwinters in the soil on affected plant parts.

Disease management:

1. Avasthi, *et.al*, (2013) recommended 0.25 × Mancozeb against leaf blight caused by Alternaria alternate.
2. The clove extract found effective against Alternaria alternata.
3. Wayne Nishizima (2010), recommended spraying of Chlorothalonil against Alternaria blight.
4. The field sanitation found effective to reduce disease intensity. Spray recommended fungicides at initial stage of disease development.

DOWNEY MILDEW OF ISABGULA

Extensive damage of the *Plantago* takes place due to downey mildew disease. The downey mildew is a serious disease of Ishabgula causing heavy loss of this medicinal plant. The downey mildew initiates at the time of emergence of inflorescence, (Desai, 1981).

Symptom

The downy mildew is also called as die back or leaf blight. The first symptom of the disease starts as a small pale yellow spot on the leaves. The gradual increase of the spot produces a large patch covering most of the leaf surface. The chlorotic patch on the upper surface of the leaf appears yellow coloured and the corresponding lower surface of leaf show the off white coloured growth of fungus. The downey growth of the pathogenic fungus consists of hyphae, sporangiophore and sporangia. The infected leaves get curled off and dry up. The infected leaves droop off by air currents. In severe cases all the leaves and twigs turn necrotic and in the advanced stage of disease the entire plant turns blighted. Kapoor and Chaudhary, (1976) observed abundance of the oospores on the infected plant debris.

The Causal Organism

The downey mildew disease of Ishabgula is caused by *Pernospora plantaginis* (Trautwein, *et.al*, 2000). The mycelium is highly branched intercellular produce haustoria. The slender hyphae which are erect, stout acts as sporangiophore. The sporangiophores are grayish yellow coloured emerging singly or in groups. The groups of sporangiophore protrude out through the stomatal opening of lower surface of leaf. The sporangiophores are dichotomously branched. Hence each sporangiophore consists of two sporangia at its tip. Patel, (1973) observed the sub-hyaline broadly elliptical to sub-globose sporangia with an average size of 35 × 22 µm. The zoospore formation was not seen. The sporangia germinate by producing hyaline germ tube. The optimum temperature for the germination was around 20 °C. The relative humidity 85 per cent favors the germination of most of the sporangia in the field. The germinated sporangia can re-infect the healthy plant or plant part.

Disease Cycle

The pathogen overwinters as systemic mycelium in affected plant part, and oospores survive in soil, which acts as most important source of primary inoculums. The oospores are also associated on surface of seed. the oospore germinate and the germ tube usually forms one aspersorium over the stomatal opening. The pathogen enters the leaf through stomata.

High humidity favors production of abundant sporangia. The sporangia remain viable for 3 or more days. The sporangia transfer from one place to other by air currents.

Disease management:

1. The spraying of recommended fungicide during early stage of disease development is essential.
2. Certain copper fungicides suggested against downey mildew of Ishabgula.
3. Most of the foliar fungicides are effective against downey mildew of Ishabgula but it should be applied before development of symptoms.

DAMPING OFF OF ISABGULA SEEDLINGS

The seedlings of Ishabgula (*Plantago ovata*) were found more susceptible than the mature plants. The damping off of seedling occurs before emergence of seedling above soil surface. That is also termed as pre-emergence damping off. In case of pre-emergence damping off, the soil borne pathogen enters the radical of the seedling. The intercellular growth disturbs the normal metabolic processes of the seedling hence the withering of seedling occurs. The withered seedlings die before they reach the soil surface. In case of post-emergence damping off disease, a small water soaked brown spots appear on the collar region of the seedlings very close to the soil surface. The blackening of collar region increases. Simultaneously the newly formed pair of leaf becomes yellowish. In advanced stage yellowing and drying of entire seedling is common. Patel, (1973) reported high temperature & humidity at the time of sowing of seeds favors the damping off disease of seedlings.

The Causal Organism

There are number of soil borne pathogens causing damping off of seedling has been reported by different workers.

1. *Pythium ultimum* trow
2. *Rhizoctonia solani* kuh.
3. *Fusarium oxysporum* (Sch) syn & Hans

- **The *Pythium ultimum*:** The mycelium is woolly, well developed, consists of coenocytic hyphae that are 2.8-7.5 µm in diameter. The sporangiophore produces lobulate, toruloid sporangia which measure 500 × 20 µm in size. At the time of germination the sporangia produces a vesicle in which zoospores are produced. The fungus produces spherical, smooth walled oospores which may be terminal and intercalary in position. The fungus produces antheridia on fertile hyphae. The antheridia are terminal or intercalary in position. The oospores are thick walled, aplerotic, mostly 15-30 µm in diameter.

- **Disease cycle of *Pythium ultimum*:** The pathogenic fungus is soil inhabitant and is capable of growing and surviving on the plant residue which is left in field soil during harvest period. The fungus produces numerous oospores on the decaying matter. The other predisposing factors are changes in the nitrogen level of soil, excess irrigation; water logging in field soil, poor physical conditions of soil promotes intensity of inoculum of the pathogen in the soil that acts as source of inoculum for disease development during next season. Younger plants were found more susceptible for infection. However lower or higher temperatures restricts the disease development. The sporangia of pathogen are disseminated by rain drops, irrigation water and by other mechanical agencies.
- **The *Rhizoctonia solani*:** The mycelium of Rhizoctonia solani is septate and branched. Hyphae are up to 12 µm wide and 250 µm long. The septa are of the dolipore type. In culture sclerotia develop within 5-6 days. The size of sclerotia ranges from 1 to 3 µm in diameters. The sclerotia consists of brown barrel shaped monilioid cells measuring up to 30 µm in width.
- **Disease cycle of *Rhizoctonia solani:*** The pathogen remains in soil on infected plant debris. The pathogen survives from one season to another in the form of mycelium or sclerotia. The sclerotia of the fungus are highly resistant to adverse environmental conditions, such as high frost and high temperature. It occurs in many types of soils and once established remains in that area for indefinite time. The hyphal threads and spores spread through wind, irrigated water or any other mechanical agencies from infected to healthy soil and host plant. In presence of favorable host and environmental conditions it causes disease.
- **The *Fusarium oxysporum*:** In culture, four different states like septate mycelium, microconidia which measure 2.5-4 × 6-15µm and macroconidia that are typically fusiform, hyaline and multiseptate which measure 3.5-5.5 × 22-25 µm in size. The fungus produces chlamydospores which are spherical and hyaline. The cultural and pathogenic variability is common in the Fusarium oxysporum.

- **Disease cycle of *Fusarium oxysporum:*** The pathogenic fungus is soil borne and also survives in the seed coat. The fungus produces thick walled chlamydospores which are drought resistant. The chlamydospores remain in soil for longer duration which acts as inoculum. The pathogen is not seed borne but it can be carried on the seed coat. The pathogen does not reproduce on living plants but produce large number of microconidia, macroconidia and chlamydospores in and on dead stems and roots. Once the pathogen enters the field it may remain for many years. The soil borne conidia penetrate the plant through root hairs. The pathogen enters through the cut surface.

Disease management:

1. The cultural practices recommended to manage Fusarium wilt of Ishabgula are crop rotation, deep ploughing to expose field soil to sunrays during summer days.
2. The disease can be reduced by sterilization of soil with recommended fumigants.
3. Dip the seeds in the solution of Carbendazim before sowing.
4. The biological control agents such as bacillus found effective against Fusarium oxysporum.

POWDERY MILDEW OF ISABGULA

The powdery mildew of Plantago has been found more common during humid temperate weather. The responsible fungus is ectoparasites that can affect the plants of all the age group. The disease first appears on the leaves as small white dots. The whitish dots of mycelium increase gradually forming a large whitish patch. In severe cases whole leaf get enveloped by the whitish growth of fungus. The whitish growth of fungus was also observed on the stem and twigs except root system. The whitish patch appears first on the upper surface of the leaf but spread all over the plant including lower leaf surface and inflorescence during favorable environmental factors. A keen observation of externally borne mycelium of fungus consists of highly branched hyphae with black dot like fruiting bodies on the affected regions of the plant. There are reports of powdery mildew diseases of another medicinal plants caused by the same pathogen i.e. *Erysiphe cinchoracearum* from different parts of country (Rathore & Rathore, 1996).

The Causal Organism

The powdery mildew of Ishabgula is caused by *Erysiphe cinchoracearum* D.C. (Anonymous, 1925). The mycelium is highly branched that occur all over the host surface. The hyphae are septate that consists of one nucleus in each cell. The pathogen grows fast and covers maximum area of the host plant surface externally within a short period. The hyphal net bears numerous straight hyphae with two to three celled that acts as conidiophores. The conidiophores are multicellular unbranched filaments produces oval conidia one after the other in basipetal succession at its tip. The pathogen produces abundance of conidia as a struggle for existence on the earth, because the pathogen is an ecto-parasite hence there is possibility of destruction of major quantity of spores.

The superficial pathogenic fungus produce black dot like fruiting bodies that are randomly distributed. The black dots like bodies are called as cleistothecium. The cleistothecium is a large globular rough walled structure with numerous hairs like appendages of unequal size hanging from the cleistothecia wall. The fruiting body enclosed a series of club shaped asci at the bottom. Each ascus consists of oval unicellular uninucleate haploid ascospores.

The cleistothecia are tough walled structures that remain in soil for a long duration. The fungus produces distinct gametes. The ascogonium is globular, terminal or intercalary with a large nucleus at the center and A elongated club shaped antheridium mostly produced near the adjacent hypha to the ascogonium. The antheridium may be terminal or intercalary. The antheridium consists of nucleus and septa at the basal region.

Disease Cycle

The powdery mildew pathogen spread from one place to other mostly by air current. The spores come in contact with the proper host plant that could develop powdery mildew if the environmental factors are favorable. The humidity favorable for the powdery mildew disease of Plantago is 90-100% observed by Mehta, *et.al*, (2005). Sometimes the seeds carry spores and cleistothecia on the seed surface hence that causes disease. The seeds of infected plant and soil act as primary inoculum for newly grown crop. The fungus produces abundance of cleistothecia. The contaminated soil is also known as sick soil. The dormancy period of fruiting bodies (cleistothecia) in soil is not exactly known. Mandal & Geetha, (2001) observed that the pathogen complete its life cycle on unwanted weed plants. Such weeds also act as inoculum of the pathogen for newly grown crops.

Disease management:

1. Field sanitation: Collection of infected plant debris before sowing reduces disease intensity in the field.
2. The fungicide like wettable sulphur is recommended against powdery mildew disease.

3. Foliar spraying of fungicides like Tridimenol has been recommended.
4. Volatile oils and plant extracts restricted conidial germination of Erysiphe.

DISEASES REPORTED ON ISABGULA (*Plantago ovata*)

Sl. No.	Disease	Pathogen
1.	Powdery mildew	*Erysiphe cinchoracearum*
2.	Downey mildew	*Pernospora plantaginis*
3.	Leaf spot	*Septoria plantaginea*

8. DISEASES OF GINGER

English name : Ginger

Botanical name : *Zingiber officinale*

Family : Zingiberaceae

Indian name : Adrak

Ginger (*Zingiber officinale Boehm.*) is a perennial herb with underground branched rhizome. The leaves possess a characteristic fragrance when cut or brushed. Rhizomes are dug out after the leafy parts are dried. It is believed to have originated from India. It is common spice in India. It is a perennial herbaceous plant; with modified stem (Rhizome). Rhizome is irregularly branched with swollen and tough surface. The leaves and Rhizome in aromatic. It is cultivated for its rhizome which is edible as spice and possesses medicinal properties. After maturity of ginger crop, the leaves start drying, at this stage the rhizomes are dug out and collected. Ginger in used as medicine from ancient time. In Sanskrit it is called as maha aushadhi means its meaning is "great medicine". It is believed that India may be the origin of ginger. The chemical composition of ginger is protein 2.3%, fat 0.9%, minerals 1.2%, fiber 2.4%, carbohydrate 121.2%, fiber 2.4%,carbohydrates 12.3 for 100 gms of ginger. The minerals present in ginger are Calcium, Phosphorous, Iron, Carotene, Thiamine, Riboflavin, Niacin, and Vit-C.

Medicinal Use

Ginger is taken internally because of its stimulating properties. The Ginger paste is effective against muscular pain. The paste of is applied over affected region. It is used against dyspepsia, flatulence, vomiting, spasms and other painful affections of the stomach and the bowels. Chewing a piece of fresh ginger after every meal is highly beneficial in disorder digestion of food. A spoonful of honey + one spoon lemon juice and 2 spoon mint juice mix in glass of drinking water. Drink it in every morning 4 evening to fight morning sickness, jaundice and piles. Ginger pieces boil in water for 10-15minutes. Filter and take the extract which is effective against colds and associated fevers. A spoonful of ginger juice with a cup of fenugreek decoction helps to reduce fever in influenza. It acts against Bronchitis, asthma, tuberculosis, of lungs and wooping cough. Ginger juice (2ml) with 5 ml of honey, at boiled egg every morning is suggested to the patients of impotency. Ginger is a very good pain killer, its decoction with slight sugar acts to get relief. Against menstrual disorders. It allays toothache when applied to the gum. In case of earache, a few drops of ginger juice give relief. Ginger is widely used as medicine in India. It is stimulating carminative and externally used as a rubefacient that is counter – irritant for relief of muscular pain. It has aphrodisiac properties. Ginger is used for the treatment of dyspepsia, flatulence, colic, vomiting, spasms and other painful affections of the stomach and the bowels. With honey it is given against nausea & vomiting. This herb is an excellent remedy for coughs & colds. The fresh ginger juice mixed with a cup of decoction of fenugreek reduces fever in influenza (Stone, *et.al.* 2004).

It acts as an expectorant in bronchitis, asthma, wooping cough and tuberculosis of lungs. Half teaspoon of ginger juice, one spoon honey with half boiled egg for a month every night tones up the sex organs & cures impotency, premature ejaculation and spermatorrhoea. It is also used to set up the menstrual disorders. Ginger in an excellent pain killer. It cures all types of pain. Headache, toothache & earache etc. The rhizome rot disease of ginger also caused by various fungal forms recorded by various authors is as follows.

RHIZOME ROT OF GINGER

The rhizome rot of ginger is a very commonly occur during long term storage durations. It is very common in all parts of India wherever the ginger is grown. The disease causes extensive damage in Kerala, Tamilnadu and Andhra Pradesh. *Dohroo* , (*2005*) reported 50% losses of produce due to the soft rot disease caused by Pythium species. The soft rot of rhizome is also an economically important disease in Pakistan, Bangladesh, Srilanka, Japan and other ginger growing countries.

Symptoms

Initially the basal portion of the rhizome turns brown. As the time increases the affected rhizome becomes watery and soft. The leaves fade up. The leaf tip turns yellowish. The yellowing progressively extends the remaining part of the leaves. The margins of the affected leaves become chlorotic while the centre of the leaf remains green. The chlorosis gradually reaches the sheath. The affected leaves dry and droop off. The basal portion of the plant where attachment of stem with rhizome is there, that part becomes translucent, discolored, soft & watery. The shoot is easily being pulled off from this region. The rot infection reaches to the rhizome from the base of attachment of shoot. The rhizomes in the soil initially become watery and brownish in colour. In severe cases decomposition of rhizome forms a watery mass of semisolid putrefied tissues which is enveloped by tough rind of the rhizome. All the buds of rhizome and the roots arise from the rhizome undergo rotting and produces semisolid soft rotted substance. The soft pulpy mass of rotted rhizome gives off a dirty smell. The incidence of this disease is very high in sick soil hence difficult to control.

The affected plants fail to produce rhizomes. The partially infected rhizomes continue to rot during transportation and storage periods. The macerated tissue of rhizome consists of all the parts of pathogen including sporangia, oogonium, & antheridia. Late in the season the thick walled globular oospores begin to develop in the rotted rhizomes.

The Causal Organism

There are reports from India and different parts world that the soft rot of ginger is caused by the following species of Pythium.

Pythium aphanidermatum

P. myriotylum

P. vexans

P. debaryannum

P. graminicolum

The Pathogenecity tests however support the importance of only two species i.e. *P. aphanidermatum* and *P. myriotylum*. The oospores of both of these species survive in soil on affected plant debris as well as rotted rhizomes as an inoculum.

- ***Pythium myriotylum***: The Pythium myriotylum causes soft rot disease of ginger. The hyphae are narrow, hyaline, coenocytic, and intercellular and less branched measuring 8.5 µm diameter. The intercellular hyphae produce abundance of knob like aspersoria. The sporangia arise from the terminal or intercalary cells of hyphae. The zoospores are 10-12 µm in diameter. The zoospores are differentiated either inside the sporangium or in the vesicle developing from sporangium. The zoospores are uninucleate, kidney shaped with two laterally attached flagella. The *P. myriotylum* produce numerous oogonia from the terminal or intercalary cells of fertile hyphae. The oogonia are smooth walled globular structures. The oogonium is 15-44 µm in diameter: The antheridia are numerous, elongated structures usually 3-6 per oogonium.

- ***Pythium aphanidermatum***: The hyphae are branched, hyaline, well developed, and coenocytic those are 7.5 µm in diameter. The sporangia are terminal or intercalary in position. Sometimes shows bud like out growths from the sporangial elements. The sporangia consist of encysted zoospores. The zoospores are 9 µm in diameter, kidney shaped, and having two laterally attached flagella. The fungus produces abundance of oogonia. The oogonium is globular, terminal or intercalary. The oogonium is 19-29 µm in diameter which is smooth textured. The antheridia are terminal or intercalary, elongated structures with 9-11 × 10-14 µm in diameter. The antheridia are mostly originated from the hyphae which are close to the oogonium. The oospores are spherical thick walled smooth or reticulate walled and are 16-25 µm in diameter (Van der Plaats-Niterink, 1981).

Disease Cycle

The disease is soil borne as well as the affected rhizome carry the born: The pathogen survives in soil on affected plant debris. The rotted rhizome and other plant parts consist of abundance of oospores that acts as primary inoculum for the newly sown crop in the next season. The oospores have also been detected from the scales of the rhizome in the store house. According to Stirling, (2008) the pathogenic fungus also transferred to other regions when the infected rhizomes used for the propagation purpose. The water logged soil favors the disease development. The secondary infection occurs during cleaning of the weeds from the crop field with the help cleaning accessories. The small injuries caused during harvest period make the rhizomes susceptible to the soft rot disease.

Disease management:

1. The cultural and chemical practices have been broadly used by the cultivars of ginger.
2. The propagating material should be selected from the disease free stock of rhizomes.
3. Water logging in the field promotes disease development hence the water logging must be avoided to restrict the growth of the pathogen.
4. Dipping of seed rhizomes in 0.25% Agallol 3 o 30 min. before planting helps to avoid soft rot disease.
5. Mixing of crop field soil with 0.3% chestnut compound reduces intensity of rhizome rot disease of ginger.
6. Dipping of the seed rhizomes in 0.25% zinc propylene bisdithiocarbamate (0.30%). Blitox-50 or copper oxychloride reduces the disease intensity.

7. The Copper oxychloride or Dithane Z-78 at the concentration of 50ppm reduces intensity of rot disease.
8. Ridomyl 5 G or Apron 35 W has given successful control of ginger rot.
9. Soil drenching with common fungicides like Bordeaux mixture (1.0%), Caresan (0.1%) or Blitox-50 (0.3-0.5%) controls the rot disease to a great extent.
10. Careful collection and distraction of infected plant residue & partially infected rhizome from the field and storehouse helps to reduce disease intensity to a great extent.
11. Use of resistant varieties like "Maran" for plantation purpose. The varieties Narasapattam and Nadia of south India found to be moderately resistant. The variety Goorubathan of Bengal was found to be moderately resistant to soft rot disease.

PHYLLOSTICTA LEAF SPOT OF GINGER

Pegg and Stirling, (1994) in Andhra Pradesh firstly discovered the disease *Phyllosticta* leaf spot of ginger.

Symptoms

The symptoms consist of small oval to elongated spots on leaf surface. Initially the spots are one mm in length with 0.5 mm width. The fully developed spot possess white coloured centre and a dark brown margin with a chlorotic halo around the spot. In severe cases of disease development the central dead tissue of the spot split open and fell off. There are numerous black coloured pycnidia of the pathogen scattered on the central region of the mature spots. Sometimes the spots may coalesce to form large necrotic lesions. The affected leave turns dark brown & dries up. The disease causes reduction of growth of rhizomes. When the disease occurs in the early stage of rhizome development causes extensive loss of the crop.

The Causal Organism

The causal organism is *Phyllosticta zingiberi* Ramakar. The mycelium is intracellular that consists of hyaline hyphal threads. Some of the hyphae act as conidiophores that produce hyaline conidia. The conidiophores are short, septate and unbranched, oblong with rounded ends, and measure 3.7-7.6 × 1.2-2.3 μm in size. The pycnidia are submerged in the leaf epidermis which may have remarkable ostiole. The average diameter of pycnidium is 78-150 μm. The pycnidiospores arise at the bottom of pycnidium which is globose to cylindrical that measure 3-12 × 3-5 μm in length. The pycnidiospores are small, unicellular, oval, hyaline structures and light in weight.

Disease Cycle

The pathogen Phyllosticta produces numerous carbonaceous pycnidia on affected leaf which remain in soil for number of months. The pathogen overwinters in the form of dome shaped conidia on infected plant residue.

Disease management:

1. The removal & burning of infected leave before maturity of spore can reduce disease intensity.
2. Spraying fungicide Zineb (0.2%) or Mancozeb (0.2%) restricted disease development.
3. Use of Bordeaux mixture (1%) also found to be effective against the disease.

PELLICULARIA LEAF SPOT DISEASE OF GINGER

The disease has been known for long time in India. The disease affects the foliage causing spotting and drying of leaves. It is worldwide in distribution and in most important leaf spot disease.

Symptoms

Initially very small water soaked spots appear either on the surface of the leaf or on the marginal region of the leaf. The lesions are few in number but occupy major portion of the leaf blade. The spot enlarge up to the leaf. The enlargement of the spot is restricted up to the leaf blade. Even the leaf sheath of severely infected leaf does not show any infection. Usually infection of the pathogen is limited up to the leaf area. The leaves of all the age group are susceptible to the disease. The infected leaves turn yellowish, loose turgidity and hang down. The severely of infected leaves split open from the region of sheath. The entire infected leaf looks like a thread hence the disease has been nominated as thread blight. The threads of loosely arranged hyphae have been observed on infected plant parts.

The Causal Organism

The causal organism is *Pellicularia salmonicolor* (Berk & Br.) Dastur. The mycelium consists of white, sparsely septate thin walled hyphae measuring 6-10 μm in diameter. It produces numerous sclerotia of dark brown colour that are scattered all over the severely infected leaf.

Disease Cycle

The soil is the main source of inoculum which retains infected plant debris on which pathogen survives for longer duration. The fungus also produces characteristics brown coloured sclerotia which remain in soil for number of months that act as source of inoculum. The pathogen lives in soil from season to season in the form of sclerotia. The sclerotia germinate over a range of 8-30 °C temperature and with an optimum at 23 °C. Many investigations have shown differences in cultural characters and Pathogenecity of isolates. There is abundant evidence of host specialization.

Disease management:

1. The Bordeaux mixture at the concentration of 1% found to be effective.

FUSARIUM ROT OF GINGER

The disease is very important; it has attracted much attention of pathologist causing heavy economical losses. It causes rapid wilt of plants in the midseason or latter which affect the yield of ginger. The underground ginger becomes dry and brown owing to a cortical decay while roots may have a soft water soaked appearance.

Symptoms

Initial the symptoms consist of change of green colour of leaves to yellow followed by rapid wilting of plant. The affected rhizome becomes creamy white. The roots get discoloured due to intercellular growth of pathogenic fungus. Especially the fungus occupy inside the vascular tissue and cortical region of the root. In severe cases the rhizomes becomes soft and watery. The affected rhizomes ooze a dirty liquid. The soft pulpy rhizomes consist of mycelium and numerous fungal spores, (Stirling, 2004). The affected plants collapse and dry. The dried plant residue carries the inoculum. The Fusarium rot of ginger occur in the patch form in the field. The patches consist of yellowish coloured plants that can be identified from the long distances.

The Causal Organism

The disease is caused by *Fusarium oxysporum* (Schl. Ex Fr.). The mycelium is cottony white that grow extensively and at maturity becomes pinkish just before Sporulation. The fungus produces abundance of conidia of two different shapes on branched conidiophores. The large sized conidia consist of 1-4 septa that are falcate & 17.2-34 × 203 × 409 µm in size and are termed as macroconidia. The small sized conidia produced by the fungus in abundance. These are small one or two celled with average size 2.5-19.6 × 1.2-4.8 µm.

The chlamydospores are also produced on the mature hyphal threads from the terminal or intercalary cells of the hyphae. The chlamydospores are the resistant spores remain in the soil as an inoculum.

Disease Cycle

The partially infected rhizomes and the field soil of previously infected crop acts as the primary inoculum for new infection to the newly cultivated ginger. The secondary spread of the disease takes place by mechanical means during cleaning of weeds. The water used during irrigation also responsible to carry the inoculum from the infected plant to healthy. The chlamydospores are highly resistant thick walled spores they can survive in soil for year after year that acts as primary source for newly sown ginger crop.

Disease management:

1. The pathogen is primarily a soil borne fungus hence crop the rotation can reduce disease intensity to a great extent.
2. There are reports of application of antagonistic organisms like *Bacillus subtilis, Memnoiella echinacea* and *Aspergillus niger* were found to be effective against *Fusarium oxysporum.*
3. Spraying of Aureofungin (0.02%) and Benomyl (0.1) controlled storage rot for great extent. It has observed that the post harvest treatment of these fungicides do not adversely affect the stored ginger.

DISEASES REPORTED ON GINGER (*Zingiber officinale*)

Sl. No.	Disease	Pathogen
1.	Leaf spot	*Cercospora zingibericola*
2.	Leaf spot	*Colletotrichum zingiberis*
3.	Leaf spot	*Phyllosticta zingiberi*
4.	Basal rot	*Sclerotium rolfsii*
5.	Leaf spot	*Septoria zingiberis*
6.	Rhizome rot	*Curvularia lunata*
7.	Rhizome dry rot	*Diploidia natalensis*
8.	Rhizome dry rot	*Fusarium sambucinum*
9.	Rhizome dry rot	*Macrophomina phaseolina*
10.	Rhizome rot	*Pythium butleri*
11.	Rhizome soft rot	*Fusarium oxysporum*
12.	Rhizome rot	*Pythium myriotylum*
13.	Rhizome rot	*Pythium graminicolum*
14.	Rhizome rot	*Pythium myriotylum*
15.	Rhizome rot	*Pythium vexans*
16.	Rhizome rot	*Rhizoctonia solani*
17.	Rhizome rot	*Rhizopus oryzae*
18.	Rhizome rot	*Pellicularia sp.*

9. DISEASES OF CASTOR

English name : Castor
Botanical name : *Ricinus communis*
Family : Euphorbiaceae
Indian name : Arandi

The castor (*Ricinus communis Linn.*) is a small plant, mostly 1-7 meters in height. The roots are well developed. Stem delicate, green or reddish in colour. The fruit is a spherical capsule with small grey seeds. The seed coat is spotted.

Castor

It is a small plant which is cultivated for its oil yielding seeds. It is a member of dicotyledonous having height of 1-7 meters. It is an annual plant with well developed root system and weak stem. Stems become hollow at maturity. Fruit is a capsule consists of 3-4 seeds; the seeds may have white to brown spots. The use of castor in India is common since ancient times, dating back to 2000 BC. In India its oil was used for lamps. Oil is highly medicinal, used in various ways according to requirement of tradition medicinal formula.

The origin of castor plant believed to be at eastern Africa. It is cultivated in warm temperate and temperate region of the world. Castor oil is used throughout the world in preparation of medicine.

Medicinal Use

Castor oil is used against the rheumatic and skin disorders. It is harmless, purgative. The paste of castor seeds is effective against rheumatic swellings. A decoction of roots of castor with carbonate of potash is beneficial in the treatment of lumbago, sciatica and rheumatism. The paste of seeds is effective against scrofulous sores and boils developed due to tuberculosis. Massage of castor oil to the breast after delivery increases flow of milk. Castor oil helps to grow hairs on head and cures dandruff. To get relief from constipation, add 10 ml of castor oil in luke warm milk and drink it. Castor oil keeps the skin healthy so used as massage oil. The paste of castor seeds effective against rheumatism. Castor is used in the treatment of rheumatism and sciatica. A poultice of castor leaves is useful as an external application to boils and swellings. Castor oil massaged over the breast after child-birth increases the flow of milk. Castor oil is a simple harmless purgative and can be used without any rigid consideration and limitation of weather and the physiological nature of the patient. Castor oil keeps the skin healthy & imports sound sleep.

GREY MOULD DISEASE OF CASTOR

It is an important disease of castor in temperate regions of the world. The pathogen causes considerable loss of yield during favorable environmental conditions. The pathogens has a wide host range can infect a variety of plants. It is a destructive disease in tropical subtropical and warmer region of the world.

Grey mould disease of castor causes heavy loss of crop yield. The disease is of major importance.

Symptoms

The symptoms consist of weathering of leaves, stem, flower and fruits. Initially small brownish blue spots appear on the branches and laterals of the spike. The affected regions split off. Gradually the disease spread to all parts of the plant. The affected flowers show wet rots symptoms. The rotted region of flower gets enveloped by mycelial mat of grey mold fungus that affects seed formation. A small blackish spots appear on the inflorescence. The interaction of pathogen and the tissue of inflorescence produce yellowish liquid hence the yellowish sticky substance comes out through the infected inflorescence. The rainy weather during capsule formation makes the disease more severe and serious. The immature capsules get rotted and fell off. The humidity up to 85% and temperature 20 °C found to be more favorable for the extensive spread of the disease.

The Causal Organism

The disease is caused by *Botryotinia ricini.* The mycelium is branched, consists of septate hyphae. The fungus produces numerous conidia especially in cluster. The conidiophores are one called about 11 × 11-15 µm in size, round to ovoid. At the end the conidiophores appear branched on which groups of conidia are produced. The fungus produces sclerotia of irregular shape, which measure about 1-5 mm in diameter. The colours of sclerotia are black in colour.

Disease management:

1. Control of disease must be done by adjustment of cultural practices.
2. Field sanitation before sowing of caster seeds, reduces disease infesting
3. Seed treatment with fungicide reduces disease in the field.
4. User resistant varieties for sowing purpose.

SEEDLING BLIGHT OF CASTOR

Seedling blight of castor reported to be a serious disease that causes severe losses of seedlings during rainy season. The disease is worldwide in occurrence. High temperature along with high moist weather favors the disease development. It is an important disease of castor in the field and can result in serious economic loss by reducing yield of castor.

Symptoms

The soil borne pathogen enters the plant through root system that expresses its sign in the form of faded greenish patches on both the surfaces of the leafy cotyledons. The spots increase in all the directions. The effected cotyledons lose its turgidity and start rotting. The seedling becomes yellowish due to loss of chlorophyll. The affected stems collapse. The tender premature leaves of older plant shows yellow patch which later turn brown. The spots encircle by greenish margin that appears brownish gray on the lower surface of the leaf. Most of the spots coalesce to form large blighted areas that cover maximum area of the leaf (Patel *et.al,* 1949). The drooping of infected leaves is common. The humidity up to 95% is highly favorable for the rapid spread of the disease. During high humid environment the patches of the disease on the lower leaf surface shows white coloured mycelial growth that consists of sporangiophore. It has observed that the cotyledons & young plant get infected and spread in moist weather. The leaves of the older plants rarely get infected. Infection on the leaves of older plant remains restricted up to the leaf that does not spread further.

The Causal Organism

The causal organism is *Phytopthora colocasiae.* The pathogen is a soil borne fungus. The mycelium is highly branched, non-septate, consists of inter and intracellular hyphae. The intercellular hyphae produce sucking organs termed as haustoria. The fertile hyphae bear unbranched sporangiophore that consists of lemon shaped sporangial sac or sporangium at its tip. The mature sporangium consists of zoospores. The sporangia are easily trnaslocated through the irrigated water or disseminate by air currents. The sporangia germinate on the surface of the host cotyledon or leaf. The zoospores germinate by producing one or two germ tubes that enter the host through injured region or stomata and produce diseased spot within a day. The process of sporangia formation is repeatedly recycled many times within a single season of crop hence the secondary infection by sporangia spread fast and responsible for great losses of seedlings.

The primary infection to the castor seedling occurs due to the presence of oospores in the soil or through the dormant hyphae present inside the seeds that are used for the sowing purpose. The Oospores is the product of fusion of oogonium and antheridium developed from the fertile hyphae mostly from the terminal or intercalary cells.

The Source of Inoculum

The soil is the very important source of inoculum. The infected stem remain in field even after harvest of crop; During rainy season or high moist weather the pathogen produce numerous sporangiophore and sporangia the sporangia acts as primary as well as secondary inoculums. The seeds of infected plant produce canker of girdle just after emergence. The plant debris of previous crop present in soil may have numerous oospores which are globose or spherical thick walled structures which act as source of inoculums.

The non-septate hyphae produce chlamydospores in unfavorable condition which causes disease when comes in contact with host plant. Pathogens survive in soil for about one year. Very low temperature and stagnant water in the crop field favors spread of disease.

Disease management:

1. Crop rotation reduces disease intensity in the field.
2. Metalaxyl is found effective against blight of pigeon pea, (Nene and Bhelva, 1976).
3. Use resistant varieties for sowing purpose.
4. Field sanitation before sowing of seeds was found effective.
5. ICRISAT (1989) suggested Fosetyl-A1 and Metalaxyl for treatment of seeds of control blight of pigeon pea.
6. Use resistant varieties for sowing purpose.
7. Field sanitation before sowing of seeds reduces disease intensity.

LEAF BLIGHT OF CASTOR

The disease has been reported from various corners of the country. It is one of the important diseases of castor. Heavy losses occur due to this disease in warm and humid areas. Under favorable weather conditions may cause yield losses by heavy premature defoliation. Losses from this disease are tremendous especially during warm humid weather. There are also reports of *Alternaria* blight as a serious destructive disease from other castor growing countries.

Symptoms

In presence of humid environment all the plant parts except root system get affected by the pathogen. Initially a very small yellowish spots appear on the cotyledons. The gradual increase of the spot takes place due to maturity of the fungus in the host tissue. The repeated secondary infection by conidia increases intensity of the disease during the same season. The heavily infected plant remains short and dries up. The infection persists on the affected plant up to the end of plants life. The disease becomes severe and serious during high humid weather or rainy seasons (Andreeva, 1979). The yellowish spots later changes to brown. Approximately the spots are spherical that consists of concentric rings inside. In advanced cases many spots coalesce to form large patches of irregular margin. The infected tissue of leaf split up and the pieces of dead tissue of the leaf easily carried away by the wind or fell off on the soil surface. The remaining tissue of the mature spots gets covered with faded grayish growth of the fungus.

The infected leaves and twigs dry up. Heavy defoliation causes wilting of the plant. During the infection the entire inflorescence turns dark brown to black in colour. It causes greatest loss of yield. When the pathogen attack at the seedling stage that restricts the leaf formation.

The infected immature capsules do not produce seeds that turn dark black in colour and droop off. The affected capsules remain smaller in size that consists of wrinkled seeds with less quantity of oil. The seeds of severely affected capsule do not produce healthy seedlings. Sometimes the fully developed capsules get infected by the pathogen. In such cases the pathogen remains restricted up to the cover of the capsule. Such capsule consists of healthy seeds. The fungus infects the seed if the affected capsule gets cracked.

The Causal Organism

The disease is caused by *Alternaria ricini.* The mycelium is septate, highly branched &olivacious in colour. The fungus multiplies by producing abundant conidia in the form of chain on the tips of unbranched septate, erect conidiophores. The conidia are olivacious in colour. The conidia are multicellular that consists of 4-20 cells due to formation of transverse and longitudinal septa within the conidium. The conidium consists of bulbous base and narrow beak like end. The beak in colourless, long, unbranched consists of only transverse septa. The conidia are retained in soil on dead organic matter of plant. The conidia are also carried by seed as well as spores found external to the seed surface that acts as inoculum for the next season crop. When the contaminated seeds used for sowing that produce infected seedlings. Pre or post emergence damping off of the seedling occurs. Agrawal and Sahni (1965) observed that high atmospheric humidity up to 90-100% and low temperature 15-22°C favors hues development of disease to the susceptible varieties.

Disease Cycle

The *Alternaria ricini* perennates on infected plant debris, in or on infected seed. The infected seed germinate into infected plant. The seeds germinate into infected plant. The seeds get infected by conidia produced on plant debris. The fungus also produces microsclerotia and chlamydospores. Wet weather is highly favorable for spread of disease. Pathogen produce abundance of spores in wet weather. Primary infection takes place by seed or air borne spores. The infected seed is the most important source of primary inoculums in cooler areas. The conidia germinate by producing two or more than two germ tubes. The germ tube enters the host by creating force or through stomata. Penetration is preceded by formation of aspersoria from the end region of germ tube.

Disease management:

1. Field sanitation before plantation is useful method to reduce disease intensity in the field.
2. Spraying of Thiram at initial stage of disease incidence reduces disease.
3. The seed borne inoculums can be treated by hot water at 50 °C for 20 controlled by spraying 0.25% Diathane M-45.

RUST DISEASE OF CASTOR

The disease occurs widely in different castor growing areas of the world and causes enormous losses by affecting leaves and twigs. It is an important disease. The disease during favorable weather conditions causes considerable losses of yield.

Symptoms

Rust symptoms appear especially on the lower surface of host leaf as a small slightly raised whitish dots. The raised rusty dots consist of a group of uredospores hence called as uredosori. The uredopustules are scattered on the lower leaf surface. In severe cases two, three or many uredopustules coalesce to form a large sized rusty patch. The fully mature pustules burst open by exposing mass of uredospores which are yellowish in colour. The exposed uredospores re-infect the healthy leaf and cause rusty symptoms. In advanced stage of the disease maximum area of the lower leaf surface get occupied by numerous uredopustules. The heavily infected leaves get shrivel and fell off. The castor plants infected in early stage of development shows severe losses of yield, (Desai and Dange, 2003).

The Causal Organism

The rust disease of castor is caused by *Melampsora ricini*. The mycelium is highly branched consists of septate hyphae. The hyphal mats mostly deposited under the epidermis of the host leaf. The branched fertile hyphae produce uredospores at its tip. At maturity of uredospores the uredosorus protrude out by rupturing the epidermal layer of the host leaf. The clusters of the uredospores exposed on the under surface of the leaf. The uredospores are oval, unicellular orange in colour that measure about 22-28 × 15-28µm in size. The uredospore possesses a small germ pore. The uredospores release from the infected leaf. The uredospores are carried away by wind or by any other mechanical agency. These spores act as secondary inoculum of the rust disease. The uredospores germinate by producing small germ tube that comes out through the germ pore. The germ tube is actively growing hyphae that infects the healthy leaves and causes rust disease.

Disease Cycle

The must fungus shown to consists of different host species. The soil borne teletospores which survive on plant debris acts as a primary source of inoculum. In presence of optimum environmental factors the teletospores germinate to from the sporidia which infects the young leaves. In India, in the hills, the teletospores are observed on infected plant debit, which acts, as a source of inoculum.

Disease management:

1. Use disease free seeds for sowing purpose.
2. Field sanitation is essential before sowing of crop.
3. Removal of weed hosts present around the field.
4. Application of Borax (60kg/hector) for the management of rust disease of castor.
5. Removal and destruction of infected plant debris, stubbles and trash from the field reduces disease intensity.

CERCOSPORA LEAF SPOT OF CASTOR

The Cercospora leaf spot is a major foliar disease of castor affecting leaves of all age group. The disease is found in all the castor growing countries of the world. It is one of the most destructive and widespread disease. The disease has been a major cause of loss of castor leaves but no approximate estimate of total losses is available. The disease has been reported from Maharashtra.

Symptoms

The first symptom of the disease is seen in the form of numerous black or brown coloured small spots on the host leaf. The spots are separately encircled by yellowish chlorotic zones. The spots are distinct on both the surfaces of the leaf. The spots increase gradually. The centre of the spot becomes irregularly angular and turns yellowish brown to grayish in colour. The grayish centre of the spot consists of dark black coloured mass of the fungus. The spot consists of group of conidiophores. In advanced stage of disease development the spot coalesce to form large patches of infected regions.

The Causal Organism

The leaf spot disease of castor is caused by *Cercospora ricinella* Sacc. and Berl. The mycelium is septate that consists of septate hyphae. The fungus reproduces by producing conidia on conidiophores. The fungus produces the clusters of the conidiophores. The conidiophores are unbranched, septate, dark brown in colour. The conidiophores possess few scars on the surface that are called as knee points. The conidiophores measure about 22-60 × 2-07.2 µ. The clusters of the conidiophores emerge through the centre of the mature spots on the leaf. The clusters of the conidiophores resemble a fruiting body. The conidia of Cercospora are elongated, colorless, tapering to the upper end and truncated below. The conidia are straight or slightly curved multiseptate arise from the knee points of the conidiophores. The conidia consist of 6-7 transverse septa. The conidium germinates by producing one, two or more than two germ tubes. The conidia get dispersed by wind or by any mechanical agency or through the seeds of infected plants. The soil seeds and air plays a important source of inoculum of the pathogen.

Disease Cycle

The organism in air, Soil and seed inhabitant. Penetration takes place at anywhere on surface of host leaf. The fungus lives through unfavorable periods in the form of sclerotia and subsists during favorable conditions as a saprophyte. The pathogens also infect several other crops on which they are also pathogenic. The spores remain in soil for a long time and attack the succeeding plants as the conditions become favorable.

Disease management:

1. Field sanitation before sowing reduces soil borne inoculums of pathogen.
2. Crop rotation for 3-4 years restricts the disease development.
3. Select disease free seeds for sowing purpose.
4. Seed treatment before sowing with recommended fungicide reduces disease in the field.

POWDERY MILDEW OF CASTOR

In India the disease was first reported by Chattopadhya, (2000). The disease was not considered as much harmful earlier, but the intensity of disease increases in humid weather and there is loss of yield due to defoliation. Damage to the plant may be very much if the disease appears during early stages of development of castor plant. It occurs in all tropical and subtropical regions of the world where castor is grown.

Symptoms

The lower surface of the leaf of infected plants gets covered with the whitish growth of the fungus that gradually spread all over the upper surface of the leaf & twigs. The affected leaves become yellow and fell off before maturity. The infected leaf shows faded green coloured patches on to the corresponding infected areas on the lower surface of the leaf, (Karan. 1966).

The Causal Organism

The causal agent is *Leveillula taurica* (Lev.) Arnaud. The mycelium of the pathogen consists of hyaline, branched septate hyphae. The pathogen is an endophytic fungus grows and spread in the intercellular spaces of the spongy parenchyma of the leaf. The fungus produces unbranched tubular sucking organs for absorption of food material from the host plant. At maturity, the fungus produce branched conidiophores that comes out through the stomatal openings of the leaf in groups, (Desai and Dange, 2003). The tips of conidiophores bear a single papillate conidium. The conidia are hyaline varying in shape and deposited extensively on the infected regions of the leaf. The conidia are light in weight that are easily carried away by air currents or washed off by rain water. The humidity up to 90% and low temperature 22 °C has been observed to be more favorable for the advancement of the disease.

Disease Cycle

The pathogen infect a broad spectrum of plants. It has a wide range of hosts i.e. wide plants as well as cultivated, which ensures the survival of fungus from one season to another. It produces numerous conidia which are light in weight hence easily blown away by air currents. The airborne conidia also play a important role as source of inoculums. The air borne conidia when comes in contact with host surface germinate in presence of moisture. The germinated conidium enters the leaf through stomata or lenticels. The hyphae grow in the intercellular spaces, which absorb food material by sending haustoria into the host cells. The pathogen produces flask shaped haustoria. The secondary & tertiary infection occurs by spread and germination of conidia on new healthy plant in the same season.

Disease management:

1. The disease can be controlled by spraying Sulphur dusts or by spraying sprays containing sodium sulphide.
2. The copper sulphate spray of recommended concentration restricts the disease development.
3. Removal and careful destruction of affected leaves in very early stage of disease development helps to avoid disease intensity.

CHARCOAL ROT OF CASTOR

The disease is cosmopolitan in occurrence. It appears in hot, dry environmental conditions. In tropical parts of the world the diseases also attack seedling stage of plant. Yield losses are very significant the fungus has broad spectrum of host range.

Symptoms

Initially the symptoms of the disease appear as small round dark brown coloured sports especially around the bases of the young branches and nodal regions. The spots are deeply seated and distinct. Gradually the spots increase in size causing large necrotic areas. The necrosis encircles the petiole of the leaf. The severe defoliation is common. In severe cases of the disease entire plant start drying from apex to the bottom. The infected capsules fade up and droop off prematurely. The affected plant shows gradual drying. The severely infected plants possess dark black coloured lesions on the stem just above the soil surface. The lesion consists of cup like pycnidia. The pycnidia are partially inserted in the host tissue.

The Causal Organism

The charcoal rot is caused by *Macrophomina phaseolina* (Tussi) Giod.

The mycelium is highly branched, septate; intercellular that produces dark brown coloured pycnidial cups made of mycelial threads (Karan. 1966). The pycnidia are cup shaped, dark brown, ostiolate borne on the infected regions of the host. The pycnidial cups are partially embedded in the host tissue. The pycnidium measures about 88.2-135.0 × 88.2-122.2 µm size. The pathogen also produces dark black coloured sclerotia of various shapes and size.

Disease Cycle

The pathogen survives in soil on infected leaf or any plant part. It survives for longer duration in plant tissue. Dry soil helps to prolong survival of sclerotia. The mycelium and sclerotia survive in wet soil for lesser duration. Soil plays important source of inoculums.

Disease management:

1. Soil solarization and deep ploughing have been found effective against reduction in soil borne inoculum.
2. Application of copper oxychloride found effective against charcoal rot of castor.
3. Use disease free seeds for sowing purpose.

SEELING WILT OF CASTOR

The affected seedlings suffer seriously which dry up at last. The disease though sporadic in nature which causes severe losses. Several soil borne fungi associated with this disease causing wilt of seedlings. It is one of the common diseases that occur throughout India where castor is grown at commercial level.

Symptoms

The initial symptoms of the disease consist of yellowing of very young leaves of the castor seedlings. The affected seedling looses the turgidity of the leaves & stem and gradually the wilting of the entire seedling takes place. In severe stage of disease development the collar region and root system below the soil surface turns dark black in colour. The water supply to the seedling get stopped due to the inter and intracellular growth of the pathogen in the root and stem tissue. The affected seedlings fell off within a short duration. The heavily infected seedlings show cottony growth of the pathogen at the collar region of the seedling.

The Causal Organism

The seedling wilt disease of the castor is caused by *Fusarium oxysporum.* The mycelium is highly branched septate that grow extensively on the affected collar regions of the seedling. The cottony growth of the pathogen is visible on the affected areas of the seedling. The whitish colour of the mycelium changes to light pink in colour after Sporulation. The pathogen reproduces by producing abundant of conidia. The conidia are of two types. The large sized conidia are called as macroconidia and small sized conidia are termed as microconidia. The macroconidia are borne on the branched conidiophores. The macroconidia are 3-5 septate, hyaline slightly curved that measure about 26.0 × 3.7 µm in size. The microconidia are abundantly produced by the pathogen. The microconidia are borne on the simple unbranched conidiophores (Chauhan, *et.al*, 1975). The microconidia consist of one to two septa that are hyaline, slightly elongated, 7.8 × 3.5 µm in size. The pathogen also produces chlamydospores from terminal or intercalary cells of the fertile hyphae. The chlamydospores are large, globose, thick walled, black coloured, one celled resistant spores.

Disease Cycle

The pathogenic fungus is a facultative parasite. In absence of proper host plant, it can survive in soil on a variety of dead organic matter in the form of chlamydospores or conidia. The disease is favored by high soil temperature and humid weather. A high dose of nitrogen favors the disease. The pathogen occurs in a variety of soil types and once it is

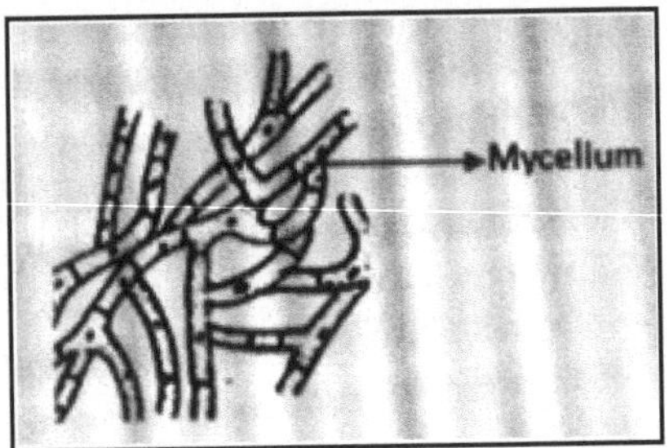

established, it remains for indefinite time. The disease spread by means of seed, soil and propagating material. The soil borne inoculums may spread through irrigated water from one place to other. The dead infected plant debris provides the substrate for asexual reproduction and formulation of numerous conidia. The spores or conidia are light in weight that can blow away by wind to long distance. The air borne spores can cause infection in contact with proper host surface.

Disease management:

1. Select seed setts from disease free cane.
2. Field sanitation is essential.
3. Soaking of seed setts in 50ppm Boron prepared in water reduces disease intensity.
4. Collect and burn plant residue from the field before cultivation.
5. Hot water treatment at 50 °C temperatures to seed setts reduces disease intensity.
6. The cane varieties like CO619 and BP 17 found resistant against wilt disease.
7. Carbendazim (0.05%) treatment to seed setts for 10 minutes reduces disease in the field.

DISEASES REPORTED ONF CASTOR (*Ricinus communis*)

Sl. No.	Disease	Pathogen
1.	Wet rot	*Choanephora cucurbitarum*
2.	Fruit rot	*Cladosporium oxysporum*
3.	Leaf spot	*Corynespora cassicola*
4.	Twig blight	*Glomerella cingulata*
5.	Stem rot	*Macrophomina phaseolina*
6.	Leaf rust	*Melampsora ricini*
7.	Powdery mildew	*Oidiopsis taurica*
8.	Leaf spot	*Phyllosticta bosensis*
9.	Fruit rot	*Phytopthora colocasiae*
10.	Seed rot	*Phytopthora parasitica*
11.	Root rot	*Pythium aphanidermatum*
12.	Spot on petiole	*Sphaceloma ricini*

10. DISEASES OF RAUVOLFIA

English name : Serpentina
Botanical name : *Rauvolfia serpertina*
Family : Apocynaceae
Indian name : Sarpagandha

The Rauvolfia (*Rauvolfia serpentina* Linn.) is a herb with smooth stem. It grows erect. The root and bark used as medicine. Leaves bright green with short petiole. Flowers are pink or white with a short peduncle. The flowers occur in clusters. The fruit shape must be round. Fruits turn blackish at maturity. It is a small erect or sub-erect perennial shrub generally 15-45 cm high. It is common on moist deciduous forest.

Medicinal Use

It is employed to relief of various disorders of central nervous system. Root is used as bitter tonic; hypnotic, sedative, specific for insanity, to reduce blood pressure. It is used as a remedy in painful affections of the bowels. Root extract used for treatment of intestinal disorder like diarrhea and dysentery. The roots stimulate uterine contraction and are used in child birth in difficult cases. The leaves are bitters in taste but stimulant for uterus, nutritive and antihelminthic. The juice of leaves is used for removal of opacities of cornea.

The herb is used to lower blood pressure. It is also useful to reduce fever. The plant is effective in treating in sanity, insomnia & hysteria. The plant useful to relive itching in urticaria. The root is the house of numerous alkaloids. The root is used in treatment of high blood pressure.

WILT DISEASE OF RAUVOLFIA

The wilt disease of Rauvolfia in the disease of major importance that causes extensive damage to the crop in the field. The disease has been reported from various parts of the world. The losses from this disease are very heavy and vary from season to season. Several workers have reported varying degree of losses from this disease. It causes potential yield reductions due to drying of branches & stem of affected plant.

Symptoms

All the plant parts of the affected plants become yellow due to scarcity of water. The water supply to the plant has been restricted due to growth of the pathogen inside the vessels of the root and stem. The yellowing or chlorosis is followed by necrosis. Heavy defoliation and drying of entire plant takes place. In advanced stage of disease development the collar region of the plant sometimes show entophytic growth of fungus. The split open stems of the host show dark brown colour of central tissue (xylem vessels) indicating presence of pathogen inside the host tissue. Similarly the infected roots become dark brown coloured. Janardhanan, *et.al*, (1964) observed disintegration of cortical region of the seedlings and young plants. Yellowish curling and drying of affected plant is common. The leaves of all the age group susceptible for the infection. Heavy defoliation occurs. Only the dried sticks of the plants without leaves remain in the field.

The Causal Organism

The causal organism of wilt disease of Rauvolfia is *Fusarium oxysporum* (Schlecht) The mycelium is branched that consists of septate hyphae. The inter and intracellular space of affected host tissue get filled by hyphal threads. The pathogenic fungus show cottony growth on the PDA (Potato Dextrose Agar) medium. The cottony growth of the fungus can also be seen at the collar region of the affected plant. The mycelium at maturity produces abundance of conidia that are of two different shapes. After sporulation the fungus turn light pink in colour. The pathogen produces abundance of microconidia and less number of macroconidia. Both the micro and macro conidia are multicellular. The Macroconidia are 3-5 celled slightly tapered at one end that is hyaline measure about 24.5 × 3.5 µm in size. The microconidia are one or two celled, elliptical or ovoid hyaline measure about 7.8 × 2.8 µm in size. The causal organism is a saprophyte fungus hence that remains in soil on dead organic matter of host plant. The fungus present on the plant residue in soil acts as a inoculum for the next crop.

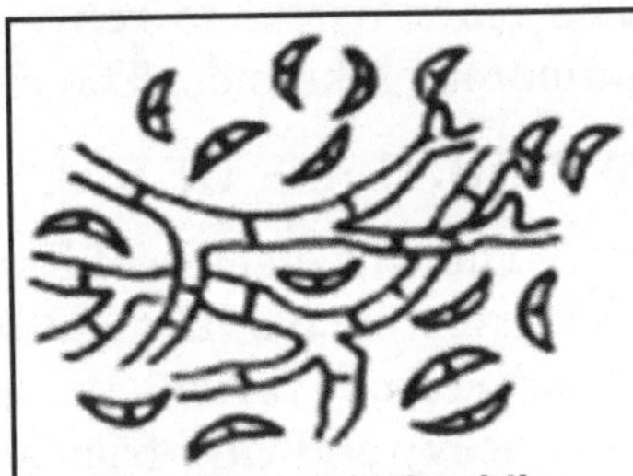

Mycelium and Conidia

During unfavorable environmental conditions, the fungal hyphae produce thick walled, round spores, one in each compartment of hyphal thread. These spores are termed as chlamydospores. The chlamydospores are thick walled spores that survive for several years on dead organic matter on plant residue in the soil.

Inoculum

The pathogen is a facultative parasite that means it is a parasite when the host is not available in the field. It survive as a saprophyte on any type of organic matter available in field soil for year after year and in the presence of proper host plant it causes disease. Such parasites are termed as facultative parasite. The soil is the main source of inoculum. The infected root system (plant residue) remains in the harvested field that acts the as the inoculum. The seeds of infected plant carry the mycoflora, in such cases seed is the source of primary inoculum.

Entry of Pathogen into the Host

The pathogen (*Fusarium oxysporum*) is a soil or seed borne fungus. Initially the fungus infects the root system of pigeon pea at the seedling stage or adult stage of host plant. The pathogen migrates slowly to the vascular tissue of the stem. Extensive growth of pathogenic fungus takes place inside the hollow space of vessels because of presence of its favorable nutrition, Anonymous, (2004). The water supply to the upper part of plant stops because of excess growth of fungal hyphae inside the vessels hence the supply of water from root to stem and other branches stops. As a result the entire plant turns yellowish and gradually dries up.

Disease Cycle

The pathogen is a soil borne fungus. This is a facultative parasite that remains in soil on plant residue for several years and in presence of host that infect the root system of pigeon pea and causes wilt disease. Mc Rae (1933) reported 8-20 years of survival of this pathogen in soil. Hence, it is highly difficult to manage disease by crop rotation method.

First of all the fungus infect root hairs from which that gradually migrate to the large vessels. The symptoms of wilt appear when infection in more than 50%. The intensity of disease is more in the field where the previous crop was the same host. After harvest of the crop, the root stalks remain in the field which acts as a source of inoculum for the next year's crop. The seed also carry the spores or hyphal threads as an inoculum.

Disease management:

1. The crop rotation to reduce disease intensity has been failed because the fungus is a saprophyte hence it multiplies continuously in soil on dead organic matter and build up the inoculum in the soil.
2. Applications of heavy doses of green leaf manure in to the field soil promote multiplication of antagonistic organisms which restricts the growth and development of the pathogenic fungus.
3. The decreased disease intensity has been obtained by mixed cropping of pigeon pea along with tobacco.
4. Chauhan, *et.al*, (1988) suggested soil solarization to reduce disease intensity.
5. Mixed cropping with Jowar also reduces disease intensity.
6. The wilt of seedling can be restricted by addition of solutions of boron, manganese and zinc during emergence.
7. Pre soaking of seed in solution of sodium chloride salt in suggested by Subramanian, (1964).

POWDERY MILDEW DISEASE OF RAUVOLFIA

The powdery mildew of Rauvolfia has been recorded in many parts of the world. It is one of the diseases of major importance. It appears first on leaves and later on spread on all parts of plant except root system.

Symptoms

In case of mildew diseases, the pathogenic fungus grows external to the host surface. The pathogen produces superficial hyphae that are inserted in the host tissue to absorb good material. The powdery mildew disease of Rauvolfia was found to be of major importance in India (Ganguly and Pandotra 1962). Initially the pathogen grows in the form of small patches on the leaf surface. The corresponding lower leaf surface show yellow patches. Gradually the patches coalesce to form large patches of irregular margin. The pathogenic fungus grows in all direction and extends all over upper leaf surface, stem, twigs and growing regions. Because of extensive growth of fungus and heavy production of spores the affected leaves curl off and dry. Heavy defoliation of the mature and immature leaves takes place. The heavily affected plant becomes powdery in appearance. The powdery mass present on the host tissue consists of abundance of microconidia, macroconidia and respective conidiophores.

The Causal Organism

The causal agent of powdery mildew of *Rauvolfia* is *Leaveillula taurica* (Lev) Atz. The mycelium is branched, septate, and produces numerous conidia on unbranched conidiophores. The conidiophores are with 2-3 septa. The conidia are hyaline spherical in shape, light in weight and produced at the tips of the conidiophores. The conidia are easily carried away by wind. The cleistothecia are not found in natured condition.

Disease Cycle

There are no reports of perithecial stage of *Leveillula taurica* from India; under field conditions. Hence the primary infection to host plant may be taken place due to ascospores of the pathogen. The air is another important source of inoculums. The fungus produces numerous conidia external to the host surface which are easily carried away by wind currents, that acts as source of inoculums. The fungus is strictly on obligate pathogen. In absence of proper host plant, the pathogen survives on collateral hosts.

Disease management:

1. Remove & burn plant residue from the field carefully.
2. Chemical Soil disinfectants and fumigants have been used by workers of certain places.

3. The infected plant parts should be pruned out and destroyed.
4. Field sanitation is effective to reduce disease intensity.
5. Collection and burning of all plant residues from the field before plantation helps to reduce disease in the field.
6. Spraying of Karathane dust restricts the disease.

LEAF BLIGHT DISEASES OF RAUVOLFIA

Leaf blights:

1. Leaf blight: *Alternaria* tenuis Nees.
2. Leaf blight: *Macrghomina phasedina* (Tussi) Gid.
3. Leaf blight: Mycosphaesella *rauvolfiae* Ramkar & Ramka.

The young plants were found to be more susceptible for Alternaria blight disease. Ganguly and Pandotra (1962) found that the pathogen is more common and destructive on one year old plants.

Symptoms

The tender leaves get affected first. A very small circular spots of brown colour appear on the lower surface of young leaves. The spots may be light to dark brown in colour with a yellowish margin around it. Gradually these spots increase in size and turns dark brown in colour. In advanced stage of the disease development many spots coalesce to form large brown patches that occupies maximum area of the leaf. The severely affected leaves dry up and fell off. In certain cases very young growing tips of the plants takes place. Drying of growing tips and axillary buds is very common. The affected plants remain stunted, unhealthy and delicate.

The Causal Organism

The causal organism is *Alternaria tennis* Nees. The mycelium is branched septate, intercellular and olivacious brown. The fungus produces multicellular conidia. The mycelium of *Alternaria tennuis* is septate, branched, light brown which turn brownish at maturity. Initially the hyphae are intercellular and later penetrating into the host cells of the invaded tissue. Many conidiophores emerging through stomata, from the center of the mature spot which appear grayish. The conidiophores are short, 50-90 µm in size and dark brown in colour. The conidia consist of certain vertical and transverse septate. The conidia possess a narrow beak like structure and basal region in rounded. Each conidiophores produce one or a short chain of conidia. The conidia measure 120-290 × 11-21 µm in size. The conidia germinate within 30-40 minutes in a drop of sugar solution at 28°-30°C temperature. On germination; each conidium produces many germ tubes in variable directions.

Disease Cycle

The Alternaria species infecting *Rauvolfia serpentina* overwinter in diseased plant debris and can persist for one to two years. The Alternaria can penetrate in cankered *Rauvolfia* stems in soil up to 14 months which is sufficient for carryover of the pathogen from one season to another. The seed borne nature of Alternaria has also been reported. The primary infection to the leaves takes place by conidia present in soil. The lowermost leaves of *Rauvolfia* which are close to soil surface get infected easily. The secondary spread of the disease occurs through conidia developed on primary spots. The conidia are transferred to healthy plants through insect's visitors, or by any mechanical agency. Mostly the pathogen enters the leaf through stomata or by direct penetration. The environmental factors such as atmospheric humidity, temperature, wind, rain, has great influence on disease development and intensity.

Disease management:

1. Field sanitation reduces inoculum potential in the field.
2. Follow suitable crop rotation which is helpful.
3. Various chemicals like, Thiram, Mancozeb, Copper oxychloride have shown good efficacy against leaf spot disease caused Alternaria.

CERCOSPORA LEAF SPOT OF RAUVOLFIA

The leaf spot disease of Rauvolfia caused by Cercospora in one of the most wide spread and destructive disease. The pathogen requires moderate temperature &humidity in the field; Disease spread rapidly resulting in widespread damage of plants, during favorable environment conditions.

The leaf spots caused by Cercospora are very important disease particularly in moderate temperature and high humidity. The disease has been reported from many countries where Rauvolfia occurs. In India the disease has been reported from almost all the states where in the recent years Rauvolfia is cultivated as medicinal plant in large scale (Bylka, *et.al,* 2003).The losses from this disease vary with disease intensity and sometimes the infection is so severe that the leaves dropdown prematurely.

Symptoms

Initially very small grayish yellow coloured spots appear on the leaves. The spots are spherical and distinct on both the surface of infected leaf. Gradual increase of spot changes its texture. The large mature spots become dark brown colour with a yellow hollow around it. There is cluster of dark brown coloured conidiophores at the centre of the mature spots. The leaf spots affect the directly the rate of photosynthesis. The affected plants remain stunted and heavy defoliation occurs.

The Causal Organism

The leaf spot disease is caused by *Cercospora rauvolfiae* chupp and Muller. Mycelium branched, septate, inter and intracellular and light brown coloured. The fertile hyphae produce few celled unbranched conidiophores which are of various lengths and curved at some places. The upper region of the conidiophores possesses narrower tapering ends. The groups of conidiophores come out through the centers of the mature spots on the host leaf. The multiseptate conidia are produced on the conidiophores. The conidia measure 3.42 × 10.28 µm. The conidia are slightly curved, 1-4 septate, olivacious brown, with blunt base and narrow tips.

Disease Cycle

The pathogenic fungus overwinters in the infected plant debris in the form of conidia. The infected plant residue remains in soil for longer duration. The fungal stromata remain in soil and also carried away by wind. The air borne conidia also acts as important inoculums of the pathogen. In the favorable environmental conditions the conidia germinate and cause infection to the specific host. The germ tubes enter the host through open stomata. The conidia which are produced on the primary spots are easily carried away by wind and causes secondary infection. There are many wild hosts are available for the fungus for its successful survival in the absence of proper host plant.

Disease management:

1. Rotation of crop is essential.
2. Use resistant varieties of Rauvolfia, for plantation.
3. Spraying of recommended fungicide can restrict disease development.
4. The useful biological control is selecting a aerated planting site & maintaining proper distance between plant helpful.

CORYNESPORA SPOTS OF RAUVOLFIA

Corynespora spotting of Rauvolfia was reported to be one of the major serious diseases responsible for extensive defoliation. Reddy, *et.al*, (1971) observed heavy defilation of premature leaves and drying of plant due to leaf spot of Corynespora species.

Symptoms

The leaves are the main site of infection. Initially reddish brown spots are formed on both the surface of infected leaf. Gradual increase of spots produces a large circular spots of average diameter 2-24 µm. The mature spots consists of concentric zones that are dark brown in colour and more distinct. Hence the spots caused by *Corynespora* sp. also called as “target spots”. The target spots on the upper the surface of the leaf turns dark brown in colour and the same spot on the underside of the leaf appear yellowish brown in colour. The spots are encircled by yellowish chlorotic zone. The leaves occur close to the soil surface get infected first and then the disease progress towards the upward region of the plant. The infected plants show stunted growth. Heavy defoliation occurs. Only the tender leaves remains at the top of the tender branches.

The Causal Organism

The causal organism is *Corynespora cassicola* (Berk & Curt) Wei.

The mycelium is branched, septate, intercellular, and grayish brown in colour. The erect conidiophores arise from the fertile hyphae. The conidiophores are simple unbranched straight light brown, septate, structures. The conidiophores measure about 108-8.45 µm in length and 3-10 µm in thickness. The conidiophores bear conidia of variable shape. The conidia may be obclavate cylindrical, elongated, slightly curved or straight. The conidia are hyaline or light yellow coloured or olivacious brown in colour. The conidia are 4-198 µm long and 9-20 µm thick at one end and 4-8 µm wide at the end. A single conidiophores comes out through the epidermal layer of the infected leaf.

Disease Cycle

The pathogenic fungus retained by the infected plant debris and in the seeds (Chowdhary, 1975). Which acts as a primary source of infection. The secondary infection takes place by air borne conidia as well as by any mechanical agency or by insects visitors. The anatomical study of seed gives evidence of presence of mycelia threads in the seeds embryo and cotyledon. The hyphal threads which are transformed through seed coat externally or internally, responsible for spread of disease. The disease appears in seasons of high humidity and on average relative humidity of 78.5% is necessary for heavy damage of plant.

Disease management:

1. Remove & burn plant residue from the field carefully.
2. Chemical soil disinfectants and fumigants have been used by workers of certain places.
3. The infected plant parts should be premed out and destroyed.

ANRHRACNOSE DISEASE OF RAUVOLFIA

Anthracnose is one of the most economically important diseases of Rauvolfia. It is the most destructive and widespread disease of Rauvolfia. In India, Anthracnose disease of Rauvolfia serpentine caused by

Colletotrichum gloesporioides was firstly discovered by (Chowdhary, 1975) from Gujarat area. The disease is widespread throughout the tropical regions of the world.

Symptoms

Initial symptoms appear as a small numerous dark spots over the leaf surface. The spots increase in size and produce large circular spots. The spots are distinct on the upper surface of the leaf. In advanced stage the circular spots coalesce to form large patches that invade the surrounding tissue. Heavily infected leaves get shriveled resulting defoliation that affects the growth and yield of the plant.

The Causal Organism

The disease is caused by *Colletotrichum gloesporioides* (Renz) sacc. (Perfect stage: *Glomerella cingulata* (Stonem) spauld).The mycelium is branched, septate, inter and intracellular. The highly infected region of the host shows numerous acervuli which are globose with an ostiole protruding out of the ruptured epidermis. The acervulus consists of a series of club shaped asci. Each ascus is filled by spindle shaped haploid ascospores.

The fungus produces conidiophores of variable length. The conidiophores are 1-4 celled, unbranched, brown in colour and slightly broad at the base and tapering towards the apex. The conidia produced at the apex of the conidiophores. The conidia are ellipsoidal with rounded apex and narrow truncate base which are hyaline uninucleate, aseptate structures.

Disease Cycle

The fungi causing anthracnose of Rauvolfia overwinter in soil on affected plant debris, as well as twigs of host plant. The spores blown in air acts as inoculums when comes in contact with proper host. Moist weather & moderate temperature favorable for the pathogen. The pathogens also survive is seed acts as source of inoculums. The infected leaves carry conidia as well as acervuli remain in soil for longer duration acts as a source of inoculum.

Disease management:

1. Field sanitation reduces disease intensity in the field.
2. No fungicidal sprays recommended against anthracnose disease of Rauvolfia.
3. Avoid overcrowding of plants.
4. Remove infected plant parts carefully and burn it away from the field.

DIE BACK DISEASE OF RAUVOLFIA

The die back disease is best known in various parts of India. It is the most serious disease. It is particularly destructive disease of affected plants. The disease has been reported from various parts of the world. The losses from this disease are very heavy that vary from season to season.

Symptoms

The die back is one of the most serious diseases of Rauvolfia. In this case drying of infected region gradually progress from top to the bottom of the plant hence the name die-back is given to the disease. Initial symptoms of the disease consist of numerous pinheads like yellowish brown spots on the leaves and stem. The acervuli are scattered all over the infected regions. The pinhead shaped spots increase to form a large circular spot. The severe infection causes heavy defoliation. The severely affected growing tops of the plant get dried. The dryness proceeds gradually towards the bottom of the plant. In this way the entire plant gets lost.

The Causal Organism

The die back disease is caused by *Colletotrichum dematium* (Pers) Grove. The mycelium of the fungus in highly branched, septate, hyaline in young stage and the hyphal wall turns dark and thick at maturity. The mature hyphae produce chlamydospores which are thick walled and intercalary in position. The thickly populated hyphae form black coloured stromata. Many acervuli are developed on stomata, beneath the cuticle by formation of a serious of short, hyaline conidiophores Setae are sterile hyphae, dark coloured occur mixed with conidiophores. Conidia are produced in acropetal succession. At the tip of conidiophores one at a time. The conidia are fusiform, hyaline, non-septate, slightly curved and obtuse at the apex and are about 3-6 to 14- 30 μm in size.

Disease Cycle

The pathogenic fungus overwinter in the infected plant parts in soil for longer duration acts as a source of inoculums for healthy crop or newly sown crop. In favorable environmental conditions the disease spread as much as possible and the conidia that are borne on the infected areas are carried away by rain drops and insect visitors. The conidia germinate in presence of proper host and causes disease.

Disease management:

1. Field sanitation: Removal & careful destruction of infected plant debris from the field before plantation of Rauvolfia.
2. The chemical fungicides such as Mancozeb and Carbendazim are suggested by workers against die back disease.

DISEASES REPORTED ON RAUWOUFIA (*Rauvolfia serpentina*)

Sl. No.	Disease	Pathogen
1.	Leaf spot	*Alternaria alternata*
2.	leaf spot	*Cercospora serpentinae*
3.	Target spot	*Corynespora cassicola*
4.	Premature defoliation	*Curvularia lunata*
5.	Leaf spot	*Epicoccum nigrum*
6.	Root rot	*Macrophomina phaseolina*
7.	Wilt	*Fusarium oxysporum*
8.	Powdery mildew	*Leveillula taurica*
9.	Leaf spot	*Mycosphaesella rauvolfiae*
10.	Leaf spot	*Rhizoctonia solani*
11.	Leaf spot	*Phomopsis sethii*

11. DISEASES OF TOUCH ME NOT (MIMOSA)

English name : Touch me not (Mimosa)

Botanical name : *Mimosa pudica*

Family : Mimosaceae

Indian name : Laywanti, Chue muae

The Mimosa (*Mimosa pudica* Linn.) plant is a trailing herb, stem straight with recurred prickles, leaves alternate, bipinnate, leaf lets 10-12 pen's, folding obliquely upwards on touching, small, sessile linear oblong, flowers tetramerous, pink, in pedunculate, polygamous, globose herb, calyx minute, corolla pinkish, 4 lobed, ovate oblong obtuse, stamens 4, filaments free, rose coloured, superior ovary, oblong, unilocular, fruit a lomentum, slightly curved with 3-5, 1-seeded points.

Mimosa Plant

Medicinal Use

It is astringent, cooling, antiseptic, alternative and blood purifier. It is used in burning sensation in the body, diarrhoea, dysentery, hemophilic conditions, leucorrhoea, and morbid conditions of vagina, wounds, and skin diseases.

RAMULARIA LEAF SPOT OF MIMOSA

The Ramularia leaf spot of chue muae (Touch me not) (*Mimosa pudica*) species is very common on red as well as white flowered Mimosa species especially in nurseries and home gardens, wherever this plant is grown. In India the disease was reported by Patel *et. al.* (1949); A considerable losses caused due to the attack of fungus has been estimated by Alam,, (1993).

Symptoms

The spore produces a vigorously growing hypha on the surface of host leaf which enters the host through injuries, wounds or stomata or the hypha may penetrate the host epidermis by its growing force. The hyphae grow, in the intercellular spaces of the host cells. The hyphal mat is deposited between the cuticle and the epidermis of the host. The epidermis at the affected region is initially visible as chlorotic patch, later it is covered by means of whitish conidia. At the initial stage the pathogen produce small circular sunken spot which gradually enlarge into a large chlorotic spots. The affected region encircled by straw coloured yellowish boarder. The infected leaves fell off before maturity. Heavy defoliation occurs during severe cases of disease development. At the end of the season mostly in unfavorable environmental conditions, the fungus produces black coloured sclerotia on the affected older parts of the plant.

The Causal Organism

The white leaf spot disease of *Mimosa pudica* caused is by *Ramularia mimosae* storvens & Dal. The branched fertile hyphal mats which are deposited between the cuticle and leaf epidermis produce simple superficial conidiophores. The conidiophores protrude out through the ruptured epidermis. The conidia may be produced in abundance. The sclerotia are also produced by fungus during unfavorable environmental conditions.

Source of Inoculum

The manner of dissemination of spores by splashing of water indicates that the great care should be exercised when the trees are watered. The affected plant residue consists of sclerotia that act as a source of inoculum for next season. The air borne conidia are also found Avasthi, *et.al*, (2013). The conidia produced early in the season may cause secondary infection.

Disease management:

1. Collect all the infected plant debris from the infected plant and field and burn it carefully.
2. The pathogen persists in soil in the form of sclerotia hence; expose the upper layer of soil to sunlight. Leave it for a year without showing that reduces the disease intensity for considerable level.

CHARCOAL ROT OF MIMOSA

The charcoal rot disease of *Mimosa pudica* was first described in India by Ashby, (1927). It is one of the severe diseases. It also occurs in other countries of the world. The disease is capable of causing considerable damage of *Mimosa pudica* plants. The pathogen *Macrophomina phaseoliina* is known in several other countries as a charcoal rot fungus.

Symptoms

The respective pathogenic fungus infects the host almost all stages of its growth. In case of seedlings the cotyledons get infected and simultaneously the infection starts at the collar region of the plant. The affected seedlings collapse and dry up. At the collar region of the plant thin dark coloured streaks are developed due to interaction of host and pathogen. The dark streaks increase rapidly during moist weather. The mature leaves found more susceptible. The infected leaves show black coloured spots especially on the marginal region as well as at the apex of the leaf. In severe cases the black spots develop on petioles, midrib of leaf and the stems. Heavy defoliation of affected leaves makes plant like a broom like. Such plants get dried. The stem shows black rotting because of extensive production of sclerotia on the affected regions of the stem. The entire roots get shredded. Partially effected plants remain stunted, leafless, do not produce flowers, or produce small and less number of flowers.

The Causal Organism

The charcoal rot disease is caused by *Macrophomina phaseolina* (Tassi.) Goid. The dry root rots disease of bean is caused by *Macrophomina phaseolina* (Tassi) Goud. The infected region of root shows sclerotial bodies which are mostly from 110-130mm in diameter. The hyphae are septate that are spread between and inside the affected host tissue (Avasthi, *et.al*, 2013). The pycnidial cups are also produced in the affected host tissue. The opening of the pycnidial cup is known as ostiole (Miller and Burke, 1974).The pycnidiospores are elliptical thin walled unicellular, elongated and are about 10-42 × 6-10 mm in size.

Disease Cycle

The pathogenic fungus survives in soil as well as in seed and a variety of organic matter present in soil. It has a broad spectrum of host range where it remains as a saprophyte and in presence of proper host plant it infects and development of disease takes place.

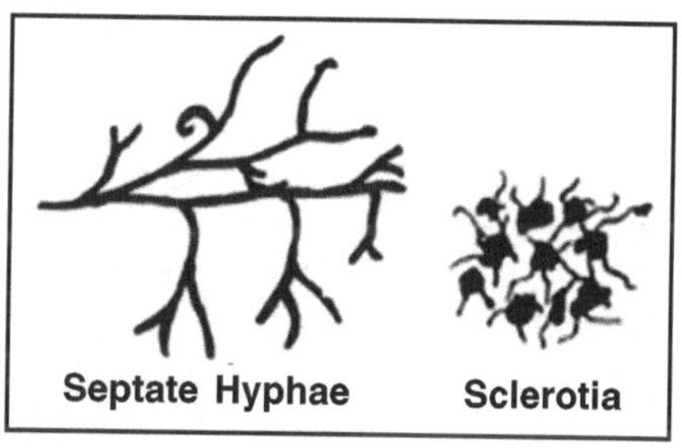

Disease management:

1. Use disease free seeds for sowing purpose.

2. Field sanitation, proper space between plants, crop rotation, drying of seeds are different methods used to control dry root rot disease.
3. Soil amendment with cotton, neem and mustard cake recommended for management of disease.
4. Prasad, (1962) suggested to use resistant varieties i.e. 109859, 163583 against the disease.
5. Seed treatment before sowing reduces disease intensity in the field.
6. Gupta, *et.al*, (1976) controlled the disease by spraying 0.2% Bavistin.
7. Dhingra and Mehrotra, (1980) observed sudden destruction of sclerotia of *Macrophomina phaseolina* in warm wet soil hence the disease can be easily controlled by keeping soil wet for 2-3 week during the temperature above 30ºC.
8. Ghosh, (1981) suggested that the application of nitrogen to the plant reduce intensity of charcoal rot for some extent.

COLLAR ROT DISEASE OF MIMOSA

It is a highly destructive disease infects the root system and collar region of the plant. The affected plant show gradual drying. It was firstly described by Kale, (1967).

Symptoms

The pathogen is a soil borne fungus. The site of infection is the root system. Initially it enters the rootlets and then transferred to the collar region of the plant. The affected roots may get covered with white mycelial hyphae during severe cases of disease development. The epiblema and the cortex of root show olivacious brown streaks indicating the presence of infectious hyphae inside.

The pathogen gets trnaslocated from root system to the collar region of plant where it spread internally into the host tissue. Externally the affected collar region show water soaked region which gradually disconnect water connection due to profuse hyphal growth in the tissue as a result the entire plant get collapsed and dry. All the stages of plant growth found to be susceptible for the disease. The young seedlings may also get infected and killed. The leaves of infected plant become yellow and fell off early before maturity.

The Causal Organism

The disease is caused by *Rosellina mimosae* kale. The mycelium consists of highly branched septate hyphae. The fungus rarely produces conidia (Kale, 1967). The intercellular hyphae deposited in the cortical region produce numerous perithecia which are dark black in colour. The perithecia are abundant on dead root and collar region of the host plant. The perithecia are variously arranged that occur singly or in-groups. The presence of numerous acervuli makes the host surface like a crust like. The perithecia are with ostiole which is supported by a short neck. The spores formed in the perithecia expel out through the ostiole. The ascospores produced by the fungus are unicellular, spindle shaped. The ascospores measure about 22 to 5µ in diameter.

Source of Inoculum

The fungus produces numerous perithecia on the affected root and collar region that purview in soil which is responsible for new infection, during the next season. The fungus persists in soil in the form of sclerotia which are produced on affected root system. The mycelial thread which remains on plant residue in soil causes new infection.

Disease management:

1. Collect the infected plant residue from the field and burn it carefully that can help to reduce disease intensity for some extent.

DISEASES REPORTED ON MIMOSA (*Mimosa pudica*)

Sl. No.	Disease	Pthogen
1.	Charcoal rot	*Macrophomina phaseolina*
2.	Leaf spot	*Ramularia mimosae*
3.	Leaf rust	*Ravenelia evernia*
4.	Leaf spot	*Rosellinia mimosae*

12. DISEASES OF BETELVINE

English name : Betel leaves

Botanical name : *Piper betle*

Family : Piperaceae

Indian name : Pan

The plant betel vine (*Piper betel* L.) is an aromatic creeper, with nodes & internodes. The roots grow from the nodal region. The leaves possess long stalks which are heat shaped and arranged in alternate manner on the stem. Each leaf possesses 5-7 ribs arising from the base. It has very small flowers and bear one seeded spherical small berries. It is an aromatic creeper, with slender stem which possesses nodes and internodes. The nodal region produces roots. It is grown for its leaves which are stalked, alternatively arranged on stem having pointed apex. The plant produce small sized flowers and spherical single seeded fruits (berries) It is believed that the central and eastern Malaysia. At present it occurs throughout the tropical regions of the world. In India it is extensively cultivated at Tamil Nadu, Madhya Pradesh, West Bengal, Orissa, Maharashtra and Uttar Pradesh. The chemical composition of betel leaves is fat 0.8% minerals 2.3%, fibre 2.3%, Carbohydrates 6.1% Protein 3.1% in 100 gms of sample. It is best source of calcium.

Medicinal Use

It is useful in arresting secretion and it is aphrodisiac. Several household remedies are prepared from betel leaf. The leaf juice with a cup of milk and a teaspoon sugar is given against obstructed or scanty urination. A spoonful of betel leaf juice along with a spoonful honey before meal helps against weakens of nerves. It is a good tonic, when taken twice a day. The leaves soaked in mustard oil and warmed and applied to the chest to relieve cough and some difficulty in breathing. The stalk of betel leaf dipped in castor oil and can be introduced in the rectum of children to relieve constipation. The leaf extract is effective in treating sore throat. Irritating cough can be cured by taking crushed fruits with honey. Betel leaves are helpful in treatment of inflammation such as arthritis. Leaf extract applied over wounds in different parts of India. It possesses healing property. A hot poultice of leaves mixed with coconut oil and can be applied to the lions, against lumbago.

The betel leaf in used as aromatic stimulant and ant flatulent. It is useful in arresting bleeding. Betel leaf juice has diuretic properties. Leave are beneficial in the treatment of nervous pains, & debility. It has analgesic and cooling properties. Leaves are useful in pulmonary affection in child hood & old age, also useful in other respiratory disorders. Leaves dipped in castor oil can be introduced in the rectum of children to relieve constipation. The leaves are effective in treating sore throat, inflammation, boils, lumbago & problems of Breast milk secretion.

The number of fungi has been recorded causing leaf rot disease of betel vine from diffident parts of India.

1. Leaf rot *Phytopthora parasitica*
2. Leaf rot *Phytopthora palmivora*

FOOT AND LEAF ROT DISEASE OF BETELVINE

Foot and leaf rot disease of piper betel is a disease of major important. It occurs in all the fields of India where betel vine is grown. It in a highly destructive disease that causes enormous losses of crop.

Symptoms

The pathogen is soil borne that infects all the parts of the plant like roots, shoot and leaves. The wet foot rot disease occurs due to wetting of betel vine for longer duration. Initially the leaves lose their turgidity for same extent and slightly droop off. In severe cases the leaves turns flaccid. The shoots of the infected plant becomes yellowish due to physiological disturbances. Chaudhary, (1944) reported shriveling of heavily affected stems. The leaf rot symptoms appear as a small brown dot especially on the leaf lamina. The spot increase during humid wet environment. The enlarged spots develop into wet rot that cover major part of the leaf. The rotted area gradually extend to the petioles and then towards the stem. The affected area on leaf lamina show distinct wrinkles.

The root system of the plants also gets infected due to soil borne pathogen. The rootlets get infected first and then the disease progress towards the old root system. The tissue of the severely affected root lets and older roots get macerated that emit a typical fishy odour. Due to the soft rot symptoms or maceration of the roots, only the fibrous portion remains back. The entire plant becomes yellow and collapse.

The Causal Organism

The causal organism is *Phytopthora parasitica* Dastur. It was firstly reported by Asthana, (1957). The mycelium is branched inter and intracellular. The pathogen does not produce haustoria. The sporangiophore are branched. The tips of the branched sporangiophore bear oval or lemon shaped sporangia of average size 30-63.3 × 20.4-40.8 µm. Each sporangia posses a prominent papilla. The sporangia are mostly spherical measuring 2.2-5.7 µm in size which are filled by biflagellate zoospores. The pathogen produce smooth walled globular that oogonia are hyaline. After maturity the oogonia turns light yellowish in colour. The oogonia measure 20.4-40.8 µm in size. Initially the antheridia are hyaline, thick walled that develop on hypha which is adjacent to the oogonium. The oogonium is globular, thick walled, hyaline or light yellow coloured that measure about 5-8µm. The oospores are resistant spores that can tolerate to adverse environmental conditions.

Pathogenecity

Dastur (1935) studied the Pathogenecity of *Phytopthora parasitica* to the betel vine crops. Chowhary, (1944) and Asthava, (1947) reported that the pathogen can survive in soil for years because of its saprophytic nature. Tewari, (1967) studied the comparative saprophytic ability of *Phytopthora parasitica* var. *piparina* and came to the conclusion that the *Phytopthora parasitica* is a week saprophyte that can easily be restricted by the growth of the other saprophytic fungi.

Disease Cycle

The infected leaves ,stem and the rotted root system remains in the field where the previous crop was grown, hence the soil acts as primary inoculum for a newly sown crop or when a stalks of infected plants were used for propagation purpose that bears diseased plants. The pathogen is soil borne. The oospores are the resistant spores of the pathogen that can tolerate adverse environmental conditions hence the pathogen remains in soil in absence of proper host plant. The pathogen survives on number of collateral hosts as mentioned below. The collateral hosts also acts as an important source of pathogen for development of disease on new crop. The oospores and chlamydospores of the fungus survive in soil year after year. Cook, (1949) reported the survival of fungus in soil. Saksena and Mehrotra, (1970) found out that the infected parts of the plant get rotted but the mycelium cannot be detected in the healthy parts. The fungus grows inside the host tissue without any symptoms outside. The cuttings of such plants used for propagation purpose produce a diseased plant.

Disease management:

1. Dasgupta, *et.al*, (2008) reported *Colocasia esculanta* is a weed plant that acts as a collateral host of phytopthora parasitica.
2. There are reports of use of Metalaxyl against foot rot disease of betel vine.
3. Soil amendment with corn straw reduces foot rot disease to a greater extent.
4. Uppal, (1937) controlled foot rot of betel vine by using *Trichoderma viridae* against the respective pathogen.
5. Chaurasia, (1968) reported the effectiveness of *Aspergillus flavas* and *Penicillium* species for the control of food rot disease.
6. Use of disease free cuttings for propagation can reduce disease intensity for some extent.
7. Dastur, (1931) recommended collection and destruction of infected plant part or entire plant for reduces disease intensity.
8. Asthana, (1947) suggested the use of upper most portion of the parental plant for the further propagation purpose to reduce disease intensity.
9. All the affected parts of the plant should be carefully collected in a sterile polythin bag and burn it away from the field.
10. Spraying of betel vine plants with recommended fungicide before and during rains gives effective protection.

11. Dasgupta, *et.al*, (2008). suggested dipping of cuttings in 1% Streptomycin solution before sowing can control rot disease of betelvine.
12. Asthana, (1957) recommended spraying of 1% Bordeaux mixture twice a month for the control of the disease.

SCLEROTIAL FOOT ROT OF BETEL VINE

The white rot or mould of betel vine is the common name of sclerotial rot, which is potentially destructive disease of betel vine under favorable environmental conditions. The crowded planting and wet weather is responsible for fast spread of white rot disease. The disease has been reported to be sporadically very severe in many areas worldwide. The white rot has emerged as a serious disease due to extensive crowded cultivation of betel vine.

Symptoms

All the stages of the plant growth are susceptible for the attack of Sclerotium rolfsii. It is a soil born pathogen attack first at the collar region of the plant. The infection spread upward as well as downward on the stem. The affected tissue of the stem shows rotting. Within a short period the rotted region get enveloped by the dense white cottony mass of hyphae of the pathogen. It is visible in severe cases of disease development. The dark black coloured spots develop on the stem. The leaves turn yellowish that loose turgidity, hang down and fell off. Ultimately the entire plants dry and die. The fungus produces very prominent brown coloured fruiting bodies (Sclerotia) on the affected regions of the plant.

The Causal Organism

The rot disease of beans is caused by *Sclerotium rolfsii* Sacc.

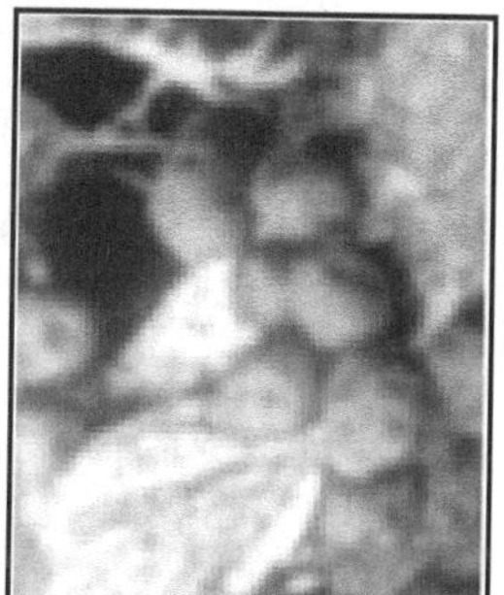

Sclerotia

The mycelium is highly branched and coenocytic. The pure culture of the respective fungus which is cultivated on potato dextrose agar medium appears fresh white. The brown coloured sclerotia are produced on the laboratory culture. The sclerotia resemble the mustard seeds. The mycelium shows clamp connections at the region of septa. Infected stems shows deep brown lesions on the stem near soil surface.

Disease Cycle

The pathogen persists in soil in the form of sclerotia. The fungus produces numerous sclerotia. The sclerotia overwinter in decaying refuse.

The fungus has broad spectrum of host range which retain fungus survive from are favorable crop period to another in the form of sclerotia in the soil. The soil borne sclerotia reach to healthy plant by agricultural tools, animals, irrigation water and through seed sets.

Disease management:

1. Maintain a proper distance between two plants.
2. Careful removal of plant residue of previous crop reduces disease intensity.
3. Use resistant varieties for sowing purpose.
4. Field sanitation reduces disease intensity. Collect and burn all plant residues from the field and burn it away.
5. Deep ploughing of field soil during summer days is beneficial.
6. Reduction in soil borne sclerotia also takes place by flooding of soil.
7. Rotation of crop of 3-4 year reduces disease in the field.
8. Soil sterilization with recommended fumigants reduces soil
9. Yadav, (2013), recommended the use of penta-chlorobenzene at the rate of 25-100 kg/ha against soil borne pathogen.
10. Tewari, (1968) suggested soil amendment with groundnut cake or safflower cake to reduce disease intensity.
11. There are the reports of application of oil cake of black sesamum restricted the growth of *Sclerotium* sp. in soil.
12. The use of biological agents like *Trichoderma harzianum, T. lignorum* and Bacillus sp. can restricts the growth of the pathogen and reduces disease intensity.
13. Collection and careful burning of infected plant residue reduces disease intensity.

ROOT ROT DISEASE OF BETEL VINE

The pathogenic fungus is soil borne. It causes serous root rot disease of betel vine. The root rot is a potentially destructive disease of betel vine under conditions of crowded growth of plants and wet weather. The disease has been reported to be sporadically severe in many areas of world. The root rot is a very serious disease of betel vine because the affected entire plant get dried and destroyed.

Symptoms

The pathogen is a soil born fungus that attacks the basal region of the stem. Decay of affected region takes place that produce reddish cankerous patch. The infection spread on the stem and roots just below the soil surface. The severely affected roots turn reddish brown and disintegrate. The infected plants above the ground level become yellow and then dry up. Chaurasia, (1980) observed extensive development of disease during the months of October-November. The affected plant can easily be identified from long distance. All the stages of plant growth are susceptible for the disease development.

The Causal Organism

The root rot disease is caused by *Rhizoctonia solani.* The mycelium of pathogenic fungus consists of septate hyphae. In young stage the hyphae looks hyaline but at maturity turn to brown. The mycelium is highly branched the size of hyphae varies from 117.7-173.5 × 6.19-9-29 µm. The fungus produces sclerotia within 5-6 days under laboratory conditions. The sclerotial are variable in size. The size of sclerotia varies from 1-3 µm in diameter. The sclerotial are barrel shaped structures which are made up of threads of hyphae which measure about 2.-35 × 10-15 µm is size. The infected foliage of betel vine possesses white crust or white mycelial net at the distal ends of severely infected leaf. In severe cases of disease development the fungus produces smooth surfaced sclerotia on affected region of plant part.

Disease Cycle

The fungus survives on number of host plants hence it is termed as polyphagous fungus. It attack of about 287 genera of monocot & dicotyledonous flowering plants. The fungus perennates in the form of mycelium or sclerotia on affected plant debris in the soil. The fungus adopted in most of the types of soil. The fungus remains in soil for indefinite period. The sclerotia also remain in soil for longer duration. The sclerotia germinate in favorable conditions and produces infective propagates, which acts as source of inoculums. The spread of fungus takes place by rain drops, irrigation or floodwater, any mechanical tools and infected plant debris. The infected plants seed sets germinate into infected plant. The soil borne. Inoculum is splashed by rain to the foliage that causes web blight. In favorable weather conditions the hyphal threads of the pathogen spread from infected part to healthy.

Disease management:

1. The *Rhizoctonia solani* is a soil borne pathogen hence it is expensive to control the pathogen by using soil sterilizing fumigants and fungicides.
2. Soil sterilization by heat is recommended to reduce soil borne *Rhizoctonia* species.

3. Spraying of Bordeaux mixture on the ridges of soil before plantation can reduce disease intensity.
4. The collection and burning of infected stems, roots and other plants can reduce the disease intensity.
5. Avoid sowing of new crop in the same field.

ANTHRACNOSE DISEASE OF BETEL VINE

Anthracnose of betel-vine is common disease occur in all the betel-vine growing areas of the country. Uppal, (1937) reported anthracnose of betel-vine in Mumbai and Mysore. (Nutan kumar, et. al, (2014). found 60% loss of crop due to anthracnose disease.

Symptoms

The symptoms consist of numerous dark brown spots with irregular margin mostly that appear on leaf lamina. The spots enlarge gradually occupying maximum area of the leaf. The disease reduces market value of betel-vine. The host tissue around the spots gets invaded. In severe cases stems get affected. The infection on stem appears in the form of dark black circular spots. Mujumdar, (1970) observed 92% relative humidity favors extensive development of disease. The infection is mainly confined to upper surface of the leaves. The severely affected leaves dry and fell off. Many acervuli occur on the necrotic regions of the affected leaves and stems.

The Causal Organism

The disease is caused by *Colletotrichum capsici* (Sydow) Butter and Bisby. The mycelium is branched that consists of narrow , sparsely septate, hyaline hyphae which turns dark brown at maturity. The fungus produces acervuli on dark brown stromata. Acervuli are formed beneath the epidermis but later become erumpent. The acervuli are round, irregular or elongated in shape of about 500 μm in diameter. There are 1-4 septate setae which are dark brown in colour and swollen at the base. The fungus produces closely packed conidiophores. The conidiophores arc unbranched and hyaline. The conidia are in the form of pinkish masses & hyaline to sub hyaline. The conidia are of variable in size and shape, mostly oblong to cylindrical, two celled having obtuse ends, slightly curved, contain 1-2 oil globules. The conidia measure about 10-25 × 3.5-7.0 μm in size. The fungus produces perithecia at maturity, which are sub-spherical, having prominent hairs at opened end or ostiole. Asci are situated at the basal region of perithecial cup, which are sub – clavate, pedicellate, and about 55-70 μm in length. Ascospores are hyaline, unicellular spores which measure about 12-22 × 3.5-5 μm.

Disease Cycle

The pathogen survive in soil on infected plant debris for longer duration. The fungus chiefly overwinters in infected plant debris as mycelium. The infected seed sets results in diseased seedling. In the spring season the mycelium present on plant debris start producing conidia which are light in weight, and easily blown away by irrigation water, air currents or by insect visitors. In presence of healthy proper host plant the spores acts as inoculum and infects the host to cause disease. The disease mostly appears in the month of November-December.

High humidity is essential pre requisite for sporulation. The conidia germinate best in the presence of free water and moderate temperature.

Disease management:

1. Remove all the infected leaves and burn it out of the field that could reduce the disease intensity during the season.
2. The disease free propagating material should be used to reduce disease in the field.
3. Application of 1% Bordeaux mixture suggested for control of the disease.
4. The Bavistin (0.2%) and Cuman (0.2%) recommended by workers to reduce disease intensity.

POWDERY MILDEW DISEASE OF BETEL VINE

The disease has been reported by Uppal, (1937) from Mysore and found about 40% loss of crop during the month of October.

Symptoms

The disease appear first in the form of whitish brown small patches on the under surface of the infected leaf. The corresponding surface of infected region turns yellow. The patches of fungal growth gradually enlarge and cover the entire leaf surface. In severe cases the powdery growth of the fungus spread all over the growing tips and stem. The affected appear unhealthy. Sathyabrata Maiti and Shivashankara, (1998) observed shedding of affected part of leaf from veins. Gradually the affected leaves become yellow and fell off. Curling and defoliation occurs; simultaneously the stems become yellowish, delicate and get withered.

The Causal Organism

The causal organism is *Oidium piperis.* The mycelium of consist of branched hyphae which are septate with 4.1-98.2 µm in size. The fungus produces conidiophores which appears emerging from the superficial fertile mycelial mat. The conidiophores are unbranched measure about 63-163 µm long and 18-22 µm wide. Each of the conidiophores produces single conidium, i.e. the conidia are borne singly or very rarely in chain of two or many.

Disease Cycle

During well growth of the betel vine the environmental factors becomes favorable for pathogen. The favorable environment activates the dormant mycelium present in infected plant debris, and abundant conidia production takes place. The conidia are light in weight that is easily carried away by insects and wind. Whenever these conidia comes in contact with betel vine causes disease. Even a single conidium enough to initial disease. The pathogenic spore perennates in intact malformed infected betel vine.

The conidia blown from these infected plant parts and there to healthy plants and cause disease. The germ tubes of fungus enter the host and absorb food material by sending haustoria inside the host tissue. Moderate temperature & high humidity are suitable factors for development of disease.

Disease management:

1. There are reports from Rajasthan about the effectiveness of Aureofungin against *Oidium piperis* causing powdery mildew.
2. Spraying of 0.2% Sulfex found to be effective against powdery mildew.
3. Spraying of 0.5% Bordeaux mixture along with 1% sulphur gives satisfactory control of the disease.
4. There are reports of one or two applications of sulphur give effective protection.
5. Careful collection and burning of all the infected plant parts and plant residue from soil surface reduces disease intensity at considerable level.

DISEASES REPORTED OB BETEL VINE (*Piper betel* L.)

Sl. No.	Disease	Pathogen
1.	Leaf spot	*Alternaria alternata*
2.	Leaf rot	*Cephalosporium acremonium*
3.	Leaf spot	*Cercospora piperata*
4.	Leaf spot	*Cladosporium pipericolum*
5.	Leaf spot	*Colletotrichum piperis*
6.	Leaf spot	*Corynespora cassicola*
7.	Wilt	*Fusarium moniliforme*

(Contd...)

Sl. No.	Disease	Pathogen
8.	Leaf spot	*Glomerella cingulata*
9.	Stem and root rot	*Macrophomina phaseolina*
10.	Powdery mildew	*Oidium piperis*
11.	Root rot	*Pellicularia filamentosa*
12.	Leaf spot	*Pestalotis piperis*
13.	Leaf decay	*Phytopthora parasitica*
14.	Root rot	*Pythium piperina*
15.	Root and stem rot	*Pythium vexans*
16.	Root rot	*Sclerotium rolfsii*
17.	Leaf decay	*Trichothecium roseum*

13. DISEASES OF ASHOKA

English name : Ashoka

Botanical name : *Saraca indica*

Family : Caesalpinaceae

Indian name : Ashoka

The Ashoka (*Saraca indica* Linn.) is a conical shaped tree with dark brown bark and compound leaves forming a dense crown. Flowers bright orange in small dense branches. Fruits flat with several smooth grey seeds.

It is a small evergreen tree with inverted hanging branches. It is cultivated as ornamental plant in gardens, lawn areas of institutes and offices. It has orange coloured flowers flat fruits. Fruit consists of several seeds of grey colour. It is one of the sacred trees of grey colour. It is one of the sacred trees of Hindus. The bark of tree possesses medicinal properties.

Twig of Ashoka

A Mesophyte, medium sized evergreen tree with aerial erect woody stems and branched tap root system. Leaves simple, petiolate with wary surface. Flowers yellowish green in colour. Flower pedicellate, bisexual, regular, Actinomorphic, stamens many, calyx with three sepals and corolla with six petals. Carpel many, Apocarpous with superior ovary. Fruit an etario of berries, large albuminous, smooth and shiny.

Medicinal Use

The decoction of bark in used for arresting bleeding. Bark extract used to cure gynecological problems. The intestinal piles can be caused by the use of bark. The decoction of bark given against dysentery. The extract of flowers prepared by grinding with drinking water which is used to cure hemorrhagic dysentery (15-20 drops enough). The powder of dried flowers useful in diabetes.

The bark is used for arresting bleeding or secretion and as a uterine sedative. It is effective for excessive blood loss during menstruation due to presence of uteri fibroids, leucorrhoea and other cause. The bark is also effective for internal piles. Decoction in useful in dysentery. The extract of flowers can cure hemorrhagic dysentery. The dried flowers of Ashoka tree are useful in diabetes. The bark in also useful entreating scorpion-sting. It is an import medicinal plant commonly grown as an ornamental plant at the gardens. It is an ever green tree.

CLADOSPORIUM LEAF SPOT OF ASHOKA

The Cladosporium leaf spot is one of the important disease of Ashoka (Saraca Indica) reported from certain parts of India. In favorable weather the spread of disease takes place very fast. It causes considerable foliage damage under favorable weather conditions.

Symptoms

The fungal pathogen *Cladosporium sphareospermum* Penz. enters the leaf through wounds, lenticels or stomata's. The mycelium is intercellular. The symptoms initially are in the form of distinct chlorotic dots on the surface of host leaf. The spots increase in size and turn brown to dark black in colour (Verma, *et.al*, 2008). The margin of the spots is highly lobed representing the growth of the fungus. The mature spots show dark black colour on the dorsal surface of leaf and the corresponding ventral leaf surface shows grayish moldy growth of the fungus which can be seen by magnifying lens. The moldy growth consists of black coloured dusty spores and mycelial threads. The disease is very common in temperate regions wherever the host is available. The infected leaves play a source of inoculum. The infected leaves droop off late after infection. The necrotic spots on the affected leaf carry the source of inoculum (Srivastava, *et.al*, 1978).

The Causal Organism

The leaf spot disease of *Saraca indica* caused by *Cladosporium sphareospermum*. It is a facultative parasite. The asexual spores of this fungus retained on the dead organic matter as a saprophyte. In presence of moisture the *Cladosporium* grow and flourish extensively on the respective host and also on the dead plant debris. The mycelium is highly branched that consists of septate hyphae. The mycelium is brown in colour. At maturity some of the fertile hyphae become erect and acts as conidiophores. The conidiophores are unbranched.

Disease Cycle

The disease is prevalent during warm weather & humid environment. The infected leaves fell off on ground acts as source of inoculums. The air borne spores when comes in contact with proper host leaf causes infection if the weather conditions are favorable. The spores of Cladosporium are very commonly present in air which acts as important source of inoculum (Kumar, *et.al*, 2013).

Disease management:

1. Careful removal and destruction of infected plant part reduces further spread of diseases in the field.
2. Spraying of Ziram and Captan are recommended against the disease.

DISEASES REPORTED ON ASHOKA (*Saraca indica*)

Sl. No.	Disease	Pathogen
1.	Leaf spot	*Cladospermum sphareospermum*
2.	Leaf spot	*Colletotrichum gloriosporiodes*
3.	Leaf spot	*Dachylium fusarioides*

14. DISEASES OF INDIAN MALLOW

English name : Indian mallow

Botanical name : Meliaceae

Family : *Abutilon indicum*

Indian name : Kanghi

The Indian mallow (*Abutilon indicum* Mill.) is an erect woody plant which appears velvety and grayish green in colour. Generally it is 1 to 11/2 meter in length. It has yellow flowers. Fruits are flat, with radiating points that are grey in colour with kidney shaped seeds. Mature plants are more aromatic. All the parts like bark, leaves, seeds & roots are used as medicine.

It is a common weed plant grows on dry open places. This herb is an erect, much branched with tap root system. Stem is aerial, cylindrical, hairy, and solid with ramal and cauline simple leaves which are arranged alternately. The leaf petiolate, stipulate, ovate, serrate and acute. The venation is multicostate reticulate. The flowers in solitary axillary inflorescence, stamens many (monodelphous), ovary superior, multicarpellary, with one ovule in each locules on axil placenta. Fruit is a schizocarp, many seeded, small non endospermic.

Medicinal Use

The root is useful as pulmonary sedative. This herb is laxative & tonic. It promotes libido. Plant is valuable in fevers, respiratory disorders. The herb is given in bronchitis, catarrh and biliousness. The seeds are very effective in curing piles. The drug has soothing effect on the skin & mucous membranes. Paste of herb applied on the affected parts in case of abscess, carbuncle, Scabies and itches. The leaf paste in effective against boils & ulcers. The decoction of herb is used as mouth wash. The seeds useful in killing thread worry.

RUST DISEASE OF INDIAN MALLOW

The Abutilon plant is a shrub that occurs as wild plant. The rust occurs on Abutilon leaves & tender stem causing drying of leaves in severe cases. The disease is favored by temperature from 15 to 22 °C. Defoliation of leaves affects the plant health. The rust is one of the very serious destructive diseases of mallow (*Abutilon indicum*). Many cycles of the disease occur within a season because the life cycle of the pathogen requires only 2-3 weeks.

Symptoms

The slightly raised brownish spots appear on the ventral leaf surface. The corresponding dorsal leaf surface shows distinct yellow spot like depressions which are circular. The spots increase in size and coalsac to form large blotches of about 1 cm in diameter. The fully mature raised spot or rust pustules burst open exposing a mass of powdery texture which consists of numerous teletospores. In severely affected cases the leaves get shriveled and droop off before maturity. The affected plants remain stunted.

The fungus *Puccinia heterospora* sometimes produces large (3/8 inch [1 cm]) blotch like dark lesions on both the surfaces of leaf but they are often more prevalent on the underside of the leaf Avasthi, *et.al*, (2013). Rust disease of mallow (*Abutilon indicum*) caused by *Puccinia heterospora*. The symptoms resemble those caused by *Puccinia malvacearum*. A fungus causing rust of other plants of malvaceae family. The disease causes extensive defoliation and makes plants delicate.

The Causal Organism

The rust is caused by *Puccinia heterospora*. The mycelium is highly branched with septate hyphae. The teletospores are dark brown that are exposed through burst open sori. The clusters of teletospores resemble a dark brown powdery mass which is easily carried by wind, water and other mechanical agencies to a long distance.

Disease Cycle

In severe cases of disease development, the teletosori burst open by exposing numerous spores in powdery form hence the spore are easily carried by wind, splashing water, insect visitors and any other mechanical agency form infected to healthy leaf of the same plant or other plants. New spores are formed within 2-3 weeks after infection hence the inoculum density increase to a great extent causing extensive damage to the plant.

Disease management:

1. Selection of the disease free plant material is essential for sowing purpose.
2. Grow plants by leaving enough space between them.
3. Collect all the affected leaves from infected plant and ground and burn it carefully.
4. Removal of leaves at a very early stage of infection may help to reduce the disease intensity to a great extent.
5. Destroy all collateral host' plants of the family malvaceae which occur as a weed around the cultivated area.
6. The non-synthetic fungicides like Ferbam, Mancozeb (Diathane M-45), Sulfur, Zineb, Copper fungicides have been recommended by the scientists as an effective chemical against the rust disease of Abutilon from different parts of India.

DISEASES REPORTED ON INDIAN MALLOW (*Abutilon indicum*)

Sl. No.	Disease	Pathogen
1.	Leaf spot	*Cercospora avicennae*
2.	Leaf spot	*C. malvaccearum*
3.	Powdery mildew	*Laveillula taurica*
4.	Leaf rust	*Puccinia abutili*
5.	Leaf rust	*Puccinia heterospora*
6.	Stem and leaf gall	*Synchytrium varanasense*

15. DISEASES OF WILD MUSTARD

English name : Wild mustard
Botanical name : *Cleome viscose*
Family : Cleomaceae
Indian name : Hulhul

There are over 150 species of cleome (*Cleome viscose*) distributed throughout the world out of which 14 species found in India. It is a common weed found all over India and it is plentifully in Bengal. It is commonly known as wild mustard. The herb is 30-90 cm tall, few branches grow from base, leaves digitate, 3-5 foliate, flowers yellow, axillary, solitary, growing into lax raceme, fruit siliqua, 5-6cm long seeds dark brown, sub-globose, with faint transverse lines. It is very common on open land and old walls &also in cultivated fields. Leaves & seeds possess medicinal properties.

Medicinal Use

It is used in scorpion sting and snake bite. The ether extract of plants is useful against anticancer. Decoction of roots is used in fever. Juice of leaves and seed oil used to cure skin diseases. Powder of seeds is a good remedy for piles. The fresh leaves are crushed in water and the paste is applied over swellings. Anemia treating medicine is prepared from its flowers in rural India.

CERCOSPORA LEAF SPOT OF CLEOME

The Cercospora leaf spot disease of Cleome (wild mustard) was firstly discovered by Russell, (1969) from the regions of Pusa and Bihar of India.

Symptoms

It is a widespread leaf pathogen of wild mustard (Cleome sp). The disease is caused by *Cercospora cleomis.* It is the main foliar disease of wild mustard. The affected leaf show elongated lesions at the marginal region of the leaf. The lesions at the on the leaf lamina appear as pin sized chlorotic spots with a small necrotic centre and a more diffused boarder. The colour of the lesion varies according to the relative humidity. During low humid environment the lesions must be tan or brown coloured but later turns dark brown in colour especially during moist weather. Many spots coalesce to form large blighted patches on the leaf; hence the disease is called as leaf blotch.

Thc Causal Organism

The fungus causing leaf blotch of wild mustard (*Cleome viscose*) is *Cercospora cleomis* Ell & Halst. The mycelium is pale brown to olivacious. The mycelium which is present in the leaf tissue accumulates just below the epidermis. Such a fully mature mycelial mat present below the epidermis gives rise to slender conidiophores. The conidiophores are hyaline to brown in colour. The conidia are long hyaline thread like with tapering ends. The conidia are borne singly and are two or more than two septate. The conidia germinate at the temperature range of 20 - 22ºC.

Disease Cycle

The infected leaves fell off on the ground that consists of mycelium and conidia. The pathogen dispersed by wind or splashing water brings about fresh infections. If the soil remains moist the mycelium in the fallen plant debris continues to extend and produce more conidia as long as moist conditions and high temperatures last. Thereafter this soil mycelium passes over into a resting condition and is said to survive from one season to the next. The disease is only epidemic under excessive moist condition and high temperatures. The plant debris acts as inoculum for new young plants.

Disease management:

The disease is difficult to eradicate. The following methods can reduce disease intensity for some extent.

1. The crop rotation.
2. The collection and burning of affected leaves during early stage of disease development helps to reduce disease intensity.
3. All leaf debris should be collected and burnt carefully.
4. Spraying of soft soap liquid prepared in water on the leaves reduces disease intensity for some extent.

WHITE RUST DISEASE OF CLEOME

The disease is common on wild mustard (*Cleome* species) in A.P., Tamilnadu and Bengal. It is common on many of the cruciferous plants like mustard, cabbage, rape, radish, cress, turnip and many weeds of the same family.

Symptoms

All the parts of the plant except the roots may show the distinct white chalky blisters of the disease hence the disease is called as white rust disease. The chalky blisters are of variable size and shape on the leaves, stem and inflorescence. Sometimes remarkable distinct swelling of infected parts takes place that is due to interaction of pathogen. The swellings occur especially in the inflorescence which becomes abnormally thickened, up to 12-14 times larger than the normal size. The whole inflorescence becomes fleshy and develops greenish-violet colour. The petals may resemble the sepals and the stamens become leaf like. The infected inflorescence does not produce normal flowers and seeds. The blisters of the pathogen develop on the swollen part of the inflorescence.

The reproductive organs of the pathogen are oogonia and antheridia. The oospores are generally found inside the swelled part of the inflorescence. Russell, (1969) reported the effect of parasite on the host tissue is profound. In affected hypertrophied leaves there is no differentiation between palisade and spongy tissue. All the mesophyll cells of the leaf enlarged two to three times the ordinary size. The stems thickened due to modification of cortex into tissue of large thin walled cells with few intercellular spaces. The affected tissue is rich in starch.

Externally the affected leaves show pale yellow coloured rust pustules of various size and shape that are situated on the lower surfaces of the leaf. During severe cases of disease the size of affected leaf and height of plant is greatly reduced. The mature leaves are more susceptible for the disease. The leaves present closer to the soil surface showed infection first.

According to Russell, (1969) during spore formation the pathogen consumes food more than the host can manufacture. Hence due to the deficiency of food the plant starved and collapse.

The Causal Organism

The *Albugo candida* is the fungal pathogen which is responsible for white rust disease of Cleome plant. The same pathogen causes white rust disease of *Boerhavia diffusa* which is an important medicinal plant.

The mycelium is intercellular that consists of aseptate hyphae. The pathogen produce very small spherical haustoria that are inserted into the host cells to absorb food material; often many haustoria are sent into each cell. Many branches of intercellular mycelium accumulate below the epidermal layer. The sporangial beds arise from these hyphae which occur below epidermis. The compact clusters of sporangiophore arise under the epidermis hence the circle is slightly raised up into a white blister. Each sporangiophore is a very thick, stout and measures about 34-39 µm thick and 15-16 µm long. The overlaying epidermal cells swell and rupture along the softened middle lamellae, exposing the sporangial beds. The sporangia are produced in basipetal chains. The first formed spore is not capable of germination, its functions being probably to aid in the alteration of the epidermis and the final break-through. The chain of sporangia held together due to sticky pads of solution (disjuncture). The sporangia are round, hyaline, multinucleate with uniform thin walls and measure about 12 to 18 mm in diameter. A sporangium may give rise to 4-8 biciliate zoospores. The zoospores release from the sporangium and then after coming to rest the zoospores germinate by producing a germ-tube which is capable to infecting the new host. Mostly the germ tube enters the host through the stomata.

The pathogen produces numerous oogonia and antheridia in some hosts and in some localities. In others they are rarely found. They occur especially in the hypertrophied parts of the stem and inflorescences. The oogonia are globose about 48-59 mm in diameter. The antheridia elongated, single, clavate mostly found adjacent to the oogonia branch. The oospores are with thick wall and brown colour which is provided with low, blunt ridges. The mature oospores measure from 38-53 µm in diameter. The oospores remain in soil and germinate after a period of rest of several months. During germination it produces a vesicle with a small stalk. Later on the vesicle is filled by many zoospores of similar size and shape. Primary infection takes place by zoospores, hence the oospores found in plant debris on soil surface acts as primary inoculum for next year's crop. Germination of oospore occurs at the range of temperature from 1 to 18°C.

Disease Cycle

The pathogen produces numerous oospores which remain in soil on infected plant debris. The weed hosts of Albugo retain the pathogen which acts as source of primary inoculums. The asexual spores of the fungus such as sporangia and zoospores carried away by wind and irrigated water which acts as secondary source of inoculums. Humid and cool environment is more favorable for the development of disease.

The pathogen survives from season to season in the form of oospores released into the soil along with plant debris. The treatment consists of a removal of all affected plant debris from soil and plants can reduce disease intensity for some extent.

Secondary spread of disease takes place by sporangia and zoospores, hence infected plant parts should be collected carefully in sterile polythin bags and burn it carefully.

Disease management:

1. The crop rotation reduces disease.
2. Use healthy seeds for cultivation of plant.
3. Destruction of collateral host also disrupts the continuity of the disease cycle.
4. Collection and burning of affected plant parts reduces disease for large extent.

16. DISEASES OF TRIDAX

English name : Tridax

Botanical name : *Tridax procumbens*

Family : Compositae

Indian name : Jakham jodi

The Tridax (*Tridax procumbens* Linn.) is a perennial herb with ascending branches and creeping base. It is a best known as widespread weed and pest plant The stem cylindrical, purple in colour. Arrangement of leaves opposite, leaf shape oblong-ovate midrib prominent reticulate venation. Mesophyte, Perennial, branched weed, herbaceous with solid cylindrical stem. Leaves simple, margin toothed, exstipulate & opposite. Head inflorescence having ray and disc florets. The plant bears daisy like yellow-centered white or yellow flowers with three toothed ray florets. The leaves are toothed and generally arrowhead shaped. Fruit a cypsela.

Medicinal Uses

Plant possesses antiviral, anti oxidant, anti biotic efficacies; wound healing a, insectificidal and inflammatory properties. It also stops bleeding, used as a hair tonic. It is also used in diarrhea and dysentery.

PHOMA LEAF SPOT OF TRIDAX

It is one of the most severe diseases of Tridax. It occurs in all parts of India where *Tridax* is grown. The leaf spot disease of *Tridax procumbens* linn. caused by *Phoma tridacis* Wehmeyer. The disease is firstly reported by Wehmeyer, (1964) from Kangra H.P. The disease is capable of causing considerable damage to *Tridex procumbens* in the area.

Symptoms

The older leaves are more susceptible for the disease. The infected leaf shows slightly sunken spots that may arise on any part of leaf blade. The spots are usually circular or angular if present at the vein. The spots vary in size up to 0.5-1 cm in diameter. The spots are mostly dirty white in colour with a light-brown or yellow margin. The keen observation shows a zone of deep green area around each spot. The lesions are also developing on the stems. The lesions on the stem resemble the lesions of leaf. In severe cases of disease the lesions were enveloped by numerous randomly distributed pycnidia.

The Causal Organism

The leaf spot of Tridax is caused by *Phoma tridacis* Wehmeyer. The pathogenic fungus enters the leaf through the stomata. This fungus also enters the host tissue by direct penetration under certain conditions. The mode of entry into the host plant is also dependant on the environmental factors. The mycelium is septate. The infected cell gets replaced by mycelial mats. The fungus produces sub-epidermal pycnidia that are globose to lenticular ranging from 120-320 mm in diameter. The pycnidia are ostiolate, dark black in colour, which are randomly distributed on the dead spots on leaf and stem of infected plant. The black coloured dotty appearance of pycnidia is necked on deadly spots of host leaf. The pycnidial cups are lined by a wall of single celled thickness. The pycnidiospores are unicellular, slightly curved 3.2 to 5 × 0.6 - 1.8mm in diameter. The pycnidiospores are hyaline. The mature pycnidium expel out the pycnidiospores in presence of moisture through ostiole. The pycnidiospores carried away by raindrops or by insect vectors. Each spore possesses a small tendril like structure which dries up during dry weather that helps spore to fix firmly on the host surface.

Disease Cycle

The pathogen *Phoma tridacis* is usually carried by affected plant debris found on the ground. It cannot live saprophytically on the fallen plant debris of other than host plant. The fungus remain on infected stems and leaves in the form of mycelium. The pycnidia persists on host plant debris which perenate the disease from one season to the next. Under the closed moist weather the mycelium on the plant debris produce oidia which are thin walled unicellular hyaline spores and other thick walled resistant spores called as chlamydospores. The chlamydospores infect the plants during next season.

Disease management:

No control measures suggested.

POWDERY MILDEW DISEASE OF TRIDAX

The tridax (*Tridax procumbence*) is severely infected by the powdery mildew fungus (Mathur and Mathur, 1971) from Jaipur, Rajasthan. It is one of the economically important disease problems of Tridax under open conditions. The disease is responsible to cause serious losses especially in warm and humid climates. The defoliation of premature leaves renders the growth of plant. It is a very common disease on Tridax spread throughout the regions of the world where Tridax occurs. The pathogen has a broad spectrum of host range.

Symptoms

The diseased plants become very conspicuous in the field because of yellow spots on the leaves and other parts of the plants. The pathogen attacks all the parts of the plant except root system. The development of numerous yellow spots on the upper surface of leaves takes place. A whitish powdery mass of fungus grow and spread all over the yellow spots. The powdery mass consists of numerous spores. The powdery mass of spores also found on corresponding area on the lower surface of the leaf. The severely affected leaves shrivel and fell off. The leaves of all the age group are susceptible for the powdery mildew disease. In severe cases the pathogen spread to leaf stalks, twigs and flowering region. The severely attacked plants remain stunted, delicate that do not flourish well; mostly they are killed. The disease becomes severe at the temperature 18-24ºC and relative humidity 70-100%.

This is the endophytic fungus. The mycelium of powdery mildew pathogen grow and spread inside the host leaf by exposing only spores on the surface of affected leaves.

The Causal Organism

The pathogen is responsible for powdery mildew disease of *Tridax procumbence* Linn is *Leveillula taurica* (Lev.) Arn. The mycelium enters the host leaf tissue and often covers the entire plant which appears like white puff. The cleistothecia are also produced within the stroma where the conidiophores and conidia are produced. The cleistothecia are embedded in the mycelium that measure about 135-250 mm in diameter. The cleistothecial wall may have numerous hyphae like freely moving appendages. The appendages are mostly short, indistinctly branched, and olivacious brown that arise from the cleistothecial wall. Usually the cleistothecium enclosed 20-35 club shaped asci. The asci may have the size of 70-110 mm × 25-40 mm. The asci are club shaped which consists of only two ascospores. The ascospores are large cylindrical to pear shaped which are slightly curved and measure about 25-40 mm × 12-22mm. The fungus produces extensive asexual spores on the short hyphal branches which act as conidiophores. The conidiophores vary greatly in size that range 25-95 mm × 14-20 mm.

Disease Cycle

The cleistothecia persist in soil for a long duration that acts as source of inoculum during next season. The pathogen produces numerous conidia which are light in weight. The air borne conidia also acts as a source of inoculum. It has a broad spectrum of host range hence there are more chances of survival of pathogen on the infected plant debris in soil.

The secondary spread of pathogen during the season takes place through insect, wind and splashing of rain drops.

Disease management:

1. Spraying of sulphur based fungicidal dust has been found most effective means of control.
2. Patil (1973) recommended 0.1% Karathane and 0.05% Morestan for control of this disease.

HEAD ROT DISEASE OF TRIDAX

The plant occurs in all parts of the temperate region of India. The plant suffers from head rot disease which is reported by Uppal, *et.al*, (1935) in India.

Symptoms

The plant gets affected at any stage of its growth. The affected plant shows die-back symptoms on peduncle as well as on the stem. The die-back symptoms are in the form of dry necrotic elongated patches that increase gradually and produce a large necrotic area on the stem. The pathogen also produces dark brown dead spots on the leaves and newly growing branches.

The leaves turn yellow due to physiological disturbance of the tissue. The ashen grey or discolored area extends on the leaf that causes premature defoliation. The twigs may show partial or complete necrosis. The affected heads becomes spotted brown and later the brown area increases along the head region and finally develops a soft rot of head. The affected head remains attached to the plant and hang down that acts as a source of inoculum.

The mycelium and fruiting bodies of the fungus occurs on all affected part of the plant. A characteristic feature of head rot disease is that there is extensive exposure of affected tissue takes place which show gradual death and drying. During moist warm weather the affected parts of the plant shows the characteristic smoky grey mycelium at the affected area.

The Causal Organism and Disease Cycle

The head rot of *Tridax procumbens* is caused by *Botrytis cinerea.* The mycelium is smoky grey in colour. It produces branched conidiophores which bear heads of conidia that are extensive in number. The conidia are carried away by insect vectors and wind. Late in the season the mycelial cushions stop producing conidia and start the formation of sclerotia. The sclerotia are hard, black, irregularly shaped structures which may remain embedded in the affected plant part or fallen heads or leaves on the ground. The sclerotia are responsible for the development of disease during next season. The sclerotia remain in the affected plant debris in soil as a primary inoculum. In presence of favorable environment and the host plant the sclerotia germinate by producing infectious hypha which again produces numerous conidiophores and conidia which are carried away primarily by wind.

Disease Management

The plants showing head rot should be removed carefully and that should be burnt very carefully.

DISEASES REPORTED ON TRIDAX (*Tridax procumbens*)

Sl. No.	Disease	Pathogen
1.	Head rot	*Botrytis cinerea*
2.	Leaf spot	*Cercospora tridacicola-procumbentis*
3.	Powdery mildew	*Leveillula taurica*
4.	Stem spot	*Phoma tridacis*
5.	Soft rot or shot hole	*Sclerotium rolfsii*

17. DISEASES OF BUTEA

English name : Bastard

Botanical name : *Butea monosperma*

Family : Papilionaceae

Indian name : Palas

There are 30 species of Butea (*Butea monosperma*); out of which only three species found in India. It is a native of the mountainous districts of India and Burma. It is very common as a wild all over Bengal. It is commonly known as flame of the forest. The Butea (*Butea monosperma*) is very common in deciduous forest of India. Because of colour of its flower, the name is called as flame. It is a medium sized tree with compound leaf having a single terminal leaflet and a single pair of leaflet. In winter season, the leaves fell off. Blooming of flowers takes place in the month of February-March. The stem is twisted, rough with fibrous bark. The leaflets with green upper surface and whitish lower surface. The flowers fire coloured, bright, calyx dark greenish black, gamosepalous, petals 5-7, long, pods very much flat. The plant produces flat pods. Pods are single seeded and very much flat. It is an indigenous plant of India. It is very common in dry deciduous forests of Western Ghats of India. The plant stem secrete red coloured gum, which is called as Butea gum. The gum is the richest source of Gallic and tannic acids. There are reports of occurrence of proteolytic and lipolytic enzymes in fresh seeds. Oil contains number of fatty acids.

Medicinal Use

The leaves are used as tonic, and aphrodisiac. Leaf extract useful in arresting secretion or bleeding. The gum is beneficial in the treatment of diarrhea and dysentery. The decoration of gum is used as a rectal enema. The powder seed recommended expelling intestinal worms. Seeds are also useful in treatment of ringworm and tapeworms. A spoon full honey mixed with a gram of seed powder and taken before meal helps to eliminate intestinal worms. The seed powder mixed with lemon juice given against skin disorders. A hot poultice of leaves can be applied to boils, pimples, ulcers, timorous piles and swelling. The crushed seeds applied over wounds. Leaves of tree reduce blood sugar. The leaves are used in treatment of leucorrhoea. The leaves used in congested and septic throat. The decoction should be used as a mouth wash in the treatment of tooth disorder. The leaves are useful in treating the difficulty of retention of urine. It is a well known tree of Indian forest which in commonly known as "Flame of the forest". It is a medium sized tree with compound leaves. The fruits are flat pods with a single seed in each fruit. The leaves are used as tonic and aphrodisiac. Gum in useful in the treatment of diarrhea and dysentery. Seed power in used to kill intestinal worms. They are useful in the treatment of round worms and tapeworms. The seeds are beneficial in the treatment of skin diseases. A hot poultice of the leaves can be applied to resolve boils, pimples, timorous piles, ulcers and swellings. Crushed seeds used for killing maggots in wounds and sores. The leaves are useful in diabetes. They reduce blood and urine sugar. The leaves are also beneficial in treatment of leucorrhoea, sore throat and are also useful in treating the difficulty of retention of urine.

POWDERY MILDEW OF BUTEA

Yadav (1963b) firstly studied the powdery mildew disease of *Butea frondosa* from Parasnath Hills Bihar, India. The powdery mildew disease of *Butea frondosa* is a common that occurs every year during the month of July-October. The pathogen having a broad spectrum of host range. It occurs extensively during warm humid weather. A variety of plants get attacked by the pathogen. The powdery mildew disease is widely reported on crops plants, forest plants and weeds in India, Canada, Australia, France, Zimbabwe, South Africa, UK and USA. The powdery mildew is economically important disease causing a serious damage of various plants mentioned above as well as the medicinal plant get attacked by the powdery mildew pathogen.

Symptoms

Small grayish-dots appear on the upper surface of the leaf. The infectious dots increase in diameter by extending growing hyphae inside the host tissue. The mature leaves get attacked first and then the infection spread to most of the juvenile foliage of the host plant. The infected young plants are either killed or their vigorousness is greatly reduced. The infection is usually associated with leaves and inflorescence. The powdery lesions on the leaf increase in size and coalesce until the entire host surface including leaves, stem and inflorescence. The infected plant parts dry up. The mycelium is superficial that absorb food from the host by sending haustoria. The mycelial threads which are in contact with the host leaf surface produce knob like sucking organs for absorption of food material. The haustoria are the sucking organs produced by the pathogenic fungus that are inserted into the host cell. The haustoria also help in absorption of food as well as to hold the superficial mycelium with host leaf surface. The superficial mycelium produces asexually as well as by sexual method. Hara (1966) reported the epidemics of powdery mildew on peas which are encouraged by prolonged warm dry days and nights with high humidity.

The Causal Organism

The causal organism responsible for the powdery mildew disease of *Butea frondosa* is *Erysiphe polygoni* DC. The hyphal mat consists of thin hyphal threads that spread randomly on the host leaf surface. The fully mature fertile hyphae act as conidiophores that produce conidial chains at its tip. The conidia develop singly at the tip of conidiophores or rarely the chains of conidium are developed. The conidium is ellipsoid measuring 31-38 mm × 17-21 mm in size. The mycelium produces globular cleistothecia that are 85-126 mm in diameter. Manoharachary, *et.al,* (2004). The fruiting bodies (Cleistothecia) are dark brown to black, tough walled with 10-30 free moving hanging appendages which arise from the wall of the cleistothecium. The appendages are made up of uniseriate cells of hyphae. The appendages are unbranched. Each cleistothecium enclosed a cluster of a series of 8 to 10 asci. The asci are sub-globose and are 50-60 mm × 30-40 mm in size. The asci consist of ascospores of size 22-27 mm × 13-16 mm. The ascospores reinfect the new host plant in presence of favorable environmental conditions. The cleistothecia fell off on the soil and remain as an inoculum.

Disease Cycle

The fungus produce conidia extensively which are easily carried away by wind, insects and other mechanical agencies. The conidia germinate in presence of proper host and favorable environmental factors. In this way extensive spread of disease takes place during the same season. The conidia are responsible for extensive spread of secondary infection. The cleistothecia act as a source of primary inoculum during next year's season. The cleistothecia are tough walled protects the ascospores during adverse environment.

The cleistothecia persist in soil for a long duration. The healthy plant is firstly infected by the ascospores which are released by cleistothecia bodies in the crop field.

Disease management:

1. It is very easy to identify infected leaves in very early stage of fungal infection. Remove and burn carefully all such infected leaves before

sporulation of the fungus. By this method the secondary spread of the pathogen can be reduced for considerable amount.

2. Uppal, *et.al*, (1936) suggested dusting of sulphur (200 mesh) to control powdery mildew caused by *Erysiphe polygoni.*
3. No control measures for powdery mildew on *Butea monosperma* has been studies still today.

DIE BACK DISEASE OF BUTEA

Sahni (1968) reported the infection of *Phomopsis buteae* to *Butea monosperma* at MP India. The pathogen attacks several forest trees including conifers. The disease is widely distributed. The disease attacks the tree in a very early stage of life. It causes die-back symptoms to the leading shoot of the young trees.

Symptoms

The pathogen causes water soaked lesions on the tender shoots and leaves. The lesions oozes amber coloured sticky substance. The affected regions become pale yellow and separates into strips. It causes death of the infected tissue. It is responsible for die back disease of the shoots of the young trees but older trees also suffer severely if the younger branches are attacked. The death of infected tissue at variable distances along the young shoots takes place that produce partial or complete girdling of dead tissue around the shoots. The large trunks of the trees get attacked and cankerous regions are formed on the affected areas. The infected trees show considerable yellowing of the foliage. Severe infection causes death of the tree.

The Causal Organism

The die back disease of *Butea monosperma* is caused by *Phomopsis buteae* Sahni. The mycelium of the pathogenic fungus is septate. It produces numerous pycnidial fructifications on the living and dead tissue of the host. The pycnidia are produced from the mycelium which is accumulated below the epidermis or bark which are densely distributed and break through the surface by the longitudinal slits in the bark. The pycnidia are dark brown to black, partially erumpent, sub-globose, 0.1 to 1.0 mm in diameter, bluntly conical and ostiolate. The pycniospores arise at the tip of the hyaline pycnidiospores. The pycnidiospores are unicellular, hyaline, measure 5.4 to 8.4 × 2.2 to 3.8mm. The mature pycniospores expel out through the ostiole. The large sized pycnidia sometimes possess two or more than two ostiole. The pycniospores are fusiform (Mishra Roli, 2013).

Disease Cycle

The surface injuries on the young shoots of leaf mostly caused due to insect bite or any other mechanical means. The injuries provide passage for the entry of the pathogen into the host. The infection proceeds in all direction and kills the whole of the current years shoot. The mycelium is present mostly in the cortex. The mycelium spread into the tissues of the stem in all directions. Every part of infected plant acts as a source of inoculum for next season. The infected regions produce numerous pycnidia.

Disease Management

The removal and burning of the infected branches can restrict the disease for some extent.

DISEASES REPORTED ON BUTEA (*Butea monosperma*)

Sl. No.	Disease	Pathogen
1.	Leaf spot	*Botryodiploidia theobromae*
2.	Leaf spot	*Cercospora buteae*
3.	Leaf spot	*Ciliochorella eucalyptii*
4.	Legume decay	*Cladosporium buteacolum*
5.	Leaf spot	*Curvularia verruciformis*
6.	Powdery mildew	*Erysiphe polygoni*
7.	Wood decay	*Favolus canadensis*
8.	Leaf spot	*Pestalotia buteae*
9.	Leaf spot	*Pestalotia theae*
10.	Leaf spot	*Phyllosticta buteae*
11.	Leaf spot	*Pseudodiploidia buteae*
12.	Wood decay	*Schizophyllum commune-radiatum*

18. DISEASES OF ASPARAGUS

English name : Asparagus
Botanical name : *Asparagus racemosus*
Family : Liliaceae
Indian name : Satavar

Asparagus Plant

The Asparagus (*Asparagus racemosus* Willd.) occur in tropical & subtropical regions of India. It is a highly branched, spiny shrub with a stout root stock bearing numerous long, fusiform, tuberous roots, leaves minute, flowers 2-6 white strong scented in solitary racemes, pedicels slender, bracts scarious, stamens 6, filaments free, apposite to the perianth segments, anthers 2 celled, ovary trigonous, 3 chambered, short style, 3 lobed stigma, fruit berries.

Medicinal Use

It is used to improve memory power, intelligence and physical strength and maintaining youthfulness. It is aphrodisiac, galactagogus, diuretic, antidysentric, and demulcent. It increases breast milk, promotes sexual vigor, cures swelling eye diseases & it is a good remedy for vaginal discharges.

WILT DISEASE OF ASPARAGUS

Wilt: The disease of Asparagus occurs in every country where this crop is grown. In India the disease was firstly reported by Chona, *et.al*, (1958). The disease is widespread and most severe disease of Asparagus in certain areas. It occurs wherever Asparagus is cultivated.

Symptoms

Asparagus plants are attacked during all the stages of growth. It has observed that the vigorously growing plants are less likely to be affected. The infected seedling shows inward rolling of cotyledons. The affected seedling becomes yellow and finally they fell off. The pathogen is a soil borne; hence root system of host plant is the first site of infection. The pathogen enters the host through root hairs; and reaches the water conducting tissue of the host, where it grows and spread inside the xylem vessels. Thus growths of fungal pathogen inside the xylem tissue blocks the water flow to the plant hence, the leaves becomes yellowish and gets shriveled. In severe cases of disease development small, dark green or brownish spots appear on the leaves and then shriveled. The affected leaves fell off. The plants get dried and the dried plants without leaves remain in the field. The split opened stems shows dark red coloured xylem indicating the presence of pathogenic fungus. The affected root hairs get rotted and discoloured.

The Causal Organism

The wilt disease of pigeon pea is caused by the fungal pathogen *Fusarium oxysporum* f.sp. *udum* (Butter) Snyder and Hansen.

The mycelium of *Fusarium oxysporum* is highly branched that consists of septate hyphae that are hyaline. It is a soil borne facultative parasite. When the infective quantity of inoculum comes in contact with root system of the host starts the infection. After entry into the host, the pathogen may be intercellular but later on it becomes intracellular. It shows extensive growth in the vascular tissues. The colour of fungal colony on PDA (Potato Dextrose Agar) medium appear whitish cottony. The sexual stage of the fungus is unknown. It reproduces by producing numerous conidia. In presence of enough nutrition and favorable environmental conditions, many of the hyphal threads act as conidiophores. The conidiophores cut off conidia at its tip. The *Fusarium oxysporum* produces two types of conidia. The small sized conidia termed as microconidia and the large sized conidia termed as macroconidia. The microconidia are small elliptical or slightly curved, unicellular with one or two septa, thin walled that measure about 5-15 × 2-4mm in size. The macroconidia are curved, thin walled 3-4 septate, which measure15-50 × 3-5mm. Sharma and Pande, (2011).

Disease Cycle

The pathogenic fungus survives in soil for years after year on dead plant residue, affected root system and hence the soil acts as important source of inoculum for newly sown crop. The Asparagus is a medicinal plant. Different types of medicines are prepared from the leaves and roots in rural areas. The raw medicine also carries pathogenic hyphal fragments or spores from one place to other. In case of Asparagus one year old crowns are generally planted. The nursery soil used for growth of the crowns should be free from pathogen and plantation must be in the fields which are free from pathogenic fungus.

Disease management:

1. The pathogen is soil borne and persists in the soil for a long duration hence avoid plantation in the same field.
2. Systematic removal and burning of all affected plants from field can reduce the intensity of inoculum in the soil.
3. Effective control measure can be achieved only by the diseases resistant varieties.

RUST DISEASE OF ASPARAGUS

The rust of Asparagus has been reported from various parts of India where Asparagus is grown in large scale. The pathogen appears to be common in the warmer regions of India, but normally causes severe losses if infection occurs at an early stage in the development of Asparagus. It causes extensive damage of medicinal plant (Asparagus).

Symptoms

The affected plant becomes very conspicuous in the cultivated area due to reddish brown elongated pustules on the affected leaves. This is due to the sori of uredospores. During severe infection the premature leaves may be killed. The dial pustules are slightly raised, elongated and red or brown in colour. The telial stage of fungus occurs late in the season. The teletosori are elongated black coloured. The pustules appear on the stem that consists of group of teletospores, (Thirumalachar, 1941 a).

The Causal Organism

The rust disease of Asparagus is caused by *Puccinia asparagi.* It is a autocious rust. The pathogen produces a Uredosori which are globoid of about 13-21 × 17-26 μm in size, hyaline. The uredospores are continuous, spherical or ellipsoid of about 18-25× 22-30 μm in size with echinulate outer wall and golden yellow in colour. The uredospores consist of 4 equatorial pores. The fungus produces stalked teletospores which are oblong or ellipsoid, two celled of about 18-25 × 30-48 μm in size. The teletospores are slightly constricted at the septum & brown in colour.

Disease management:

1. The fungus is heterothallic hence require two host plants to complete its life cycle. Hence, removal destruction of collateral host helps to reduce disease intensity.
2. There are certain fungicides recommended against the rust disease are Maneb, copper oxychloride, Mancozeb.

BOTRYTIS BLIGHT OF ASPARAGUS

This is widely distributed disease of Asparagus and sometimes appears in severe dimensions. It is a very common and destructive disease of Asparagus. It is a very important disease particularly in moderate temperatures and high humid conditions. The disease causes substantial damage in the field.

Symptoms

Initially the affected plant shows drying of branches from top to bottom. On the affected regions brown coloured spots are seen which are having dark brown boarders. The spots may have chlorotic zone around the spot. The complete plant gets killed by drying. In severe cases the dry affected region of plant shows grayish hyphal mat along with numerous spores.

The Causal Organism

The pathogen responsible blight disease of Asparagus plant is *Botrytis cinerea.* The pathogen Botrytis spread rapidly during hot moist environment.

The mycelium is branched septate that produce abundance of conidia as a result of asexual reproduction. The conidia are born at the apex of conidiophores which are branched grey in colour; arise from the fertile mycelial mat in the host tissue. The pathogen also produces sclerotia which are highly resistant to adverse environment. The sclerotia persist in soil and acts as inoculum for next season. The conidia are easily carried away by wind, insects, and rain drops to a long distance that causes new infection to the respective hosts (Shreemali, 1973 c).

The pathogen has a broad spectrum of host range. A considerable genetic variability in different *Botrytis cineria* strain has been observed from different parts of the world. Infection by Botrytis spread very fast during cool, rainy season usually around 20-27°C temperature and humidity.

Source of Inoculum

The pathogen survives in soil on deed affected leaves. The sclerotia are highly resistant to adverse environment that survive in soil up to next favorable environmental conditions in the infected plant debris. The fungal hyphae may also survive in blighted regions of the stem.

Disease management:

1. Several antibiotics recommended against Botrytis rot of Asparagus.
2. Deep ploughing during summer days helps to make filed soil sterile. This method helps to reduce inoculums potential in the field.

PHOMOPSIS ROT OF ASPARAGUS

The asparagus plant is affected by *Phomopsis.* It is a worldwide in occurrence. Thirumalachar and Mishra (1953) reported the disease of Asparagus *Phomopsis* from Karnataka India. The infection progress slowly and lesions are formed on the affected stems. The spots are mostly oval to elongated patches of dead tissue. The centre of the spot is brown with dark brown coloured margin. The affected stems get dried sometimes may show shriveling. The centre of the fully mature spots becomes white due to growth of hyphae and remaining patch is covered by black dot like structures which are filled with fungal spores and mycelium.

Symptoms

Initially small water soaked spots appear on the stem during warm season with high humidity. The younger plants were found more susceptible. In fact the *Phomopsis* blight occurs at any time when the younger foliage appears on the stems. The infectious hyphae and spores which are present is infected part of previous crop cause infection immediately. The prolonged moist weather favors the disease development hence severity of disease occurs during moist weather. Avasthi, *et.al,* (2013). The highly susceptible species show cankerous growth around girdling region of the affected plant. The unhealthy region of affected plant becomes reddish brown due to inter and intracellular growth of fungus.

These are reports of 2 years survival of spores of Phomopsis on infected plant debris from different parts of the world.

The Causal Organism

The causal agent is a fungus called *Phomopsis asparagi.* (Sacc.) Bubak. The mycelium is septate, highly branched hyaline and intracellular. It is a worldwide in occurrence. The intercellular mycelium gathers under the epidermal layer of the stem which produce black dot like pycnidia which are filled with spores. The spores are hyaline, fusiform unicellular and 5.6-7.2 × 2.1-2.8 mm in size.

Source of Inoculum

The infection to the new plant occurs due to wind borne spores. The affected plant parts persist in soil that carries a source of inoculum. The pycnidia produced on the infected stem of previous crop survive in soil as inoculums. The spores are abundantly found on infected tissue of host plant. The spores require hundred percent (100%) humidity for a short period for germinate. The spores discharge and new infection occurs during wet environmental condition.

Disease management:

1. Collect all the infected plant parts and destroy it by burning away from the field.
2. Destroy the collateral weed hosts present around the crop field.
3. Complete irradiation of the disease is impossible hence, for the control of the disease, care should be taken especially avoid contact of fungal spores with newly grown plants.
4. Avoid growing plants in crowded manner.

DISEASES REPORTED ON ASPERAGUS (*Asparagus racemosum*)

Sl. No.	Disease	Pathogen
1.	Stem blight	*Phomopsis asparagi*
2.	Leaf spot	*Cercospora asparagi*
3.	Rust	*Puccinia phyllocladiae*

19. DISEASES OF WITHANIA

English name : Withania

Botanical name : *Withania somnifera*

Family : Solanaceae

Indian name : Ashwagandha

This plant of Withania (*Withania somnifera* Pauq.) grows on waste lands in sub-tropical regions of India. Plants erect, grayish, under shrub, long tuberous roots, alternate leaves, broadly ovate, sub acute, entire, flowers small, greenish, axillary, gamosepalous calyx, 5lobed, corolla campanulate, greenish yellow, lobes 5, triangular-oblong, 5 stamens, ovary ovoid or globose, glabrous, many ovules, style filiform, bilobed stigma, fruit berry, orange red at maturity which is enclosed by calyx, seed many.

A Twig of Ashwagandha

Medicinal Use

The drug of this plant used in the treatment of anxiety, neurosis and it possesses anti-tumor activity. According to Aayurveda scientists, this plant is used for importing long life, youthfulness, vigor and good intellectual powers. The root posses' germicidal, aphrodisiac, diuretic properties. It cures fever, ulcers, cough, dropsy, impotence, rheumatism, toxicities and leucoderma. It improves physical strength. Mirjalili, *et.al*, (2009) explain "Withania somnifera, as an Ancient Plant for Novel Medicine". According to Ahmad, *et.al*, (2010) "*Withania somnifera* improves semen quality by regulating reproductive hormone levels and oxidative stress in seminal plasma of infertile males".

SOUTHERN BLIGHT OF WITHANIA

Damping off disease of Ashwagandha (*Withania samnifera*) was reported to be a serious disease that cause extensive damages the seedlings. Heavy destruction of seedlings reduces the number of plants that directly affect the quantity (root yield) of product. Hence the disease has become more and more important.

Symptoms

Initially a small brown spot appear on the cotyledons l as well as on young leaves of seedling. The affected leaves get folded. The affected seedling appears yellowish and delicate. The heavily affected leaves droop off. According to Gupta, *et.al*, (1980) burning of entire seedling takes place during severe cases of infection. The disease becomes serious during high humidity and moderate temperature. The environment during the month of mid July – September was found to be highly favorable for the extensive spread of infection. In fact, the plant population is reduced to a great extent.

The Causal Organism

The Southern blight disease of Withania is caused by *Sclerotium rolfsii.*

Disease management:

1. The infection can be reduced by the use of seeds collected from disease free plants for sowing purpose.

2. Avoid repeated sowing of the seeds in the same field.
3. Timely sowing of crop also helps to restrict disease development.
4. Jain, *et.al*, (1980) recommended use of fungicides like Diathane – M.45, Bavistin and Brassicol fungicides against damping off seedlings.
5. Pandey, *et.al*, (1981) suggested spraying of Bayletan and then Brassicol for the successful control of disease.
6. Nema and Mishra (1965) treated seeds with Diathane M – 45 at 3g/ kg seed and found successful control of damaging off disease.

LEAF BLIGHT OF WITHANIA

The leaf blight disease of Ashwagandha (*Withania samnifera*) occurs in India wherever this crop is grown. The pathogen is responsible for enormous losses of the crop. The damages are considerably high.

In India the disease was first reported by Sharma and Pati, (2011). It is one of the destructive diseases of Withania.

Symptoms

The first symptoms of the leaf blight disease of Ashwagandha (*Withania samnifera*) are very small light brown coloured sports on leaves and flowers. The spots increase gradually in size and then coalesce to form large a sized necrotic patch on the affected parts of the leaf and flowers. The necrotic patches consists of distinct concentric rings of dark brown colour and later on the twigs of plant become yellowish and get dried. In this way the tops of all the branches of infected plant withered. Pati, *et.al*, (2009) observed grayish brown colour of heavily infected twigs.

The Causal Organism

The causal organism is *Alternaria alternata* (Fr.) Keissler. The characteristics of pathogen explained earlier. The pathogenic hyphae are branched, septate, which produce simple or branched conidiophores which measure about 50 × 3-6 µm in size. Mostly conidiophores arise in clusters or singly. The conidiophores are straight or flexuous, sometimes geniculate or smooth. The fungus produces conidia in a long strait or branched chains. Each conidium consists of eight transverse septa and several longitudinal septa. Each conidium is obclavate, ovoid to ellipsoidal, pyriform having a small short beak of 2-5 µm thick which is one third long than the parental conidium. The mycelium appears carbon black in colour.

Disease Cycle

The uredospores of rust disease causing fungus are easily carried away by air currents. These spores when comes in contact with healthy leaf or fruit causes rust disease.

Disease management:

1. The first prerequisite for checking this disease is to choose seeds form disease free plant for sowing purpose.
2. Saroj, *et.al,* (2012) suggested seed dressing with suitable fungicidal dust before sowing for excellent control of disease.
3. The affected plants should be sprayed with Diathane M-45 (0.5%).
4. Avoid repeated cultivation in the same field.

DISEASES REPORTED ON WITHANIA (*Withania somnifera*).

Sl. No.	Disease	Pathogen
1.	Leaf spot	*Aecidium withaniae*
2.	Leaf spot	*Cercospora withaniae*
3.	Leaf spot	*Colletotrichum capsici*

20. DISEASES OF TURMERIC

English name : Turmeric
Botanical name : *Curcuma longa*
Family : Zingiberaceae
Indian name : Haldi

The turmeric (*Curcuma longa* Linn.) is a perennial herb, having 60-90 cm height. The rhizomes are short, & thick.

Turmeric is cultivated in large scale in tropical regions of the world. The turmeric is originated from India. besides India, it is extensively cultivated in Thailand, Pakistan, Japan, Korea Malaysia, West Africa, Myanmar, Vietnam, , China, Sri Lanka, Nepal, East & South Pacific Islands, America and Philippines,. In India, the areas cultivating turmeric as a major crop are Maharashtra, Kerala, Andhra Pradesh, Orissa, Tamil Nadu and Karnataka. Turmeric is cultivated in large scale in tropical regions of the world.

The turmeric is known as important spice, throughout the world. The stem is short with raised branches (Ravindran, *et.al,* 2007). The underground rhizome is a modified stem, which is thick, irregularly branched, highly commercial. It is a common spice of everyday use in Indian kitchen. It is the native of southern and South Eastern Asia. Today it is known throughout the world. It has been extensively cultivated in India as a commercial crop. It is used in various formulations in Aayurveda, Traditional medicine and in homeopathic medicines. Chemically it consist of 13.15 moisture, fat 5.1% protein 2.6% Carbohydrates 69.4% in 100 Gms of total weight. The mineral & vitamins presents in turmeric calcium phosphorous, iron, carotene, niacin and thiamine.

Medicinal Use

The rhizomes are aromatic which is atomic and stimulant. It is beneficial in relieving flatulence. It helps to restore the normal function of digestion. It also helps to prevent attack of hysteria. It is the best medicine for intestinal disorder.

The juice of raw rhizome or powder in mixed in butter milk or plain water is highly beneficial in intestinal problems, especially chronic diarrhea. The juice of raw rhizome (6 drops) with cup of water recommended to expelling worms from body. Turmeric is the richest source of Iron hence beneficial in anemia. Turmeric with honey beneficial in anemia. The herbs are useful in treatment of measles. The juice of bitter gourd leaves with few ml of honey and 2 gms of turmeric powder is recommended against measles. Turmeric is used as remedy against bronchial asthema. Turmeric possesses antiseptic properties, which is effective against throat irritations. A spoonful turmeric powder with a glassful of milk twice a daily recommended against asthma. Turmeric powder with ajwain seeds is highly beneficial against colds in infants and children. Turmeric is skin cleanser. It is very effective in the treatment of a variety of skin diseases, such as skin rushes, scabies, ringworm etc. Turmeric powdery is boiled in water for half an hour; the water is used as eye drop, against sore eye problem. Prepare fresh every time. It is common spice in India and most of the countries of the world.

Rhizome is stimulant and a tonic. It is useful in reliving flatulence. It is useful in curing periodic attacks of hysteria. It is useful in intestinal antiseptic, chronic diarrhea. Raw turmeric juice with pinch of salt is given for expelling worms. Turmeric in a rich source of iron so valuable in anemia. It cures bronchial asthma, cough and cold; for treating sprains or swellings, boils, skin disorders & sore eyes.

LEAF SPOT DISEASE OF TURMERIC

Usually the disease becomes severe during the months of July-September in different parts of India. It is firstly recorded by Ramkrishnan, (1954).

Blotch is a type of leaf spot that consists of large sized elongated area of necrotic tissue with irregular margin. The blotches are especially developed due to mixing of many small spots. Example: *Colletotrichum capsici* causes blotches on the leaf surface of Turmeric (*Curcuma longa*).

The disease is common in all states of India where turmeric is extensively grown. All the stages if plant growth is susceptible for infection of *Colletotrichum*. It causes heavy loss of leaves. Leaf spot disease reduces photosynthetic area of leaf that affects the yield of crop. It is a very common disease occurs at Orissa and Andhra Pradesh area of India. During continuous rainy seasons 100% plants gets infected by the respective pathogen. The pathogen also survives on other host like *Zingiber.* The fungus *C. capsici* is reported to reduce dry rhizome yield by 62.7%.

Symptoms

The disease causes extensive damage of the leaves. The leaves are main site of infection. A characteristic spots appear on the leaves. Initially very small spot appear on the leaf lamina. The spots increase gradually attaining a length and width of spot up to 3-5 × 2.4 mm. mostly the spots are elliptical or elongated in shape. The centre of the spot turns grayish due to the intercellular growth and sporulation of the pathogenic fungus. Two, three or more spots may coalesce to form a large necrotic spot with irregular margin. The necrotic patches spread over leaf surface; hence the affected leaves get dried and fell off. The severely affected grayish region of leaf consists of small dot like acervuli which are abundantly produced by the fungus. The affected leaf shows arrangement of acervuli in the form of concentric rings. The spots and large patches surrounded by a dark brown coloured margin, on the leaf surface and next to it a yellow halo occurs. The spots are more distinct on the upper surface; the lower surface of corresponding spots appears to be yellowish green coloured. The leaves of all the age group are equally susceptible to the infection. In case of advanced stage of disease development, most of the leaves dry up. The loss of yield is estimated up to 50% by Kumar *et.al,* (2010). Disease development is severe during high humid conditions.

The Causal Organism

The disease is caused by *Colletotrichum capsici.* The mycelium consists of branched, septate, both inter and intracellular hyphae which are light brown in colour. The hyphal mats accumulate under the epidermis of the affected leaf. The acervuli are dark black dot like structures along with numerous setae formed by the fungus which are tapering at the ends and scattered all over. The setae measure about 50-150 mm in length. The conidiophores are septate that are blunt that produce conidia at its tip. The conidia are crescent shaped narrow at ends, unicellular, hyaline and they are about 17-32 × 3.4 mm in size. The clusters of conidia are produced which are held together in bunches of large number. The affected dried leaves fell off along with bundles of conidia, acervuli and mycelial threads in soil. The conidia separated from bundles in presence of water drop.

Disease Cycle

The infected leaves fall on the soil hence the acervuli are retained in soil that acts as primary inoculum for the newly grown crop. The dispersal of pathogen also takes place during irrigation of water. There are reports of presence of acervuli below the scales of rhizomes of affected plant.

Disease management:

1. Rao, *et.al*, (2012) reported Propiconazole (0.1%), Hexaconazole (0.1%), Tricyclazole (0.1%) and Carbendazim + Mancozeb(0.1%) for the management of leaf spot disease caused by *Colletotrichum capsici* of turmeric.
2. Rhizome treatment with Carbendazim + Mancozeb (0.1%) gave the best results for germination (90.52%).

LEAF SPOT OF TURMERIC

It is a best known disease in turmeric (*Curcuma longa*) growing areas. There are reports of its common occurrence along the coastal regions of Orissa and Andhra Pradesh. It is very common in the turmeric growing areas of Mumbai, Gujarat, and Madras. The disease is considered as a destructive causing considerable loss of produce.

The disease initiates in rainy season. It is very common throughout India. There are reports of epiphytotic from the regions of Orissa and Andhra Pradesh. The disease is prevalent in the field during rainy season. The disease reduces the yield of crop.

Symptoms

The disease is produced in the form of numerous small spots all over the leaf surface. The spots are produced on both the surfaces of the leaves but more prominent and distinct on the upper surface of leaf. The spots are comparatively small and numerous. Initially the spots appear yellowish but later changes to dark yellow colour. The spots measure about 1-2 mm in diameter. The spots are abundantly produced hence occupied larger area of leaf that affects the rate of the photosynthesis. In severe cases many spots coalesce to form brown coloured larger spots. Drying of leaf lamina takes place. The affected leaves become reddish brown in colour. The affected plant is not killed, but yield is reduced at great extent.

The lesions appear on both the surfaces of leaf. Initially spots are visible at lower surface of leaf. Mostly the spots are 1-2 mm in diameter. The spots are rectangular in shape. The spots are formed in a series parallel to the veins of the leaf. The spots gradually increase in size and get mixed to form irregular patches, Ahmad, *et.al*, (2010). The infected leaf turns reddish brown. The infected leaves droop off before maturity.

The Causal Organism

The responsible pathogenic fungus is *Taphrina maculans* Butler. The mycelium is highly branched, inter and intracellular. The mycelial mats are especially occupied between the cuticle and epidermis of the host leaf. The fungus produce branched haustoria (food sucking hyphal branches). The lobes of haustoria inserted in the host cells for absorption of food material. The penetration of hyphae restricted up to 1-2 layers of host cells below leaf epidermis. When the spots are fully formed, their central portions are occupied by an almost continuous layer of fungal hyphae (Ben-Shalom, *et.al*, 2003). The outermost layer of this continuous layer of fungal hyphae grows into finger like or elongated sac like projections which are called asci. The asci are thin walled club shaped structures. The asci measure about 20-30 × 6.5-10m in size that consists of ascospores. Mostly eight ascospores are present in each ascus. The ascospores are hyaline, avoid, unicellular, light in weight and measure about 4-6 × 2.2.5 mm in size. The ascospores are discriminated by wind or irrigated water. The ascospores multiply within the ascus by budding process forming sprout conidia.

Disease Cycle

The mode of reoccurrence of disease is not known exactly known. The possibility is that the affected leaves retain the pathogen and the air born spores might be able to infect the newly sown crop.

Disease management:

1. The disease is of minor importance. It can be controlled by careful removal and burning of affected leaves from the field.
2. Spraying Bordeaux mixture (1%) has been recommended for control of *Taphrina* leaf spot of Turmeric.
3. Collect plant residue and burn it carefully before sowing.
4. The recommended fungicides for the control of leaf blotch disease of turmeric are Fytolan, Blitox-50, Diathane-Z-78 and Bordeaux mixture etc.
5. Seed treatment with Mancozeb (3 gm /liter of water) and Carbendazim (1 gm/liter of water) restricts the disease, Kumar Balwinder and Gill, (2010).
6. Spraying with Copper oxychloride (3gm/liter of water) is recommended.

RHIZOPUS ROT OF TURMERIC

Initially the symptoms of the disease became evident on leaves due to which leaves turn yellowish in colour. Leaf yellowing progresses slowly in coerce of time and covers the leaf completely. The infected leaves of plant exhibit drying of marginal region. The central lamina of affected leaves remain green. The leaves dry up completely within short period. In severe cases of disease development, the basal regions of shoot shows water soaked regions that later causes soft rot symptom (Chawda, 2012).

The rhizomes get affected; initially the affected rhizomes becomes wet watery and fade up the original texture. The water soaked patches are formed on the rhizomes that causes soft rot disease. The affected rhizomes remain small and get destroyed due to degeneration of tissue due to interaction of pathogenic fungus. The root system of affected plant gets reduced to a great extent. The soft rot of rhizome affects the yield of crop to a great extent. The yield from such plant is practically zero. The rotted rhizomes get mixed in soil hence the soil as well as partially infected rhizomes acts as primary source of inoculum. Sometimes the healthy rhizomes get infected during harvest period (Uday Kumar, and Usha, 2010). It is also difficult to identify partially infected rhizomes during harvest. The soft rot disease remains in continuation during transport or storage periods.

The Causal Organism

The soft rot disease is caused by *Rhizopus* sp.

The hyphae of responsible fungus are branched, hyaline, inter and intracellular. The fertile hyphae produce abundance of sporangia from terminal or intercalary cells. The sporangia measure about 22-40 µm in size. The oospores are globular, tough walled measure 17-30 mm in diameter.

Disease Cycle

The healthy rhizomes get contaminated during harvest period. The oospores are easily carried on the surface of the rhizome. The oospores are also retained in soil for longer periods that acts as primary inoculum. The secondary spread of disease occurs by spread of zoospores during irrigation of water or any other mechanical agencies during weed harvest process.

Disease management:

1. Select seed rhizomes from disease free parental rhizome.
2. Avoid repeated cultivation in the same field.
3. Drenching of chestnut compound around the affected plants reduces the disease intensity.
4. Dipping of seed rhizomes in Agallol (1%) found to be effective against rhizome rot disease.

LEAF BLIGHT OF TURMERIC

The Rhizoctonia blight of turmeric appears to be more common in tropical regions of the world. It is one of the serious diseases of turmeric causing heavy burning and defoliation affects the yield of crop.

Symptoms

The water soaked small spots appear on the leaves. Initially the spots are round but later turn irregular in shape. The spread of infection is very fast. The affected leaves turn reddish brown in colour within a short period of 3 to 4 days. Finally the leaves turn straw coloured with narrow dark brown margin. A distinct chlorotic margin can be seen around the spot since early stage of its development. The lower leaves get infected earlier than the leaves of upper region. (Sathiyanarayanan Anusuya and Muthukrishnan Sathiyabama, 2014).

In severe cases, the spots coalesce to form large patches of dead tissue occupying large area of the leaf lamina. The leaves dried up and shrivel for some extent. The dried leaves remains attached to the plant up to harvest and they are removed by some mechanical agency.

The Causal Organism

The pathogen responsible for this disease is *Rhizoctonia solani* Kuhn. It consists of septate hyphae, which are about 12 µm wide and 250 µm long. In culture, fungus produces sclerotia within 5-6 days. The size of sclerotia ranges from 1 to 3 mm in diameter. The sclerotia made up of brown barrel shaped which measure about 3 mm in width.

Disease management:

1. Application of excessive use of nitrogen fertilizers should have to be avoided to avoid disease intensity.
2. Spraying with Zineb (0.5%) can control *Rhizoctonia* blight.

BASAL ROT DISEASE OF TURMERIC

The basal rot of turmeric is one of the common problem in turmeric growing areas. This is one of the serious and widespread diseases because of saprophytic nature of fungus. It is one of the common diseases in tropical regions of the world. It is highly destructive diseases of turmeric which causes considerable losses. The disease occurs in the end of monsoon.

Symptoms

The disease initially manifests as pale yellow coloured area especially at the tips of the upper younger leaves. The yellowing of tips gradually progress towards remaining part of leaf blade and then to the leaf sheath. In severe cases the entire plant turns yellow and becomes delicate and looks unhealthy. In severe cases of disease development the water soaked spots near the basal region of the plant just above the soil surface. The affected area turns yellow to brown and then dark brown in colour due to rotting of affected tissue. Due to severe infection the affected plants fell off. The rhizome in the soil remains uninfected. It does not show any symptoms of the rot. The pathogenic fungus remains on the scales of the rhizome. The mechanical injures to the fresh rhizomes takes place during harvest, packing and transportation. The injured rhizomes get infected and the infection continued during the storage periods (Ramakrishnan and Sowmini, 2014). The visible mycelial growth is seen on the surface of affected rhizomes which also contain the fruiting bodies of fungus called sclerotia. The sclerotia are granular dark coloured structures which measure about 100-250 mm in size.

The Causal Organism

The basal rot disease of turmeric in the field is caused by *Sclerotium rolfsii.*

Disease Cycle

The sclerotia survive in soil in dormant stage for longer duration which acts as source of primary inoculum.

Disease Management

Treatment of rhizomes and with organo-mercury fungicide has been recommended before sowing and storage. The humid environment with low light of store houses promotes the disease development. The affected rhizomes show sunken areas and dry up at the infected site hence; partial drying of rhizome is common. If the infected rhizome cut open, a cavity is seen in the centre because of degeneration of central tissue of rhizome due to fungus. Sometimes a white coloured mycelial growth is seen on the affected areas.

DISEASES REPORTED ON TURMERIC (*Curcuma longa*)

Sl. No.	Disease	Pathogen
1.	Leaf spot	*Alternaria tenuissima*
2.	Leaf spot	*Cercospora curcumae-longae*
3.	Leaf spot	*Colletotrichum capsici*
4.	Leaf blight	*Corticium sasakii*
5.	Leaf spot	*Leptosphaeria sp.*
6.	Leaf spot	*Myrothecium roridum*
7.	Leaf spot	*Phyllosticta zingiberi*
8.	Leaf spot	*Pyricularia grisea*
9.	Leaf rust	*Puccinia curcumae*
10.	Rhizome rot	*Pythium graminicolum*
11.	Storage rot	*Sclerotium rolfsii*
12.	Leaf spot	*Sphaceloma curcumae*

21. DISEASES OF GOOSBERRY

English name : Indian gooseberry

Botanical name : *Emblica officinalis*

Family : Euphorbiaceous

Indian name : Amla

The gooseberry (*Emblica officinalis* Gaertn.) is a small sized deciduous tree. Leaves 10-13mm long. Branches feathery. Flowers pale green in a small dense clusters below the leaves. Fruits fleshy, round, with indistinctly marked into 6 lobes, about 1.5 to 2-5 cm in diameter & pale green or yellowish in colour. Seed three angled.

Medicinal Use

Indian goose berry contributes greatly towards health & longevity. In Aayurveda this fruit is used to prepare medicine of heart problems. The root bark of the tree useful in arresting secretion or bleeding. Regular use of honey with amla powder in the morning promotes vigor in the body within few days. Fruit is useful in respiratory disorders, asthma, Tuberculosis of lungs, & bronchitis. it is effective in controlling diabetes. A teaspoon of fruit juice of Amla with cup of fresh sweet bitter guard juice taken daily for two months will stimulate the pancreas and enable it to secrete insulin, thus reducing the blood sugar in diabetes. It also prevents eye complications in diabetes patient. Amla tones up all the organs the body & builds up health. It also renews energy, eyesight, it is useful in rheumatism, diarrhea, dysentery, ageing. It strengthens the heart, hair & different glands of the body.

RUST DISEASE OF GOOSBERRY

In India the rust of Amla reported form Maharashtra, Uttar Pardesh, Madhya Pardesh and Rajasthan. The infected leaf possesses small concentric rings on the leaflets and immature fruits. The affected fruits show black spots which increase gradually covering entire surface and result in premature fruit drops. The plant gets attacked severely.

Rust is one of the important diseases of amla. The disease affects the quality of fruits hence the market value of the fruits decline.

Symptoms

The disease appears in the form of small reddish brown pustules on leaves and fruits. The pustules on fruits are skin deep that can easily removed by needle. Later on the rust pustules become dark brown. Each pustule consists of cluster of spores. Ramakrishnan, (1952) reported the susceptibility of Deshi variety was more in comparison to the variety like Banarasi and Chakiya.

The Causal Organism

The pathogenic fungus responsible for rust disease of amla (*Emblica officinalis*) is *Ravenella emblica* Std. The mycelium is septate consists, of branched, hyphae which are sub-epidermal erumpent; the fungus produces sub epidermal pustules. The pustules consist of uredospores that are smooth walled. The uredospores may have pedicel or sessile measuring about 9.10 × 6.7µm in size. The teletosori are sub epidermal in origin, erumpent, bearing pedicellate compound teliospores.The teletospores measure about 42-54.4 × 20-28.8µm in size. The uredospores are easily carried away by wind which successively.

Disease Cycle

The uredospores of rust disease causing fungus are easily carried away by air currents. These spores when comes in contact with healthy leaf or fruit causes rust disease.

Disease management:

1. Spraying of trees with Diathane Z – 78 (0.2%) can control rust disease.
2. Pathak, *et.al*, (1970) recommended Wettable sulphur against rust of amla.
3. The sulphur dust also recommended against the disease.

ASPERGILLUS ROT OF GOOSBERRY

Aspergillus rot of Amla during storage and transport is a common problem. This is one of the serious and widespread diseases because of saprophytic nature of fungus. Rough handling of amla during harvest, packing and transportation causes mechanical injuries and the injured fruits are highly susceptible to Aspergillus rot disease.

Symptoms

Initially the symptom of the disease was in the form of purplish brown necrotic spots especially at the injured region of the fruit. The brown spot are slightly depressed with circular margins. As the spot increases the affected region appears wet within a short period of time. The growth of the *Aspergillus niger* takes place on the depressed spot that becomes visible. Gradually the whole fruit get covered with dark black coloured mycelium and spore of *Aspergillus niger*. The affected fruit becomes soft, pulpy, that emit foul odour. It has observed that the complete maceration of fruit takes place within 8-10 days of infection. The growth of the fungus is extensive on the affected fruits hence little movement of infected fruit shed off thousands of spores. The adjacent fruits get contaminated (Srivastava, *et al*, 1964).

The humid air free go downs with poor light promote disease development. Sorting of spotted fruits during packing in essential otherwise the Aspergillus rot disease develops during transportation and destroy large quantity of fruits due to rot development.

The Causal Organism

The rot disease of amla is caused by *Aspergillus niger* van Tiegh.

The pathogen consists of septate branched hyphae. The conidiophores are borne singly. The apical region of conidiophores is large spherical structure on which a many bottle shaped sterigmata are produced. The sterigmata are sterile and supportive in function. The tip of each sterigmata bears a long chain of conidia. The conidia measure about 2-5 µm m in size which is very small, black and light in weight.

Disease Cycle

The pathogen has wide spectrum of hosts. It also causes black rot disease of number of fruits and vegetables, hence the fungal flora retained extensively in air, soil and surfaces of fruits and vegetables. It grows extensively in humid environment but normally it can grow in all types of environment. Only the low temperatures restricted the growth of this fungus for some extent. The soil, air and partially infected fruits act as inoculum. Carelessness during harvest of fruits is also responsible for the spread of disease. It is highly essential to collect infected fruits during harvest. At the time of harvest the harvested healthy fruits are mostly kept on the soil surface in large bulk. This is very dangerous for health of fruits. The soil is the source of numerous fungal floras. The fruits which come in contact with soil get infected (Srivastava and Tandon, 1968). The soil borne fungi also carried along with the fruits. The fungus also enters the fruit through stalk end regions. The dark and less ventilation of store houses retains the spores of *Aspergillus* hence responsible for spread of the disease.

Disease management:

1. According to my opinion, there should be a law to make compulsory training to the workers who work in the fruit yards about the methodology and essential precautions during harvest packing, transportation and storage. Such law can restrict spread 1. o f number of diseases of fruits, vegetables and other plant product for a great extent. Definitely such a law can uplift the economy of India by avoiding post harvest losses of various fruits.
2. Avoid keeping harvested fruits on soil surface.
3. Collect the infected fruits separately and destroy carefully.

4. Keep the store houses well aerated with enough sunlight. Store houses should be clean and dry.
5. Bhargava and Singh (1978) recommended washing of fruits with Benomyl (1500 ppm) before storage.
6. Dipping of fruits in hot water for 5 minutes also recommended reducing disease intensity during storage.
7. Careful handling of fruits is very essential factor to avoid disease caused by Aspergillus. Any small injury or little bite of insect to fruit also enough to grow the pathogen.
8. Confirm all the fruits should be uninjured during packing to avoid *Aspergillus* rot.
9. Use soft textured packing material to avoid injuries to the fruits.

PHOMOPSIS ROT OF GOOSBERRY

Storage disease of amla is due to Phomopsis is one of the most important disease and most commonly reported. The rot is responsible for 5-2% losses during storage period. In certain parts of India the disease is quite serious where almost 96% fruits have been found infected due to infection. The *Phomopsis* fruit rots also responsible in reduction of ascorbic acid, sugars, proteins and total phenols.

Symptoms

The fruit rot of amla initiated in the form of water soaked spots on fruit surface. Gradually the spot becomes sunken and dark brown to black in colour in advanced stages of infection. Sometimes, such spots are encircled by white raised tissues. The affected area turns soft and pulpy. It is also known as soft rot disease. The rot percentage depends upon the pathogen involved.

The Causal Organism

The mycelium consists of branched thin walled septate hyphae. The pycnidia are globose to sub-globose, conidiophores numerous, branched up to 20 μm long. The fungus produces two types of conidia. The first type of conidia are fusiform , elliptical that measure 5-9 × 2 μm in size and the second type of conidia are slightly curved that measure 15-20 μm long.

Disease Cycle

The fruit rot fungus overwinters in the infected rotted fruit in the form of mycelium. In case of severe rot development, the affected fruit shows pycnidia of the fungus. The infected fruit may severe as a substrate for the survival of pathogen. The pathogenic fungus also permeates as mycelium and spores in the soil for longer duration which acts as a source of inoculums. It has observed that the inoculums. It has observed that the inoculums of fungus remain viable for about 14 months in soil on rotted fruit tissue. The mature pycnidia of fungus release numerous spores through ostiole. These spores are disseminated by rain drops or irrigation water and wind currents; the pathogen requires warm weathers for successful infection.

Disease management:

1. Careful handling of fruits during harvest and transportation reduces diseases intensity.

DISEASES REPORTED ON GOOSBERRY (*Emblica officinalis*)

Sl. No.	Disease	Pathogen
1.	Leaf spot	*Alternaria alternata*
2.	Leaf spot	*Cercospora phyllanthi*
3.	Leaf spot	*Cuothospora phacidioides*
4.	Fruit rot	*Cladosporium cladosporoides*
5.	Leaf spot	*Colletotrichum sp.*
6.	Leaf spot	*Glomerella phyllanthi*
7.	Powdery mildew	*Oidium phyllanthi*
8.	fruit rot	*Pestalotia cruenta*
9.	Leaf rust	*Phakospora phyllanthi*
10.	Fruit rot	*Phoma putaminum*
11.	Leaf spot	*Phyllosticta sp.*
12.	Fruit rust	*Ravenelia emblicae*
13.	Stem gall	*Synchytrium phyllanthi*
14.	Leaf and stem gall	*Synchytrium phyllanthicola*

22. DISEASES OF ALOE

English name : Indian Aloe

Botanical name : *Aloe vera*

Family : Liliaceae

Indian name : Ghee Kanvar or Musabbar

Alove vera Plant

The aloe (*Aloe vera* Linn.) is a small erect wild plant; in the recent year it has been Cultivated as extensively in various parts of our country for its medicinal values. it is 30 to 150 cm in height with smooth, pale green, fleshy leaves which are convex below, tapering to a blunt point; The margin of leaf appear toothed because of Horry prickles.

Medicinal Use

The leaf juice is used as medicine. It is used to cure multiple health problems. The leaf juice is given for restoring the disordered processes of nutrition. Leaf juice promote libido and arrest secretion. It is useful in liver and spleen disorders. It is given against Jaundice, Enlargement of liver, spleen, cough, cold, rheumatism, stomach disorders, indigestion, constipation & flatulence intestinal worms and skin disorders.

RUST DISEASE OF ALOE

The rust disease is common in India in aloe growing areas. Recently in Maharashtra state cultivation of aloe has been started for its medicinal value. The rust is very rarely found on aloe grown as wild plant. The damage is considerably high in aloe cultivated fields.

Symptoms

Just below the epidermal layer a cluster of fertile hyphae acts as uredospore. The tips of uredospore produce uredospore. Many such uredosori (group of uredospore) comes out through the ruptured epidermis and are freely scatted all over the leaf surface. The uredosori are mostly cinnamon brown in colour. The teletosori are produced late in the season after formation of uredosori. The teletosori are dark brown in colour.The infected plants become very conspicuous in the field because of pinkish brown coloured distinct pustules on the leaf blades. The pustules are small, round or oval which increase in number and are distributed randomly on both the surfaces of leaf. The pustules consist of bulks of urediospores. In severe cases numerous uredosori spread all over the plant except root system. The heavily affected leaves shrivel and die before maturity. The teletosori appear late in the season.

The Causal Organism

The causal agent of rust disease of aloe is *Uromyces aloes.* The mycelium of the pathogenic fungus is branched, septate, intercellular and pale yellow. The uredia are hypophyllous that consist of clusters of yellowish brown uredospores which are globose to subglobose in shape and are 20-26 μ in diameter with 2-3 μ thick wall. The uredospores are echinulate that consists of 4 germ pore at peripheral region. The teletosori are dark brown in colour that consists of cluster of teletospores of variable shape. The teletospores are oval which are 16-28 × 16-22 μ in size with transparent spot at the apex (thin wall). The pycnidial and aecidial stages are not known.

Disease Cycle

Shubhi Avasti, *et.al*, (2015) reported occurrence of rust disease of Aloe leaf from Madhya Pardesh, India. This is macro cyclic rust. The teletospores which are scattered in soil initiate the primary infection. The teletospores germinate to form the sporidia which acts as inoculum. The sporidia infects the young leaves. The urediniopores can also over summer and perpetuate the fungus. The uredospores are disseminated by wind to long distance. The spread of pathogen is favored by humid cloudy environmental factors and temperature between 21-26° C favors the disease.

Disease management:

1. Careful removal destruction of collateral host helps to reduce disease intensity.
2. There are certain fungicides recommended against the rust disease are Maneb, Copper, (Akinbode, 2010).

RING SPOT DISEASE OF ALOE

Avasthi, *et.al*, (2011) reported a ring spot disease of Aloe vera. He observed spots in the form of ring on leaves of potted seedlings in Hachigogima and Chichigima Islands, Tokyo. The inoculation of infected tissue on PDA (Potato Dextrose Agar) medium produced conidia resembling the conidia of Fusarium species. After one month reddish cups of perithecia of fungus are formed on the mature colonies of this isolate on PDA. Typical ring spot lesions were produced by artificial inoculations using single ascospores and single conidium isolates.

LEAF SPOT DISEASE OF ALOE

Roy, (1974) reported leaf spot of aloe due to infection of *Pestalotiopsis* Bihar, India. The spots caused by *Pestalotiopsis versicolor* were internal remaining within the host or beneath the epidermal layer. Both the surfaces of leaf show greenish brown spots which are roughly circular and slightly sunken. The acervuli are generally sub-epidermal. The conidiophores and conidia arise in the acervulus. Each conidiophores consists of single conidium at its tip. Shubhi, et. al, (2015).

Control:

1. Spraying with systemic fungicide reduces disease intensity.
2. Regular applications of recommended fungicides beginning in the seed bed should continue through the growing season.
3. The Bordeaux mixture is effective against *Pestalotiopsis* leaf spot disease.

4. There is need of development of resistant varieties against the disease (Jat, *et.al.* 2013).

DISEASES REPORTED ON ALOE (*Aloe vera*)

Sl. No.	Disease	Pathogen
1.	Leaf spot	*Colletotrichum gloesporioidess*
2.	Leaf spot	*Pestalotiopsis versicolor*
3.	Leaf rust	*Uromyces aloes*

23. DISEASES OF MESUA

English name : Mesua

Botanical name : *Mesua ferrea*

Family : Clusiaceae

Indian name : Nagkeshar

There are three species of Mesua (*Mesua ferrea* Linn.) in the world only one occurs in India. This tree is common on the mountains of Eastern Bengal, the Eastern Himalaya, Burma and the Andaman's. It is cultivated in gardens as an ornamental plant in Bengal. In India it is commonly known as Nagkeshar. It is a small -sized evergreen tree. The stem cylindrical with smooth bark. Leaves simple, arrangement opposite, margin entire, shape of leaf narrowly elliptical, reticulate venation. Flowers bisexual, terminal or axillary, inflorescence solitary or open panicle. Flowers pedicellate with a pair of bract. Calyx consists of four sepals that are persistent. Petals four, white or pink. The stamens many, free, ovary superior, bicarpellary, style a slender, stigma four lobed, fruit a capsule.

Medicinal Use

Root bark is astringent and aromatic used in rheumatism. It is useful in burning sensation, blood dysentery and bleeding piles. Leaves are used as poultice for postural eruption applied on forehead in several colds. Flowers are astringents, useful in gastric troubles. The oil of Mesua extracted by traditional method is used against rheumatism. The oil also used against skin diseases and in preparation of soap.

STUMP ROT DISEASE OF MESUA FERREA

The stump rot is a common disease in the forests of Bengal and in the forests of Silong and Meghalaya. It is also one of the destructive rot diseases of living *Mesua ferrea.* It is very common in temperate and tropical regions of India. It causes stump rot in which the heart wood is deteriorated by the fungus. At the initial stage of attack a white streaks formed on wood which separate the wood into oblong pieces (Dreistadt, *et.al*, 2004). Gradually the infection extends deeper causing whitish soft spongy rot. The hyphae inserted into the solid wood and deteriorate the cells of wood where growth of fungal hyphae makes their space permanent. The hyphae penetrate in all direction and destroy the wood cells. The fungus is a wound parasite entering the tree trunks through the wounds caused by any mechanical agency or man himself. In the final stage of disease development the infected tree trunk becomes yellowish and useless. The affected trunk may show internal decay hence loses its strength and quality. The disease is reported by different plant pathologist from different parts of India.

The Causal Organism

The pathogen responsible for stump rot disease of Mesua Ferrea is *Ganoderma lucidum* (Leyss) Karst. The mycelium is olivacious brown, septate and extensively branched. The hyphae penetrate the cortical region as well as hard wood of the host plant. The fertile mycelial tuffs produce fruiting bodies which come out through the crack open space of the trunks. The fruiting bodies or sporophores show rings of growth. They are thinner at the peripheral region and thicker at the central region. The sporophores are made up of numerous compactly arranged fertile and sterile hyphae. The fertile region produce numerous spores which are small unicellular, dusty in appearance which are of two different strain. Jalalpure, (2011).

The fruiting bodies are flat, arranged one above the others unsystematically. The upper surface of the fruiting bodies possesses mostly light yellowish colour and the lower region is carbon black in colour. The sporophores are of various size and shape. The fruiting bodies show growth regions which are distinct at the upper region of the sporophores (Fruiting body).

A species *Ganoderma lucidum* also causes stump rot disease of *Terminalia ballerica.*

Disease Cycle

The pathogen occurs in soil as well as its spores occur in air. Both soil &air acts as source of inoculums. It is more prevalent and more destructive during rainy season. The infected stem of mesua carries infection and retain for number of years. Once the tree stem or branches get infected, the infection spread very slowly for numbers of years. The mesua is a perennial plant, after infection acts as source of inoculums. The air currents and insect visitors responsible for transfer of inoculums from one place to other.

Disease management:

1. Application of biocontrol agent such as *Trichoderma harzianum* along with organic amendment.
2. Removal of affected branch can reduce spread of disease.

TRUNK ROT DISEASE OF MESUA FERREA

The tree *Mesua ferrea* Linn is an important medicinal plant in India because of its use in preparations of Aayurvedic, unani and local medicines. The trees are attacked by *Fomes dochmius* Berk and Br. causing deterioration and rotting of tree trunks. The hyphae of *Fomes dochmius* enter the tree trunk through wounds. The mycelium grows deep into the cortical regions of the wood. The affected region turns faded reddish brown. The affected wood split into cubical regions. The cracks are formed on the affected trunks in which profuse growth of fungus is seen that forms a tough mat. From the mycelial mat the fruiting bodies of *Fomes dochmius* develops which emerge through the cracks present on the affected trunks which are easily identified with necked eyes. The cracks on the trunk are formed because of disintegration of cellulose wall of affected cells by the action of enzymes secreted by the pathogenic hyphae.

The Causal Organism

The trunk rot disease of *Mesua* species is caused by *Fomes dochmius* Berk and Br: The mycelium is septate, highly branched olivacious brown in colour. It is extremely prevalent and destructive in nature, causing serious damage in the forests, Hassan, *et.al*, (2006). It is most wide spread of all the wood rotting fungus in Bengal forests. During severe attack the rot may extend into the sapwood. The sporophores arise from the oldest mycelium occur inside the affected region of the trunk. Infection usually brings about great loss of mechanical strength of wood. The heartwood is usually first to show signs of decay in living trees; but the sapwood also destroyed by the fungus at an equal rates. Sometimes it causes vertical furrowing of the truck. The mycelium develops chiefly in the medullary rays and vessels of the wood, often completely filling the vessels. There are different species of *Fomes* responsible for rot diseases of trunk of wider range of economically important trees.

The sporophores are lobed pale brownish found on the affected region of tree trunks. The sporophores are the store house of millions of fungal spores.

Another species of *Fomes* that causes trunk disease of medicinally important trees like *Terminalia chebula, Terminalia arjuna, Terminalia Billerica.* These are the extremely important plants used in preparation of variety of medicine preparation in India. The Fomes *dochmius* cause stump rot of *Terminalia chebula.*

Source of Inoculum

The dikariotic hyphae which spread under soil surface acts as source of inoculum. The pathogen has a broad spectrum of host range. Most of the hosts are perennial plants which retain dormant mycelium and spores for year after year play s very important role in spread of disease in every favorable season. The spores and fungal threads are easily carried away by air currents or by other mechanical agencies. These spores when comes in contact with healthy host causes disease in presence of favorable environmental conditions.

Disease management:

1. Application of paste of Burgundy mixture or Bordeaux mixture restricts the development of disease.
2. Careful removal and destruction of affected branch reduces further spread of disease.

DISEASES REPORTED ON MESUA (*Mesua ferrea*)

Sl. No.	Disease	Pathogen
1.	Stump rot	*Ganoderma lucidum*

24. DISEASES OF VITEX

English name : Vitex

Botanical name : *Vitex nigundo*

Family : Verbenaceae

Indian name : Shiwari

A Twig of Vitex Nigundo

There are 250 species of Vitex (*Vitex nigundo.* Linn.) found in the world out of which only 13 occur in India. It is common in all states of India. The plant is extensively grown as wild plants in Bengal and Southern India. It is a shrub of 3-5 feet in height that commonly grow in deciduous forest. It is branched shrub with grayish green leaves. Flowers are of light violet coloured. It is a shrub, leaves compound , leaf lets lanceolate- acuminate, entire, green above, grey-bubs cent beneath, terminal, blue flowers, grey panicle: Gamosepalous, calyx corolla, irregular gamosepalous corolla, 2-lipped, Stamens 4, didynamous, epipetalous, filaments hairy at base, ovary 2-4 celled, 4-ovuled, stigma bifid, fruit ovoid drupes, 1cm long.

Medicinal Use

It is possesses germicidal properties. The drug cures cough, asthma, eye diseases, inflammatory, glandular and rheumatic swellings, intestinal worms, fevers, fever, ulcers, skin diseases, nervous disorders & leprosy. The leaves aromatic, vermifuge, and are very efficacious in dispelling inflammatory swellings of the joints in acute rheumatism; the root in used in dyspepsia, colic rheumatism, worms, boils & piles.

WHITE TIP DISEASE OF VITEX

The white tip disease is common on the Vitex grown in open lands of various districts of high spring rainfall and humidity. It has been closely investigated by Sydow (1914) from Tamilnadu, India.

Symptoms

The pathogen infects the leaves causing typical spot at the tip region. The spot increase in size. The spot consists of whitish growth of fungus. The affected tissue of leaf tip destructed because of white moldy growth of fungus. The lowermost young leaves are more susceptible for the attack of the fungus. On the affected leaves small sunken grey streaks may be seen near the tips of the leaves. The streaks enlarge in size and become yellowish brown. The spots get covered by thick mycelial and conidial mass of fungus which is white in colour hence the disease called white tip. The secondary spread of disease occurs by dispersing spores from infected to healthy leaves.

The affected leaf loose natural green colour hence may be easily detected. With the advancement of the season the affected leaves start drying simultaneously at that time the black coloured small sclerotia are produced on the affected part of the leaf. The sclerotia are numerous, easily carried away by wind.

The Causal Organism

The white tip spots disease of *Vitex* species is caused by *Ramularia vitis* Syd. The pathogen consists of septate mycelium. It is a highly polymorphic fungus. During its parasitic career it the pathogenic fungus produces two or more than two types of conidia.

The conidia penetrate the leaf through stomata, lenticels or through injured spaces or wounds. The infectious germ tube of spores enters the stomatal passage. The germ tube of the fungal spore slightly gets swelled in the sub-stomatal region of stomata and produce branched mycelium which spread in the intercellular space of the leaf mesophyll. At this stage the infected leaf shows yellow discoloured zone. In severe cases the affected mesophyll cells collapse and disintegrate. The pathogenic hyphal threads spread to other parts of the epidermal cells of the leaf. In severe cases the mycelial mats get aggregated below the epidermis which produces numerous conidia.

Disease Cycle

The fungus produces unlimited spores of two to three types that can persist on affected plant debris in soil; hence the soil acts as the primary inoculum. The air currents also carry numerous spores which that act as source of primary inoculum.

Disease management:

1. The pathogenic fungus survive in soil on infected plant residue, hence the disease can be managed by using cultural methods such as field sanitation.
2. Collection and destruction of infected leaves reduces disease intensity.
3. Singh and Pavgi (1971b) recommended fungicides against Ramularia are Carbendazim.

DISEASES REPORTED ON VITEX (*Vitex nigundo* L)

Sl. No.	Disease	Pathogen
1.	Leaf spot	*Alternaria alternata*
2.	Leaf spot	*Asterina sphaerotheca*
3.	Leaf spot	*Cercospora viticis*
4.	Leaf spot	*Curvularia lunata*
5.	Leaf spot	*Drechslera sp.*
6.	Leaf spot	*Glomerella cingulata*
7.	Sooty mould	*Meliola sakawensis*
8.	Leaf spot	*Ramularia viticis*

25. DISEASES OF BALIOSPERMUM

English name : Baliospermum

Botanical name : *Baliospermum montanum*

Family : Euphorbiaceae

Indian name : Danti

There are about ten species of Baliospermum (*Baliospermum montanum* Bl.) on the world out of which six found in India. Plants are shrubs, simple leaves, and alternate. Two glands present at the base of leaves, shape & size of leaves variable. Long petioles, flowers unisexual, small greenish, in axillary monoecious perianth, stamens many. Female flowers with 5 lobed calyx, lanceolate, ovary hairy outside, 3 celled, 3 ovules, style 3, each 2-fid, fruit a capsule.

Medicinal Use

The plant is purgative, anti-helminthes, carminative, and anodyne. It is useful in abdominal pain, constipation, calculus, piles, helminthes manifestation, scabies, skin disorders & ulcers. Leaves used to cure asthma, seeds used in snake bite.

LEAF SPOT DISEASE OF BALIOSPERMUM

Pawgi and Singh (1965b) from sahdol MP (India) reported leaf spot disease of danti (*Baliospermum montanum*) caused by *Cercospora baliospermi* Pawgi and Singh. It is one of the serious diseases of danti responsible for reduction of quality of leaves which are used for preparation of medicine. The disease incidence is responsible for drooping of leaves and early maturity of plants.

Symptoms

The pathogenic fungus *Cercospora* causes distinct spots on all parts of the plants above ground level. Initial symptoms appear on the leaves which are closer to the soil surface. The spots are dark brown in colour that is surrounded by yellow hollow. Approximately the spots are circular. Numerous spots appear on the leaves of affected plants. The spread of the pathogen from lower leaves to upper ones takes place by wind, insects or any other mechanical agencies. The fully mature spots turn dark brown with grayish centre. The spot appear intensely darker on the upper leaf surface and light dark on the lower surface. During the severe infection the stem and petioles get infected. Less number of spots observed on the stem and petiole in comparison to leaves. Sometimes two or more than two spots coalesce to form large sized lesion that causes drying and shriveling of affected leaves. Such an infected leaves fell off. Severe infection causes stunted growth, delicacy of all branches and at last the death of plant occurs. The total effect is the loss of quality of the plant product.

The Causal Organism

The leaf spot of Danti plant is caused by the attack of *Cercospora baliospermi.* The mycelium branched intercellular that absorb food material by sending haustoria in to the host cells. The branched hyphae occupy in the intercellular space of spongy and palisade tissue of the host leaf. During sporulation the fully developed fertile mycelium forms stromata of compactly arranged hyphae. The conidiophores arise from the stromata in groups. The group of conidiophores protrudes out by rupturing host epidermis. The conidiophores consist of 2-6 septa. It produces cylindrical conidia on lateral walls. The conidia are hyaline to light olivacious with 2-12 septa. The conidia are slightly curved measuring 20-87 μm in length and 2.4 μm in width.

Disease Cycle

The newly sown plants get infected due to presence of pathogen on the plant debris of earlier crop in the field soil. The airs also play an important source of inoculum. The air borne spores of pathogenic fungus also produce disease when comes in contact with the leaf in presence of all favorable environmental factors. The temperature range between 24°C to 84°C with high humid environment has been found most favorable for a successful development of the disease. The conidia of the pathogen mostly enter the leaf through stomata or by direct penetration force. The mycelium of fungus form stromata beneath the epidermal layer just before formation of conidiophores and conidia.

The conidia re-infect the healthy host plants or healthy leaves of the same plant hence act as a secondary inoculum. The inoculum of the pathogen is disseminated by insect visitors, wind and rain drops and also through some other mechanical agencies or through propagating material or seeds.

Disease management:

The control measures of the *Cercospora* leaf spot disease of Baliospermum has not been reported in India but in general the leaf spot disease can be checked by following methods.

1. The careful collection and burning of infected plant debris can reduce disease intensity to a considerable amount.
2. The methods of crop rotation can reduce disease intensity by eradicating pathogenic flora from soil.
3. Use of healthy propagating material reduces disease.
4. The spread of inoculum by collecting and burning of infected leaf reduces severity of the disease.

26. DISEASES OF SWEET FLAG

English name : Sweet flag
Botanical name : *Acorus calamus*
Family : Araceae
Indian name : Safed bach

The sweet flag (*Acorus calamus* Linn.) is an aromatic marshy herb. There are about 5 species on the world out of which two found in India. Mostly the plant is distributed in West Bengal (Calcutta), Jammu and Kashmir, UP, Nilgiri hills and Tamil Nadu. It is a perennial herb with long aromatic creeping rhizomes bear sprouting leaves. The shoot bearing flower is a large leaf like structure which is known as spathe. The flowers are yellowish-green, small, 5-10 cm long cylindrical spikes and yellowish fruits. The rhizome is used as medicine.

It is commonly as sweet flag. It is a perennial herb. It is having long aromatic rhizome. It is a modified underground stem. The flowering shoots are supported by spathe. Spathe is a leaf like structure. The flowers are pale green in colour which is small in size. Fruits yellowish the rhizome is used in preparation of Aayurvedic medicine. The dried rhizome yield oil which is yellow and aromatic.

In India it is known as safed bachh.

Medicinal Uses

The rhizomes used as medicine which is aromatic, bitter tonic & expectorant. It is useful in flat lance, counteracts spasmodic disorders and induces vomiting. It is useful in regulation of menstrual periods. Rhizome is useful in stomach disorder. It is effective in chronic diarrhea and chronic dysentery. In the treatment of asthema, Acorus calamus rhizome is useful. The boiled extract of rhizome given to children against whooping cough. A pinch of rhizome powder given with honey. It is effective against intestinal worms. A pinch of powder in given with water or worms. The herbs are beneficial in treating mouth ulcers.

The rhizome is stimulant, bitter tonic, expectorant, it regulars menstrual periods. It is used against stomach disorders, diarrhea, dysentery, Asthma, common cold, wooping cough, intestinal worms & Mouth disorders.

LEAF SPOT DISEASE OF SWEET FLAG

The leaf spot disease of safed bach (*Acorus calamus*) reported firstly by Robenhorst, (1878) from West Bengal. The disease has been reported to cause considerable damage in India. The disease is noticed on leaf, twigs & young stems. It was observed extensively during humid warm weather. The damage to the plant is mainly through partial or complete drying of infected leaves and defoliation.

Symptoms

It has found that the mature leaves were more susceptible for the infection of *Cryptosporium* leaf spots. Initially the spots were in the form of small, more or less circular, discoloured brown areas. The mature spots appear grayish in colour. During the entire favorable environment conditions many spots coalesce to form a large blighted patch on the leaf with an irregular margin. The severely affected leaves fell off. The affected plants get seriously damaged. Sometimes the young shoots and stem may be affected. In severe cases most of the leaf blades get affected. Initially the upper leaf surface shows spots later on the spots appear on both the surfaces of leaves. The large blighted areas show narrow concentric bands of alternate lighter and deeper shades especially near the margin sometimes it might be seen on the upper surface.

The Causal Organism

Robenhorst, (1881) isolated *Cryptosporium calamy* from leaf spot of sweet flag from Calcutta. The mycelium is branched sparingly septate, hyaline and intercellular. Just below the epidermal layer the acervuli are formed. The pathogenic fungus bears conidiophores. The conidia are produced at the tips of the conidiophores. The fully developed conidia release along with small stalks. The stalks remain as an appendage at the basal region of the conidium. The epidermal wall of infected leaf rupture by exposing ruptured acervuli liberating the conidia.

The conidia are multiseptate; spindle shaped consists of four septa. At one end of the conidium there are small three hairs like colourless, appendages are seen and the other end is having tail like extension of conidial cell. The appendages help in dissemination of the conidia.

The five celled conidium consists of two regions, i.e. the central three cells of conidium appear dark coloured and the cells present at the polar region of conidium are transparent bud like colourless cap to both the ends of the conidium. The conidia measure 16-29 μ in length and 4-8 μ in width. The appendages are 8-12 μ long. During germination the lowermost cell of conidium produce germ tube during germination. The waterlogged areas make the host more susceptible.

Disease Cycle

The infected leaves of *Acorus calamus* fell off on the soil which carries the source of inoculum that acts as primary inoculum. The dispersal of conidia of pathogen also takes place during irrigation of water.

Disease Management

Remove the blighted leaves from the field and infected host plants and burn carefully that helps to restrict blight disease to a considerable extent.

RUST DISEASES OF SWEET FLAG

The quality of *Acorus* plant greatly handicapped by the incidence of rust pustules on the lower surface of the leaf. The disease is particularly important since the *Acorus* plant is proved one of the important medicinal plants. The rust pustules appear mostly in the month of February.

The rust disease reduces the amount of foliage. The pathogen is an obligate parasite. The secondary and tertiary infection reduces quality and quantity of foliage and seriously affects the health of the plant.

Symptoms

The affected plants easily are identified because of the dark brownish orange coloured pustules on the lower leaf surface. The pustules consist of uredospores. In severe cases the uredopustules occur in large number on both the surfaces of leaves and other parts of the plant. The affected leaves die and fell off early hence final stage appear late in the season on the stems. The teletosori are dark black coloured that appear as a crust.

The Causal Organism

The pathogen causing rust disease of Acorus is firstly by Butler and Bisby, (1931). The disease is caused by *Uromyces acori*. The rust of Acorus seems to be heteroceous but the pycnidial and aecidial stages of this rust are unknown (Mukherjee, 2009). The uredosori are more distinct dark brown in colour. The uredospores are approximately globose with colourless papilla and thick reticulate wall. The teletosori resemble uredosori but they develop late in the season and dark brown in colour. The teletospores vary in size and shape those might be roundish, angular or oval in shape with thin walled hyaline apex and short stalk. The teletospores measure 28 × 15-24 µm in size.

Disease Cycle

Very little information is available about the rust disease of Acorus. The rust appears to survive on collateral hosts. The weed plant on which rust occurs retains the pathogen which serves as primary or secondary source of inoculums. The fungus is an obligate parasite and perennates on weed hosts.

Disease management:

1. Remove the entire plant residue present in the field before sowing to reduce disease intensity.
2. Seed treatment with recommended fungicides restricts the disease.
3. Sanitation and crop rotation should be practiced.
4. Use certified seeds for sowing purpose.

27. DISEASES OF TINOSPORA

English name : Tinospora

Botanical name : *Tinospora cordifolia*

Family : Menispermaceae

Indian name : Guloh

There are about 40 species of Tinospora (*Tinospora cordifolia* Miers.). Out of which three found in India. It is a weed plant grows on waste land. It is very common in deciduous forests. It is a twining herb, stem terete, sparsely lenticellate, produce filiform aerial roots, green when young, leaves simple, alternate, long petiolate, laming broadly ovate-cordate, shortly acuminate at apex, flowers unisexual, green, mostly in the axils of fallen leaves, sepals 3+3, free; petals 6,stamens 6, carpel's 3. Fruits drupaceous, ovoid or ellipsoid.

Medicinal Use

The aqueous extract used to reduce blood sugar, It is anti-pyretic and anti-inflammatory. It in used to remain eternally young. In Aayurveda it in used for youthfulness, vitality & longevity. It is a best digestive tonic. It cures fever jaundice, thirst, burning sensation, diabetes, piles, skin ailments, respiratory disorders, neurological diseases & improves intellect. Iyer & Kolammal, (1963) reported to use this plant against rheumatic complaint.

CESCOSPORA LEAF SPOT OF TINOSPORA

Rao, (1970) observed spots of *Cercospora* on the Tinospora leaves in Andra Pradesh. *Tinospora* suffer from leaf spot disease characterized by the dark brown coloured spots of dead tissue. The *Cercospora* leaf spot was the most common and destructive disease of *Tinospora* in Andhra Pradesh. It was extensive in areas that are relatively humid or get regular raining during the growing of the *Tinospora* plants. It was observed that the *Cercospora* spots on *Tinospora* plants were totally absent in dry seasons.

Symptoms

The infection by *Cercospora* to the leaf produces roughly circular darker spots with a distinct yellow coloured boarder of chlorotic tissue. The spots were 2-12 mm in diameter. At the centre of the spots are brown coloured. The centre of the mature spot sometimes shows grayish coloured mycelial mat and spores. In severe cases of disease development the spots coalesce to form large patches of the dead tissue. The mature leaves were more susceptible than the younger leaves. Ajrekar and Kamat, (1923) reported leaf spot disease of *Tinospora* caused by *Cercospora tinosporae* at Allahabad, Gujarat. Munjal, (1960) studied leaf spot of *Tinospora* due to *Cercospora tinosporae* from Jammu and Kashmir area. Mundkur and Thirumalachar, (1946) leaf spot of *Tinospora* by the *Cercospora tinosporae* from Kashmir. Thirumalachar and Chupp, (1948) observed leaf spots of *Tinospora* due to *Cercospora tinosporae* in Bangalore, Karnataka.

The Causal Organism

The pathogen responsible for the leaf spot disease is *Cercospora tinosporae.* The mycelium is septate with characteristic long, thin and septate spores borne at the tip of the short conidiophores. The developing conidiophores and conidia break the host epidermis or arise from the stomata.

The *Cercospora tinosporae* produces conidial masses just below the epidermal layer of the host leaf which probably acts as the source of inoculum. The spores which are borne at the centre of the mature spots were easily be carried away by wind that acts as the secondary inoculum. The plant debris fell off on the soil ground that consists of conidia that germinate in presence of high humidity. The leaves closer to the ground surface get infected first. The fungus enters the leaf through stomata or penetrates the epidermis through injuries. The fungus spread rapidly in the host tissue and produce to spots on the leaf.

Chandra, (1957) reported another leaf spot disease of *Tinospora* caused by *Cercospora verruculosa* from Allahabad, India. The spots caused by *Cercospora verruculosa* are quite circular and usually have a whitish centre. The spots occur extensively during high humidity in the environment.

Disease Cycle

The pathogenic fungus overwinters in infected plant debris in the form of mycelium or conidia. During rainy season , the fungus present on infected plant debris start germinating conidia which are easily carried by wind currents, insects agricultural tools and irrigation water. The fungus is soil borne in nature. The conidia also suspended in air, which causes infection when comes in contact with host leaf.

Disease management:

1. Field sanitation: Removal of infected plant residue from the field before sowing reduces disease intensity.
2. The protectant fungicides such as Bordeaux mixture (4:4:50) found effective against Cercospora leaf spot.
3. Other recommended fungicides against Cercospora are Diathane Z-78(0.2%) & Diathane M-45 (0.2%).
4. Removal of weed host suggested managing Cercospora leaf spot.

The other leaf spot diseases of *Tinospora* reported from different parts of India by different workers. Bakshi, *et.al,* (1970) reported leaf spot disease of *Tinospora* species caused due to *Glomerella cingulata* in the region of Maharashtra. Butler and Bibsy, (1931) also found the leaf spot by the same pathogen in Maharashtra. Agrios, (2005) observed and studies leaf spot of *Tinospora* caused due to attack of *Hymenula indica* in Gujarat. Tar spot disease of *Tinospora* is found wide spread caused by *Phyllachora dolichospora.* It has found in the regions of Maharashtra, (Rajakumar and Shivanna, (2010) reported another leaf spot disease of Tinospora caused by *phyllosticta tinosporae,* which was very common in Gujarat and UP. Shivanna and Rajakumar, (2010) was also reported leaf spot of *Tinospora* due to infection of *Phyllosticta tinosporae.* Rajakumar and Shivanna, (2009) published a report of one of the new leaf spot of *Tinospora* caused by *Ramularia tinosporae* in Bihar.

28. DISEASES OF CITRUS

English name : Citrus

Botanical name : *Citrus medica* Linn.

Family : Rutaceae

Indian name : Kagzi nimboo

Citrus (*Citrus medica* Linn.) is a very common fruit with a distinct and pleasant aroma. It is a small evergreen tree. Fruits are the best source of vitamin-C, which is native of Asia. It is extensively cultivated in tropical and subtropical regions of the world. India ranks fifth in production of lemon. The states of India grow lemon trees in large scale are Gujarat, Tamil Nadu, Karnataka, Haryana, Assam, Bihar, Punjab, Andhra Pradesh and Rajasthan. Sumia Fatima and Meenakshi Mahajan, (2013). It is the best source of minerals like Calcium, Phosphorous and Iron. It possesses medicinal properties. The fruits are susceptible for fungal infection.

Medicinal Use

The paste of seeds applied over scorpion stings to relive pain.

It possesses liver stimulating properties.

It is used to prepare several Aayurvedic medicines which are useful against nausea and piles. The leaf paste is applied externally against pain.

Citrus Medica

PINK DISEASE OF CITRUS

It is one of the common diseases in tropical regions of the world. It is one of the highly destructive diseases of citrus, which causes enormous losses. The disease occurs in the end of monsoon and infects all parts of plant except root system. Initially the pathogenic fungus occur on surface of host later on penetrates the bark causing necrotic spots. The infection reach the xylem of wood. Once the disease girdles the trunk, the affected tree dies quickly. The warm wet weather is highly favorable for disease spread and development.

Symptoms

The disease is more prevalent during monsoon. The infected plant shows wilting of leaves, drying and hardening of bark. The affected region oozes gummy substance. The mycelium mats of fungus becomes thick and form sterile pin head shaped pustules which are slightly embedded into the bark. In the advanced stages of disease, girdling of trunk and branches takes places. The affected regions appear presence of salmon ping pustules, which are numerous

The Causal Organism

The disease is caused by *Pellicularia salmonicolor* (Berk, and Br.), the mycelium is highly branched consists of spetate, hyphae. The hyphae are hyaline, thin walled and sparsely septate, that is 7-15 µm in diameter. The mycelial nodules from sterile pink coloured pustules which are highly resistant to adverse environmental conditions. The pustules may be partially or wholly embedded in affected bark. The pustules looks like pycnidia but are not pycnidia. The sexual spores of the fungus are hyaline, thin walled, angular or round of about 8-15 × 5-10 µm in size. The spore germinates in presence of moisture. The basidial stage has not been observed on citrus.

Disease Cycle

The disease spread takes place by insect vectors, wind borne spores and rain drops. The mycelial aggregates which retain in the affected region acts as primary source of inoculums. Warm humid weather is favorable for disease development. The asexual spores present on infected part of plant acts as source of inoculums.

Disease management:

1. Remove infected branches and the cut ends should be painted with paste of Bordeaux fungicide
2. The removed branches should be burnt carefully far from the field.

FOOT ROT DISEASE OF CITRUS

The phytopthora infections have been considered as one of the major cause of citrus decline in the world, as well as in India. Kapoor and Choudhary, (1976) reported 14-18% of decline of citrus due to foot rot disease.

Symptoms

The pathogenic fungus causes root rot, foot rot or collar to or stump rot, gummosis, etc. During rainy seasons the pathogen infects the leaves. However root rot can be severe during any time of year under irrigated conditions.

The soil borne fungus Phytopthora infects the root hairs. The infected root system consists of few members of root hairs. In severe cases of disease development the infection extend to lateral roots and develops bird eye spots or big roots. In severe cases, complete root system get rotted. When the tip of main tap root shows rotting, the entire plant gets destructed.

The collar region of root gets infected and gradually the infection reaches to the bark on the trunk. Due to foot rot the bark gets damaged, and the growth of plant is affected, leading to death. In case of severity of disease the entire plant gets dried.

The dead areas on stem secrete sticky brownish substances which contain numerous fungal threads and sporangia.

The Causal Organism

The foot rot of citrus is caused by *Phytopthora nicotine* var *parasitica* (Dastur) Waterhouse (Syn. *P. parasitica* Dast.).

Mycelium highly branched consists by septate hyphae. The hyphae are with irregular in width. The sporangiophores are slender which are irregularly or sympodially branched. Sporangiophore produces lemon shaped sporangia having papillate, broadly avoid, ellipsoid to spherical, of about 50 × 40 µm , in size with short stalk. The pathogen produces oogonia of 24-26 µm in diameter in size. The oogonia size is about 24-26 µm in diameter. The oogonia are thick walled, designed turn yellowish brown at maturity. The fungus produces abundant chlamydospores which turn brownish at maturity. The temperature above 30 °C is optimum for fungus.

Disease Cycle

The fungus phytopthora is soil born which is a weak saprophyte. It survive in soil for several months, in the form of chlamydospores or oospores. In presence of favorable environmental conditions the zoospores are released , which infect the root hairs. After infection, the pathogen produces sporangia. The sporangia release numerous biflagellate zoospores which are carried by irrigated water to new host roots. The damaged roots under soil surface acts are best source of inoculums (Gottwald, and Graham, 2000).

Disease management:

1. Avoid water stagnation in the field
2. Removal and careful destructed of affected plants from roots reduces disease intensity.
3. Spraying of Bordeaux mixture (4:4:40) recommended by workers.
4. The recommended fungicides against foot rot disease of citrus are Captan (0.2%) Chlorothalonil (0.2%), Copper oxychloride (0.3%) etc.
5. Application of Metalaxyl (0.25%) recommended.

CITRUS CANKER DISEASE

The disease was firstly obtained in Japan. Now it is common in all the countries where citrus is grown. It is a worldwide disease. The disease stated to have originated from South China, Indonesia and India. In India it is one of the most destructive diseases. All the species of citrus get affected with the bacterial pathogen. Losses are caused due to reduced size of fruit, rough appearance of fruit skin and premature fruit dropping. It has observed that 80% to 90% of fruits get infected. It is regarded as the disease of international importance.

Symptom

All the parts of plant get affected except roots. Heavy infection occurs on leaves, twigs, young branches and fruits. The infected leaf may have small watery translucent spots which are dark green in colour; mostly developed on the lower surface of the leaf which are 1 to 2 µm in diameter. On young leaves in the beginning lesions (spots) appear as small white speck, difficult to be seen with necked eyes. After few weeks it becomes mature dark brown which can be easily seen. The mature lesions are slightly raised forming a spongy white eruption. The lesion enlarges gradually which shows brown depressions in their central region. At maturity the lesion turns grayish white, hard and appears corky, dead tissue with a rough surface surrounded by brown to dark brown raised margins. The lesions are surrounded by yellow halo. More or less similar lesions develop on twigs, stem and fruit. The lesion size varies from 1-9 µm in diameter on leaves and up to 1cm in diameter on twigs and fruits, Anonymous, (2004).

The lesion enlarges gradually and many lesions coalesce to form large patches of necrosis on leaves, twig and fruits. There is no effect on fruit juice because the infection is only skin deep, that do not affect the juice of infected fruits.

Citrus Canker

The Causal Organism

The citrus canker disease is caused by the bacterial pathogen such as *Xanthomonas citri.* It is a straight rod shaped, gram negative bacterium which is 1.5-2.0 × 0.5-0.75 µm in size with a single polar flagellum. It occurs in chains, it is non spore forming, and aerobic oxidase test negative and catalases test positive, milk colour changes to blue, positive to hydrolysis of starch, Casein and Tween-80. It is an obligate parasite which can survive only on living host plant. It does not multiply in soil. It can survive for 2-3 months on infected plant debris under dry conditions. There are many weed plants on which the bacterium occurs. The pathogen enters the host through stomata, natural openings or through wounds or insect bite holes. Gottwald, The bacterium multiply into the intercellular spaces that secrete enzymes which dissolve middle lamella and spread into the cortex region, as a result cankerous growth occurs on the affected plant part.

Disease Cycle

The pathogen *Xanthomonas citri* transferred from one season to another chiefly through infected leaves, twigs and fruits of living host plant. It enters the host through stomata or wounds. Several cycles of infection can occur on fruits and thus fruits have lesion of different size. High humidity and strong wind favors the spread of the disease.

The bacterium multiplies and the cankers outgrowth develops. The disease is disseminated by wind, rain and insects, (Brown and Eckert, 2000). Citrus leaf miners are very important for the dissemination of pathogen from field to nursery trees.

The optimum temperature for the better growth and development of pathogen is 30C°, and free moisture of 20 minutes is enough for the infection of leaves. The pathogen survive in infected leaves for up to 6 months; in sterilized soil for 52 days and in unsterilized soil for 9 to 17 days, (Everett, and Rees-George, 2006).

Disease management:

1. Use disease free nursery stocks.
2. Careful removal and destruction of infected plant material helps to control disease for some extent.
3. Spraying of trees with Copper fungicide before disease occurrence prevent disease occurrence.
4. Dewdney and Timmer, (2009) recommended spraying of Streptomycin 500-100 ppm at interval of 15 days for disease management.
5. Phytomycin at 2500 ppm has also been reported to be effective against canker disease.

6. Use resistant varieties for sowing purpose. The resistant varieties of *Citrus reticulata,* including Tangerines, King Mandarin and Satsuma oranges are resistant to *Xanthomonas citri* pathogen.
7. Pruning of shoots bearing canker lesion is also effective in reducing the inoculum load.
8. Collect and burn all the infected leaves, to avoid spread to adjacent trees.

DISEASES REPORTED ON CITRUS (*Citrus medica* Linn.)

Sl. No.	Diseases of Citrus	Pathogen
1.	Leaf spot	*Alternaria citri*
2.	Fruit rot	*Aspergillus niger*
3.	Grey mold of fruit	*Botrytis cinerea*
4.	Soft rot	*Cladosporium sphareospermum*
5.	Die back	*Curvularia tuberculata*
6.	Stem end rot	*Diplodia indica*
7.	Powdery mildew	*Oidium sp*
8.	Fruit rot	*Penicillium digitatum*
9.	Leaf fall	*Phytopthora colocasiae*
10.	Fruit rot	*Rhizoctonia bataicola*
11.	Soft rot of fruit	*Rhizopus nigricans*
12.	Leaf spot	*Septoria cattanei*
13.	Fruit rot	*Trichothecium roseum*
14.	Leaf rust	*Uredo citri*

29. DISEASES OF ROSE

English name : Rose

Botanical name : *Rosa domestica* Linn

Family : Rosaceae

Indian name : Gulab

There are about 250 species of rose (*Rosa domestica* Linn.) and Probably about 12 species found in India. It is a mesophyte, perennial, prickly shrub with branched taproot system. Stem erect, woody, cylindrical, solid with sharp prickles. Leaf petiolate, stipulate, alternate, compound, leaflets 3-7, serrate margin with unicostate venation. Inflorescence solitary axillary. Flowers pedicellate, bracteates or ebractiate, complete, actinomorphic, bisexual, perigynous. The thalamus is cup like. Calyx with 5 sepals, gamosepalous, imbricate aestivation. Corolla with 5 free petals, imbricate aestivation, stamens indefinite, free, unequal ovary semi-inferior. Polycarpellary, Apocarpous arising from the floor of the thalamus cup. Fruit is etario of achene, exalbuminous.

It is a medicinal as well as ornamental plant. It is cultivated in temperate, tropical and subtropical regions of the world for its beautiful flowers. A variety of rose crop available in market; it is cultivated in India as a cash crop. The essential oil prepared form rose is useful in variety of medicines, beauty products, perfumes and soap makings. It is cultivated throughout India.

A Twig of Rose Plant

Medicinal Use

The rose water is mixed with sandalwood power and applied over face to avoid pimples. The rose oil is used to prepare perfumes, cosmetics and skin softening soaps. Eating five grams of fresh rose petals in the morning before meal reduces body heat and burning sensation.

POWDERY MILDEW DISEASE OF ROSE

It is a very common disease of all kind of roses, which was firstly discovered by Wajid Khan (1972) in Germany. It is prevalent throughout Europe, America, Australia, India and many other countries.

The disease has been reported from all parts of India. The losses vary from 20-30% depending upon the favorable environmental conditions. Nursery plants are damaged more than the adult plants.

Symptoms

Powdery Mildew of Rose

It is a fungal disease initially it appears on the younger foliage in the form of whitish sparsely spread small spherical superficial powdery mass. The leaf show crinkling. The powdery spots increase in size coalesces to form large irregular patches. The patches are heavily covered by necked mass of hyphae and spores. The fungal hyphae produce sucking organs (haustoria) which are inserted into the host tissue for the absorption of food. During the severe infection the stems, buds, twigs except root system show the white powdery growth of fungus. The powdery mildew pathogen produces millions of small spores on unbranched conidiophores which are carried away easily by air current. During the moist weather spores or conidia spread very fast causing deformed blighted leaves enveloped by loosely layered fungal filaments and numerous spores. The disease becomes very serious during dry weather with cool moist nights. The spores germinate in presence of small amount of moisture. The poor air circulation promotes the disease development and fast spread of the pathogen.

The pathogen *Sphaerotheca pannosa* especially attack the young shoots and leaves. In favorable environment it can cause some economic loss by reducing flower quality and quantity. The infected leaves fell off or fail to develop normal size. The young affected shoots become thin and delicate. All the affected plant parts coated with fungal hyphae. The mature leaves have been found to be resistant to powdery mildew pathogen. The affected buds do not open that gets shriveled.

The Causal Organism

The mildew disease of is caused by a fungal pathogen *Sphaerotheca pannosa* (Erysiplaceae) which usually occur on variety of roses. The pathogen is an ectoparasites; its mycelium is superficial which produce haustoria. The haustoria penetrate the host epidermis to absorb food material. The mycelium produce conidiophores which are septate, erect which cut off 6 to 8, elliptical or barrel shaped conidia that are 22-92 to 13.63 to 15.8µm in size. The perithecia or cleistocarps are found on the bases of thorns or felted patches of persistent mycelium and are usually to be found mostly on the petiole and at the back of the midrib. They are globose to pyriform, 85 to 120 µm in diameter; the cleistocarps possesses appendages or no appendages. If present, they are short, tortuous, pale brown and septate; Cleistocarps consists of a group of Asci, each ascus is broadly oblong to globose,88 to 115µ averaging 100 by 60 to 75 µm, Ascus contains 8 ascospores which measure from 20 to 27 by 12 to 15µm.

After separation of conidia from their host, the conidia are very sensitive to environmental conditions. They are not adapted for long survival and lose their germinative capacity in less than 24 hours. They are wind borne and are no doubt, dispersed for short distances; during mild winters conidia are probably enabled to survive in sheltered places in the open, or on another wild hosts. In the spring, the ascospores from the overwintered cleistocarps bring about fresh infections in the spring. The mycelium survives in the buds.

Germination of Conidia

The conidia may germinate on either side of the young leaf, producing several germ tubes; the superficial mycelium forms dense white spiny patches of interwoven hyphae which are thick walled, refractive and somewhat rigid. Later the colour becomes grey, dingy-buff or rarely pale brown, Karlik, (2008).

Mildew appears to break out under most diverse conditions of the environment; the disease is more severe in warm humid weather. The disease may develop rapidly but it varies considerably in intensity from season to season and is severe during the dry summer. The conditions under which the conidia and ascospores germinate and attack the host are not fully known.

The favorable temperature for the growth and germination of conidia is 21°C. The relative humidity of about 80-90 percent is very good for germination of conidia and ascospores.

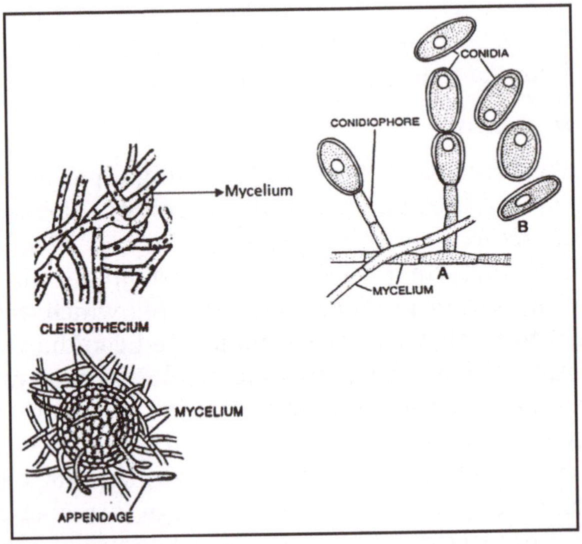

Disease Cycle

During the unfavorable environmental conditions the pathogen survive in the affected young twigs and buds in the form of hyphae. When the branches of host start growing simultaneously the dormant fungus situated in the host tissue get activated and start growing inside the host tissue. The pathogenic fungus produce conidia, which are disseminated by wind and air that, can cause new infection to the plants. The disease is favored during dry warm environment with high moisture. New symptoms are formed within 8-10 days of infection. The spores or conidia germinate at the relative humidity between 40-100%.

The following factors encourage the powdery mildew disease:

1. Cloudy moist weather with cool nights.
2. Crowded plantation.
3. Susceptible variety.
4. Improper sanitation.

Disease management:

1. The excess use of nitrogen fertilizers increases disease intensity.
2. Remove infected leaves in very early stage and destroy carefully.
3. Grow resistant varieties of rose.
4. Avoid crowded plantation.
5. Good control over rose mildew may be obtained by spraying with copper oxychloride in oil.
6. Sulphur and lime sulphur may also be used on roses in the open but is inclined to leave a deposit on the foliage and has a tendency to harden young growth under certain conditions.
7. Water sprays on plants every day can reduce disease intensity for some extent.

RUST DISEASE OF ROSE

Rose rust is a worldwide in distribution. Extensive damage of rose leaves takes place due to rust disease. Sydow and Sydow, (1903) reported the rust disease of rose from India. Cook, (1872) reported rust of rose due to *Phragmidium disciflorum* from champa ghat Himachal Pradesh, India. Mundkur and Ahemad, (1946) published a report on rust disease of rose from Simla India. Arthur and Cuminis, (1933) published a report on rusts of the north and west Himalaya in which rust of rose was due to the fungus *Phramidium kamtschatke*. Barclay, (1886) also reported *P. rosae-moschatae* on rose leaf as a rust pathogen from Simla, Missouri, India.

Symptoms

The rust causing fungus is autocious. It completes its life cycle on one host only. The uredosori and teletosori are produced on the leaves and the aecidiospores mostly found on buds, stems, leaves and petioles. The infected leaves and branches becomes hypertrophied and abnormally changed for some extent.

The uredosori develop first on the lower surface of the leaf which are small, slightly raised, yellow in colour, and these are surrounded by circle of clavate hairs. The uredospores are oval to ellipsoidal, echinulate, double walled measuring about 21-28 × 14-20 μm in size with many germ pores. The uredospores germinate and spread secondary infection. Panwar and Vyas, (1971) reported production of teletospores in the same sorus where uredospores were formed earlier. The teletospores are black, bulbous having long septate stalks. The septa in the stalks may be 6 – 8 μm. The terminal cell acts as teletospores which has pointed top region called papilla. The teletospores measure about 65-120 × 30-45mm. The teletospores germinate after a period of rest.

The aecidium may occur singly or joined together and break through the epidermis exposing the mass of bright-orange coloured sorus of aeciospores. The aeciospores are in present in the form of chains. The spores are usually 24-28 × 18-21 mm in size.

The Causal Organism

As already mentioned that there are reports from different parts of India that the rust disease is caused due to different species of *Phragmidium* disciflorum.

Disease Cycle

The infection during next season is possible through perenating mycelium which produce mycelial mat below infected leaf epidermis (fructification) remains in soil which acts as source of inoculum.

Disease management:

1. All the stems showing coenomata (mycelial made fructification) should be cut out as soon as observed.
2. All the infected leaves and cuttings should be collected and destroyed.
3. Panwar and Vyas, (1971) suggested spraying of 2% lime sulphur for the control of rust disease of rose.
4. The colloidal sulphur with soft soap also gives good control (Karlik, 2008.)

BLACK SPOT DISEASE OF ROSE

The black coloured spots on the rose leaves are very commonly seen in the home gardens and social gardens of the cities in India. In severe cases extensive defoliation makes plants like a broom. The affected plant becomes delicate and short. Such plants produce small and less number of flowers. The flower producing tendency gets reduced year after year. The black spots causing pathogen attack all the varieties of rose plants. In India it is studied in detailed by Bordoloi & Ganguly (1963) from Jammu & Kashmir, India. It is firstly observed by Patel, et. al, (1949) from Mahabaleshwar Maharashtra, India.

Symptoms

In Jammu & Kashmir the disease breaks out usually during the month of June in the form of small, brownish-black coloured spots on the upper surface of the leaf. Sometimes the spots also found on the lower surface of leaf. The spots are mostly round with a radiating fringe-like margin. The mature fully developed spots may reach up to 1cm in diameter. During severe stage of disease development most of the area of the leaves becomes black and the leaves get killed. Defoliation makes plant leaf less. The flower buds of infected plant remain closed for a long duration or rarely open. The weekend trees fail to produce flowers. There are many small spots develop on the stem and stalks of infected flower.

Black Leaf Spot of Rose

Septate Hypha

Spores

The Causal Organism

The pathogen responsible for black leaf spot disease of rose in *Diplocarpan roase* wolf. According to Dreistadt, (2004) the fungus has three types of reproductive structures which are as follow:

1. The acervuli containing conidia that occur on the leaves and young shoots.
2. The cleistocarpic stage occurs on overwintered leaves.
3. The spermogonial stage occurs on the older leaves.

All three fructifications are developed between cuticle and epidermis that appear as tiny raised specks within the blackened areas especially towards the fringe like margin of the spots. The conidia are oval to elliptical, hyaline, two celled and constricted at the septum. The cells sometimes breaking apart at the septum to function as separate spores. The conidia measure from 18-25 × 5-6 μm in size. The tiny spermogonia contain spermatia of 2 to 3 mm long and sometimes bicellular conidia in addition to spermatia.

The cleistocarps are situated deep into the tissues of the dead leaves which are globular and 100-250 mm in diameter that consists of sub-clavate asci which are intermixed with septate unbranced uniseriate paraphysis. The ascospores closely resemble the conidia. The ascospores are hyaline and bicellular. The cleistocarps open at the top and release asci and ascospores. The cleistocarps are the product of sexual reproduction.

Disease Cycle

The cleistothecia survive in the soil for longer duration. The healthy uninfected plants or branches get infected by ascospores during next season. The conidia also persist on the infected leaves of plant or on ground acts as primary inoculum. Another source of inoculum is development of conidial acervulus on the young woods late in the season that also acts as primary inoculum. Most of the conidia and ascospores are probably disseminated when the rose plants are splashed with rain or irrigated water. The insect visitors also carry spores from one plant to another. The younger leaves are more susceptible than the older leaves. The pathogen penetrates through cuticle or enters through stomata. The high humidity up to 92-97% and temperature between 20°-26.5°C is highly favorable for disease development.

The conidium germinates on leaf surface. The germ tubes form aspersoria after insertions into the epidermal cells. The hyphae produce haustoria after entry in to the host cells; soon the epidermal wall of leaf turn brown due to death of its cells and by the time turns dark black. When acervuli are about to develop on such black areas the spot become dotted with small blisters due to the formation of conidia or acervuli. The conidia or spermatia develop from thin stromata of mycelium situated between cuticle and the epidermis. The stromata of mycelium also developed in young shoots are somewhat thicker than the stromata found on leaf but the development is in the same way as in the leaf spot. The stromata of mycelium are a compact mass of fertile mycelium from which conidiophores are developed. The conidiophores produce conidia at its tip. These conidia are also similar to the conidia of leaf acervuli and they are liberated late in the season and remain in visible masses on the surface of the affected twigs which also act as important source of inoculum.

Disease management:

1. The dissemination of spores takes place by splashing rain water during irrigation of plants hence a great care should be taken during watering techniques.
2. The collection of all the infected leaves and branches and careful burning of such material can reduce the disease intensity.
3. The removal of one layer of soil (½ feet) from infected plot can reduce disease intensity for some extent.
4. Salem, *et.al*, (2008) suggested spraying of dust of sulphur plus copper on the leaves for control of black spot disease of rose.
5. Pemberton, (2007) recommended two to three applications of pyrethrum oil against the black leaf spot disease of rose with the interval of 7 to 10 days.

DISEASES REPORTED ON ROSE (*Rosa domestica* Linn.)

Sl. No.	Diseases	Pathogen
1.	Leaf Spot	*Alternaria alternata*
2.	Leaf Spot	*Cercospora panderi*
3.	Leaf Spot	*Colletotrichum capsici*
4.	Leaf spot	*Curvularia lunata*
5.	Black spot on leaf	*Diplocarpon rosae*
6.	Leaf Spot	*Pestalotia seiridioides*
7.	Stem spot	*Pestalotia suffocata*
8.	Leaf Rust	*Phragmidium butleri*
9.	Leaf Spot	*Phyllosticta rosae*
10.	White rot	*Sclerotium rolfsii*
11.	Leaf spot	*Septoria rosae*
12.	Powdery mildew	*Sphaerotheca pannosa*

30. DISEASES OF PYRETHRUM

English name : Castor

Botanical name : *Chrysanthemum indicum*

Family : Euphorbiaceae

Indian name : Arandi

Pyrethrum (*Chrysanthemum indicum Linn.*) is a small ornamental herb plant. It is a perennial plant.

Medicinal Use

The leaves having pungent efficacy in relieving toothache and in promoting a free flow of saliva. It is used in relaxing usual and partial paralysis of the tongue and lips. It forms a good snuff to cure chronic catarrh of the head and nostrils. It is a Remedy for toothache. The plant is poisonous hence without prescription of doctors does not use any type of medicine made by use of Pyrethrum.

SEPTORIA LEAF SPOT OF PYRETHRUM

The Septoria leaf spot disease of Pyrethrum (*Chrysanthemum indicum*) has a wide geographical distribution including the Asian and European continents as well as the western hemisphere. This is a common disease in the limited states since 1891 and has been reported from most of the Chrysanthemum growing areas of United States (Pavgi and Upadhyaya, 1964). The pyrethrum is one of the most important medicinal plants. It is also grown as an ornamental plant for its beautiful flowers.

Symptoms

Initially the spots appear on the leaves. The mature leaves are more susceptible in comparison to younger leaves. The leaves found close to the ground show first symptoms of Septoria. Initially the affected leaf shows very small water soaked spots which are approximately circular in outline. The spots are randomly distributed over the leaf surface. Gradually the spots increase in size forming roughly circular large blotches of the size of about 1/20 to 1/4 inches in diameters. The blotches are surrounded by dark black margin and whitish grey coloured centre. The whitish grey colour consists of fungal hyphae, spores and fruiting bodies. Hence, the fully mature Septoria spots show dark black coloured fruiting bodies. The fruiting bodies filled with numerous spores of fungus. The heavily infected leaves drop off. The heavy defoliation reduces the growth of the plant.

The spots are sometimes surrounded by a narrow yellow halo. The leaf spot vary in size and shape. Large sized blotches formed due to intermixing of many small spots covering about one third of the leaf surface. The spots increase in size and become more abundant. The affected leaves turn yellow and fell off. Many such leaves persist on the plant and many of them fall down.

The Causal Organism

There are two species of Septoria causing leaf spot disease of pyrethrum (*Chrysanthemum indicum*), *Septoria socia* Syd. and *Septoria chrysanthemi* Sacc: The pathogen becomes destructive at the temperature (68-89 F) and high humid environment. The fungus persists in soil on affected plant debris. The black fruiting bodies which are produced on severely affected regions of leaf are carried by wind or rain drops to healthy leaves. Then fruiting bodies of fungus also removed from leaf blotches due to splashing rain drops and during the process of irrigation in the cultivated fields. The fruiting bodies of fungus persist in soil on affected plant debris for up to 4 months. After that during favorable environment that germinate on the plant debris and produce spores which act as a source of infection for next healthy plants (Pethybridge *et.al*, 2004).

Disease Cycle

The pathogenic fungus survive on infected plant material in the field soil for longer duration The fungus has a broad spectrum of host range, including many types of weeds and crop plants. The temperature at 20-25 °C and 75-92%. Relative humidity is highly favorable for disease development. The pathogen overwinters on infected leaves in the form of mycelium or spores. The spores germinate in presence of moisture and infect the plant.

Disease management:

1. Pethybridge *et.al*, (2004) suggested weekly applications of fungicidal sprays such as Zineb (1/2 lb 75% WP) mixed with Captan (3/4 lb 50% wp) or Zineb alone (1 lb 75% WP) in 100 gal water. After development of disease symptoms the spray applications should be made daily.
2. The lower leaves of plants get infected first hence spray a protectant in order to ensure adequate protection.
3. Collect and destroy infected leaves by burning or by burying them carefully.
4. Avoid new plantation in the same field.
5. Keep enough space between two plants to increase air flow and to decrease humidity.

DISEASES REPORTED ON PYRETHRUM (*Chrysanthemum indicum*)

Sl. No.	Disease	Pathogen
1.	Leaf spot	*Alternaria chrysanthemi*
2.	Leaf spot	*A. tenuis*
3.	Leaf blight	*A. tenuissima*
4.	Leaf spot	*Cercospora chrysanthemi*
5.	White rot	*Sclerotium rolfsii*
6.	Root rot	*Fusarium solani*
7.	Powdery mildew	*Leveillula taurica*
8.	Leaf spot	*Phoma herbarum*
9.	Leaf spot	*Phyllosticta chrysanthemi*
10.	Soft rot	*Phytopthora cambivora*
11.	Collar rot	*Rhizoctonia solani*
12.	Leaf spot	*Septoria chrysanthemi*
13.	Wilt	*Verticillium albo-atrum*

Bibliography

1. Agrios, G.N., (2005). Plant Pathology. 5th Edition. Elsevier Academic Press, Burlington, USA Ahmad, F., Ali, M., Alam, P. 2010. New Phytoconstituents from the Stem Bark of Tinospora Cordifolia Miers. Natural Product Research. 24: 926-34.
2. Alam, M.M.; Anis M., (1987). Ethno Medicinal Uses of Plants Growing in the Bulandshahr Distract of Norter India. Journal of Ethnopharmacology p. 202.
3. Alam, M.M., (1993). Bioactivity Against Phytonematodes. In NS Randhawa and BS Parmar (eds.). Neem Research and Development. Pub. No. 3. Society of Pesticides Sciences, India, 123-143.
4. Ahmad, M.K.; Mahdi, A.A.; Shukla, K.K.; Islam, N.; Rajender, S.; Madhukar, D.; Shankhwar, S.N.; Ahmad, S., (2010). "*Withania somnifera* Improves Semen Quality by Regulating Reproductive Hormone Levels and Oxidative Stress in Seminal Plasma of Infertile Males". *Fertility and Sterility* 94 (3): 989-996.
5. Avasthi S, Gautam AK, Bhadauria R., (2011). First Report of Anthracnose Disease of Aloe Vera Caused by *Colletotrichum gloeosporioides.* J. Res. Biol 5: 408-410.
6. Avasthi, S., Gautam, A.K., Bhadauria, R., (2013). First Report of Phoma betae on *Aloe vera* in India. Arch Phytopathol. Pl. Prot. 46: 1508-1511.
7. Akinbode, O.A., (2010). Evaluation of Antifungal Efficacy of Some Plant Extracts on Curvularia lunata, the Causal Organism of Maize Leaf Spot. African J Environ. Sci. Technol. 4: 797-800.
8. Alam, M.S., (1993), Some Fungal Disease of Leaf of *Azadiracta Indica.* Abstract in "World Neem Conference." Held at Bangalore India, 55-25.

9. Anonymous, (1917). Proceedings of the Mycological Conference held at Pusa on 5th February, 1917 and Following days, Supdt. Govt. Printing, Culcutta.
10. Ajrekar, S.L., (1912) and M.N. Kamat, (1923). The Relationship of the Species of Fusarium Causing Wilt and Dry Rot of Potato in Western India. Agri. J. India, 18: 515-20.
11. Ashby, S.F., (1927). *Macrophomina phaseolina* (Maubl). Comb. Nov. Pycnidial Stage of *Rhizoctonia bataticola* (Tavb). Butl. Trans Buit. Myc. Soc, 12: 141-47.
12. Arthur, J.C. and G.B. Cummins, (1933). Rusts of the North West Himalayas. Mycologia, 25: 397-406.
13. Asthana, R.P., (1957a). Incidence of Wilt Disease (On *Linum usetatissimum*) in M.P. Nagpur Agric. Cole. Mag. 31: 16-17.
14. Ajrekar, S.L. and B.R. Tonapy, (1923). A Note on the Life History of Uromyces Aloes (cke). Magn. J. Indian Bot.Soc. 3: 267-69.
15. Anonymous, (2004). Annual Report. Dept. of Forestry, CCSHAU, Hisar, pp. 34.
16. Abou-zeid A.M., Altalhi, A.D. and Abd El-fattahk R., (2008). Fungal Control of Pathogenic Fungi Isolated from Some Wild Plants in Taif Governorate, Saudi Arabia Mal. J. Microbial. 4 (1), 30-39.
17. Abhijit Ranware, Vijendra Singh and Nandini Nimbkar, (2010). *In Vitro* Antifungal Study of the Efficacy of Some Plant Extracts for Inhibition of *Alternaria carthami* Fungus, Indian. J of Natural Products of Resources Vol. 1(3) pp. 384-386.
18. Aragaki, M. and J.Y. Uchida, (1978). A New Papaya Fruit Rot in Hawaii Caused by *Phytopthora capsici*. Plant Disease Reporter 62: 765-768.
19. Agrawal, G.P. and Sahni, V.P., (1965). Fungi Causing Plant Diseases at Jabalpur (MP) 1. Mycopath. Et. Mycol. Appl. 27: 136-143.
20. Andreeva, L.T., (1979). *Fusarium* wilt of *Ricinus communis*. Zashchita Rastenil, 7: 22.
21. Ashby S.F., (1927). Macrophomina Phaseolina (Maubl.) Comb. Nov. the Pycnidial stage of *Rhizoctonia bataticola* (Tanb) Butl. Trans. Br. Mycol. Sco. 12: 141-147.
22. Bilgrami, K.S., (1963), "Leaf Spot Diseases of Some Ornamental Plants", Proc. Natl. Acad.Sci., India, 33: 429-452.
23. Bylka. W., Czyrski, A., Witkowska-Banaszczak, E. Olejki eteryczne stosowanew lecznictwie, (2003). Herba Pol.,; 49: 369-70.
24. Bakshi, B.K., (1976). Forest Pathology; Principles and Practices. New Delhi, India. Controller of Publications, 1976.

25. Balasubramanian, P. And P. Narayanswami, (1980). A Note on a New Blight Disease of Groundnut Caused by *Phoma microspora* sp. Nov. Tamilnadu. Indian Phytopathology, 33: 133-36.

26. Balasubramanian, R. and K.S. Bhama, (1977). A New Leaf Sport Disease of *Catharanthus roseus* in India. Indian Phytopathology, 30: 556-57.

27. Bilgrami, K.S. (1963), "Leaf Spot Diseases of Some Ornamental Plants", Proc. Natl. Acad. Sci., India, 33: 429-452.

28. Bhat, S.S., Sateesh M.K. and Devaki, N.S., (1998). A New Destructive Disease of Neem (*Azadiracta indica*) Incited by *Phmopsis azadirachtae*. Current Science, 71(1): 17-19.

29. Bhattacharyya, G., Pandya, S.N., (1996). Distribution Studies on Exotic Weeds of Seurashtra (India). Advances in Plant Sciences, 9: 29-32.

30. N. Ben-Shalom, R. Ardi, R. Pinto, C. Aki, and E. Fallik, (2003)."Controlling Gray Mould Caused by Botrytis Cinerea in Cucumber Plants by Means of Chitosan," Crop Protection, Vol. 22, No. 2, pp. 285-290, 2003.

31. Brown, G.E. and Eckert, J.W., (2000). Anthracnose. In Timmer, L.W., Garnsey, S.M. and Graham, J.H. (eds.), (2011). Compendium of Citrus Diseases. APS Press, St. Paul MN. pp. 37-38.

32. Bulter, E.J. and G.R. Bisby, (1931). The Fungi of India Imp. Coun. of Agr. Res. India Sci. Mono, 1, XVIII, Culcutta.

33. Butter, E.J. and G.R. Bisby, (1931). The Fungi of India Imp. Coun. of Agr. Res. India Sci. Mono 1, XVIII Calcutta.

34. Bhatnagar, M.K., (1966c). An Oidial Stage on *Xamthium strumarium* L. Sci. & cult, 32: 422.

35. Bakshi, B.K., P.C. Pandey, R.M., A. Reddy and S. Sing, (1970). Disease Situation in India Forest and Stem Disease of Some Enotis due to Corticium Salmonicolor and Monochaetia Unicoruis. Indian for., 96: 826-26.

36. Bordoloi, D.N. and D. Ganguly, (1963). Black Spot of Roses Caused by Diplocarpon Rosae Welf. Indian Phytopathology, 16: 255-59.

37. Chauchan, M.S.D. Surayanarayana and D.P. Singh, (1973). *Myrothecium* Leaf Spot Disease of Cotton in Haryana. Viability of the Fungus and Role of Seeds in Disease Development. Sci. & Cult., 39: 215-16.

38. Cooks,W.B., (1949). Western Fungi-1. Mycologia, 41: 601-622.

39. Chattopadhyay, S.B. and P.K. Basn, (1957). Wilt of Bhindi (*Abelmochus esculentus*). Sci. &. Cult, 23: 320-21.

40. Chona B.L. and R.L. Munjal,(1951). A New Smut of Sugarcane. Curr. Sci, 20: 301-302.

41. Chona, B.L, R.L. Munjal and B.S.Bajaj, (1958). An Undescribed Specues of *Sphaerulina* on Ivy. Indian Phytopathology, 11: 172-74.

42. Chowdhury, S., (1944b). A Leaf Spot of *Carica papaya* L. Caused by a New Species of *Phyllosticta*. Indian J.Agric. Sci., 14: 395-98.

43. Chaudhary, S. (1975). Fruit Rot of *Trichosanthes dioica* L.Caused by *Pythium cueurbitacearum* Takimoto in West Bengal. Curr. Sci. 44:68.

44. Cooke, M.C., (1872). Blights on Tea and Cotton. Grev, 1: 90.

45. Chawda, S.K., (2012). Epidemiology of Turmeric (Curcuma longa L.) Leaf Spot *Colletotrichum gloesporioides* (Penz. and Sacc.). The bioscan 7(2): 441-443.

46. Cooley, K.; Szczurko, O.; Perri, D.; Mills, E.J.; Bernhardt, B.; Zhou, Q.; Seely, D., (2009). "Naturopathic Care for Anxiety: A Randomized Controlled Trial ISRCTN78958974". In Gagnier, Joel. *PLoS ONE* 4 (8): e6628.

47. Chattopadhyay, C., (2000). Seed Borne Nature of *Fusarium oxysporum* f.sp. *ricini*, and Relationship of Castor Wilt Incidence with Seed Yield. J. Mycol. Pl. Pathol., 30: 265.

48. Chauhan, L.S., Swarup, I. and Saksena, H.K., (1975). Studies of *Myrothecium* Leaf Spot of Castor. Indian J. Farm Science. 3: 111.

49. Chandra, V., (1957). Leaf Blotch Disease of Rauvolfia Serpentina Benth. Sci. And Cult., 23: 99.

50. Desai, A.G. and Dange, S.R.S., (2003). Effect of Soil Solarization Fusarium Wilt of Castor Agric. Sci. Digest, 23: 20-22.

51. Dasgupta, B. Mohanty, P.K. Dutta and Satyabrata Maiti, (2008). "Phytopthora Diseases of Betel Vine (*piper betle.*) A Menace to Betelvine Crop", SAARC Journal of Agriculture, Vol. 6, No. 1, pp. 1-19.

52. Daodu T., (2000). Aloe vera, the Miracle Healing Plant. Health Field Corporation, Lagos.

53. Dreistadt, S.H., J.K. Clark, and M.L. Flint., (2004). Pests of Landscape Trees and Shrubs. Oakland: Univ. Calif. Agric. Nat. Res. Publ. 3359.

54. Dewdney, M.M. and Timmer, L.W., (2009). Citrus Production and Diseases in Ghana. Citrus Industry 90(5): 10-13.

55. Dreistadt, S.H., (2004). Pests of Landscape Trees and Shrubs. Oakland: Univ. Calif. Agric. Nat. Res. Publ. 3359.

56. Dohroo, N.P., (2005). Diseases of Ginger. In 'Ginger, the Genus Zingiber'. (Eds. P.N. Ravindran, K. Nirmal Babu) pp. 305-340. (CRC Press: Boca Raton).

57. Desai, S.A., (1981). A Note on the Occurrence of Twig Blight and Stem Canker of *Gossypium herbacceum* L. In India Curr. Sci, 50: 282-83.

58. Everett, K.R. and Rees-George, J. , (2006). Species-specific PCR Primers for *Guignardia citricarpa* and *Guignardia mangiferae*. New Zealand Plant Protection 59: 141-145.

59. Evans, H.C., (1995). Pathogen–weed Relationships: The Practice and Problems of Host Range Screening. *Proceedings of the 8th International Symposium on Biological Control of Weeds* (eds E.S. Delfosse & R.R. Scott), pp. 539-551.

60. Evans, H.C. (1995). Pathogen–weed Relationships: The Practice and Problems of Host Range Screening. *Proceedings of the 8th International Symposium on Biological Control of Weeds* (eds E.S. Delfosse & R.R. Scott), pp. 539-551.

61. Fokkema, N.J., (1993). Opportunities and Problems of Control of Foliar Pathogens with Microorganism. Pestic Sci. 37: 411-16.

62. Flint, M.L., and J.F. Karlik. September, (2008). Pest Notes: Roses in the Garden and Landscape—Insect and Mite Pests and Beneficial. Oakland: Univ. Calif. Agric. Nat. Res. Publ. 7466.

63. Falloon, P.G., *et.al*, (1987). First Report of *Stemphylium botryosum* Causing *Stemphylium* Leaf Spot of Asparagus in Greece, Phytopathology 77: 407.

64. Garner, D.E. and C.S. Hodges, Jr., (1989). The Rust Fungi Uredinales of Hawii. Pacific Science 43: 41-55.

65. Goyal, G.P. and P.N. Patel, (1967). Host Range of *Cercospora medicaginis* from Alfalfa (*Medicago sativa*) Indian Phytopathology, 20: 378-79.

66. Grewal, J. S.M. Pal and D.D. Kulshrestha, (1974). A New Record of Wilt of Gram Caused by *Fusarium solani*. Curr. sci., 43: 767.

67. Garibaldi, A, Gullino, M.L, Minuto, G., (1997). Diseases of Basil and Their Management. Plant Dis. 1997; 81: 124-32.

68. Groenewold, M., *et.al*, (2006). Host Range of *Cercosposa apii* & *C. beticola* & Description of *C.apicola*, a Novel Species from Celery Mycologia 98: 2.

69. Gottwald, T.R. and Graham, J.H., (2000) . Bacterial Spot. In Timmer, L.W., Garnsey, S.M. and Graham, J.H. (eds.) Compendium of Citrus Diseases. APS Press, St. Paul MN. pp. 7-8.

70. Gupta, A.; Mittal, A.; Jha, K. K.; Kumar, A., (2011). "Nature's Treasurer: Plants Acting on Colon Cancer" (pdf). *Journal of Stress Physiology & Biochemistry* **7** (4): 217-231.

71. Gupta, R.B.L., G. Singh and G.C. Dalela, (1972). Occurrence of Drechslera Rostrata on Cowpea in India. Indian J. Mycol. Pl. Path., 2: 86 Gupta D.B, Padhi and P.N. Chowdhury, (1980). Two New Species of *Mycosphaesella* from India. Indian Phytopathology, 33: 500-502.

72. Gradner, D.E., and C.S. Hodges, Jr. (1989). The Rust Fungi (Uredinales of Hawaii, Pacific Science 43: 41-45.

73. Ganguly, D. and V.R. Pandotra, (1962). Some of the Commonly Occurring Disease of Important Medicinal and Aromatic Plants in in Jammu & Kashmir. Indian Phytopathology 15: 50-54.

74. Hara, H., (1966). The Flora of Eastern Himalayas. University of Tokyo, Japan.

75. Haines, H.H., (1961). The Botany of Bihar and Orissa.Vols. I-III. Bot. Survey of India, Calcutta.

76. Horst, Kenneth, Rev, By R.. Cynthia Westcott, (2001). Westcott's Plant Disease Handbook, Boston Mass; Kluwer Academic Publisher pp. 245-678.

77. Hassan, T.M., Ali, M.S., Alimuzzaman, M., Raihan, S.Z., (2006). Analgesic Activity of Mesua Ferrea Linn. Dhaka Univ. J. Pharm. Sci. 5: 73-75.

78. Hickman, G.W., and E.J. Perry, (1997). Ten Common Wood Decay Fungi on Landscape Trees—Identification Handbook. Sacramento: Western Chapter, ISA.

79. Jalalpure, S.S., Yuvaraj, D., Mandavkar, Pallavi, R., Khalure, Gulab, S., Shinde, Pournima, A., Shelar, Amol, S., Shah, (2011). Antiarthritic Activity of Various Extracts of Mesua Ferrea Linn. Seed. J. Ethnopharmacology. 138: 700-704.

80. Jamaluddin, Goswami, M.G. Ojha, B.M., (2004), Fungi of India. Scientific Publisher (India) Jodhpur.

81. Joseph Jose and Rayalakshmi, R. (2005). Medicinal and Aromatic Plants (Essential Oils and Pharmaceutical Uses). Pub. By Discovery Publishing House, New Delhi.

82. Jat, R.N., Jat, R.G., Nitharwal, M., (2013). Management of Leaf Spot of Indian Aloe (*Aloe barbadensis* Mill.) Caused by *Curvularia lunata* (Wakker) Boedijn. J. Pl. Sci. Res. 29: 89.

83. Jandhanan, K.K. Ganguly and A. Hussain, (1964). *Fusarium* will of *Rauvolfia serpentina* Curr. Sci., 33: 313.

84. Kalra, A., Singh, H.B., Pandey, R., Samad, A., Patra, N.K., Kumar, S., (2004). Diseases in Mint: Causal Organisms, Distribution and Control Measures. J Herbs Spices Med Plants; 11: 71-91.

85. Kumar, Y. *et.al.*, (2011). Plant Pathol., 60; 1040.

86. Kotzé, J.M., (2000). Black Spot. In Timmer, L.W., Garnsey, S.M. and Graham, J.H. (eds.) Compendium of Citrus Diseases. APS Press, St. Paul MN. pp. 23-25.

87. Karlik, J.F., (2008). Pest Notes: Roses in the Garden and Landscape—Cultural Practices and Weed Control. Oakland: Univ. Calif. Div. Agric. Nat. Res. Publ. 7465.

88. Karan, D., (1966). Some Diseases of Castor Bean (*Ricinus communis*) from Hyderabad. Mycopath. Mycol. Appl. 30: 187-189.

89. Keane, P.J., Kile, G.A., Podger, F.D. and Brown, B.N., (2000). Diseases and Pathogens of Eucalypts. (SIRO Publishing).

90. Khanna, K.and Chandra, S., (1977). Some New Leaf Spot Diseases –II pro C. Natl. Acad. Sci. 47 B, 251-253.

91. Kapoor, J.N. and D.K. Agrawal, (1972). Indian Species of *Ravenelia* on *Abrus* and *Albizzia*. Indian Phytopathology, 25: 551-54.

92. Kale, S.B., (1967). The Genus *Rossellinia* in India. Sydowia 21: 132-35.

93. Kumar, A. and Mall, T.P. (2013). Three New Foliacious Fungi on Sacred and Potent Ethno Medicinal Plant Indian Banyan from Shrawasti (U.P.) India. Species, 6 (15): 6-12.

94. Kirk, P.M. Cannon, P.F. Minter, D.W. Stalpers, J.A., (2008). Dictionary of the Fungi. 10th ed. Walingford CABI P.22. ISBN. 085199826-7.

95. Lawrence, D.P., Park M.S., Pryor, B.M., (2013). Nimbya and Embellisia Revisited with Nov. Comb. for *Alternaria celocaceae* and a Perpunctulata, Mycological Progress Vol.11 No. 3, 799-815.

96. Mukherjee, M., (2009). Studies on Major Diseases and Biochemical Investigations of Some Important Medicinal Plants in West Bengal with Special reference to Senna (Cassia angustifolia). Ph.D (Plant Pathology) Dissertation, BCKV, Mohanpur. pp. 6-7.

97. Mandal, K. & Geetha, K., A., (2001). Floral Infection of Downy Mildew of Isabgol. J. Mycol. Pl. Pathol. 31: 355-357.

98. Mehta, N., Sangwan, M.S. & Saharan, G.S., (2005). Fungal Diseases of Rapeseed–Mustard, pp. 15-87. In: Saharan G.S., Mehta N. & Sangwan, M.S. (eds.), Diseases of Oilseed Crops, Indus Publishing Company, New Delhi.

99. Mirjalili, M.H.; Moyano, E.; Bonfill, M.; Cusido, R.M.; Palazón, J., (2009). "Steroidal Lactones from *Withania somnifera*, an Ancient Plant for Novel Medicine".

100. Manoharachary C., I.K. Kunwar and P. Ramesh Microxyphispora, (2004). A New Sooty Mold Genus (Order Dothidiales) from India.

101. Mishra Roli., (2013). Studies on Fungal Disease of Butea Monosperma with Special Reference to Sootymold Ph.D. Thesis Rani Durgavati University, Jabalpur.

102. Mumtaz Baig anf Sumia Fatima, (2015). A Survey Report of Leaf Spot Diseases of Certain Medicinal Plants of India", Journal of Medicinal Chemistry and Drug Discovery pp. 559-563.

103. Mundkur, (1946). Revisions and Addition to Indian Fungi 1. Mycol. Pap. Imp. Mycol. Inst. 16: 1-2-7.

104. Misra, R.P., M.N. Khare, S.C. Mandloi and J.N. Chand, (1969). Studies on the Black Point of Wheat in Madhya Pardesh. Proc. 8th All India Wheat Research Workshop, Indore, pp. 434-37.

105. Mukherjee, P.K., (2003). GMP for Indian Systems of Medicines. In: GMP for Botanicals: Regulatory and Quality Issues on Phytomedicines (P.K. Mukherjee and R. Verpoorte. eds.), Business Horizons, New Delhi. pp. 99-112.

106. Mohanty, N.N. and S.N. Das, (1958). Leaf Spot of Safflower. Sci. & Cult., 24: 284-85.

107. Mohanty, N.N and S.N. Das, (1958). A Leaf Spot Disease of Safflower (*Carthamus tinctorius*). Caused by *Cercospora carthami.* Nov. SP Agric. J. India, 23: 383-89.

108. Mumtaz Baig and Sumia Fatima, (2015). A Survey Report of Leaf Spot Diseases of Certain Medicinal Plants of India", Journal of Medicinal Chemistry and Drug Discovery pp. 559-563.

109. Mc Roe (1933). India, New Diseases Reported during the year 1932. Int. Bull. Pl. Prof., 7: M79.

110. Mehrotra, B.S., (1960). Studies on Mucorales-III. *Piptocephalis debaryana* sp. Nov. proc. Natl. Acad. Sci. Indian, 30: 370-72.

111. Mathur, B.L. and R.L Mathur, (1971). A Wet Rot of *Chenopodium* by *Choanephora cucurbitarum.* Indian Phytopathology, 24: 407.

112. Nema, K.G. and R.P. Mishra,(1965). The Uredineae of Jabalpur (M.P). Mag. Agril. Coll, 6: 7-9.

113. Nene, Y.L., (1972). Viral Disease of Pulse Crops in Uttar Pradesh, Univ. Agric. & Tech. Pantogar.

114. Nagata, N.M. and M. Aragaki, (1989). Etiology and Control of Phytopthora Leaf Blight of Golden-fruited Palm. Plant Disease 73: 661-663.

115. Nutan Kumar, S. Jane, Prof. Mrs. Anupama, P. Deshmukh, Prof. Mrs. Madhavi, S. Joshi, (2014). Study of Different Diseases on Betel vine plant and control measure, International Journal of Application or Innovation in Engineering & Management (IJAIEM), Volume 3, Issue 3, Page 560.

116. Oram, R.W., (1984). Register of Australian Herbage Plant Caltivers.B. Legumes. 20. Cassia, Journal of the Australian Institute of Agricultural Science, 50, 195-196.

117. Patel, K.S., (1973). A Cercospora Leaf Spot Disease of Bajra (*Pennisetum typhoides*, stapf) in Gujarat.curr.Sci 42: 34.

118. Pegg, K.G., Stirling, G.R., (1994). Ginger. In 'Diseases of Vegetable Crops'. (Ed. Persley D) pp. 55-57. Information Series QI93024. (Queensland Department of Primary Industries, Brisbane).

119. Pati, P.K.; Sharma, M.; Salar, R.K.; Sharma, A.; Gupta, A.P.; Singh, B., (2009). "Studies on Leaf Spot Disease of *Withania somnifera* and its Impact on Secondary Metabolites". *Indian Journal of Microbiology* 48 (4): 432-437.

120. Pethybridge, S.J. Jones, R.G. Shivas, F.S. Hay, C. R. Wilson[3] and T. Groom, (2004). Tan Spot: A New Disease of Pyrethrum Caused by *Microsphaeropsis tanaceti* sp. nov. Volume 57, Issue 6, pp. 1058-1065.

121. Pati, P.K. Monika Sharma; Rajkumar, (2008). Studies on Leaf Sport Disease of Withamic Somnifera and its Impact on Secondary Metabolites, Indian J. Microbiol, 48: 432-437.

122. Pemberton, H.B., ed., (2007). Proceedings of the Fourth International Symposium on Rose Research and Cultivation. Acta Horticulturae No. 751, International Society for Horticultural Science.

123. Pandit, S.; Chang, K.W.; Jeon, J.-G., (2013). "Effects of *Withania somnifera* on the Growth and Virulence Properties of *Streptococcus mutans* and *Streptococcus sobrinus* at sub-MIC levels". *Anaerobe* 19: 1-8.

124. Pawgi, M.S. and U.P. Singh (1965a). Parasitic Fungi from North India-III. Mycopath. Et. Mycol. Appl., 23: 355-61.

125. Pawgi and Singh, (1950). List of Common Names of Indian Plant Disease, Indian J. Agric. Sci. 20: 107-142.

126. Pawgi, M.S. and U.P. Singh (1964a). Parasitic Fungi from North India-III. Mycopath. Et. Mycol. Appl., 23: 188-96.

127. Patel, M.K., M.N. Kamat and V.P. Bhide, (1949). Indian Phytopathology 2: 142-55.

128. Pandotra, V, R. And D. Ganguly (1964). Fungi on Medicinal and Aromatic Plants in the North West Himalayas-II. Mycopath. et. Mycol. Appl., 22: 106-16.

129. Papas, A.C., Elena, K., (1997). Occurrence of *Fusarium oxysporum* f. sp. *cumini* in the Island of Chios, Greece. J. Phytopathol. 145: 271-2.

130. Patel, M.K, M.N. Kamat and V.P. Bhide, (1949). Fungi of Bombay. Suppl.I. Indian Phytopathology, 2: 142-55.

131. Panwar, K.S. and N.L. Vyas, (1971). *Pleospora passeriniana* Berl. A New Ascomycetes from India, Causing Leaf Spot Disease of *Citrus aurantifolia* swingle.sci.cult, 37: 392-93.

132. Pangi, M.S and H.P. Upadhyaya, (1966), Parasitic Fungi from North India - VI. Myco. Path.et. Mycol. Appl, 30: 257-60.

133. Patel, M.K., M.N. Kamat and Y.P Bhide, (1949). Fungi of Bombay, Suppl. Indian Phytopathology 2: 142-55.

134. Prasad, S.S., (1962). Two New Leaf Spot Disease of *Nephelium litchi* Comb.Curr.Sci., 31: 293.

135. Patil, A.S., (1973). Anew Species of Trichospharia from India. Syodia, 36: 91-92.

136. Pathak, V.V., N. Prasad and D.D. Shukla, (1970). A New Physoderma from Rajasthan (Indain). Sydowia, 24: 79-80.

137. Parndekar, S.A., (1964). A Contribution of the Fungi of Maharashtra J.Univ. Poona, 26: 57-64.

138. Rajakumar, N., and Shivanna, M.B., (2010). Traditional Herbal Medicinal Knowledge in Sagar Taluk of Shimoga District, Karnataka, India. Indian J. Natural Product. Resour.1: 102-108.

139. Rajakumar, N., and Shivanna, M.B., (2009). Ethno-medicinal Application of Plants in the Eastern Region of Shimoga District. J. Ethnopharmacol. 126: 64-73.

140. Ramakrishnan, T.S. and C.K. Sowmini, (2014). "Rhizome and Root Rot of Turmeric Caused by *Pythium graminicolum* sub," Indian Phytopathology, Vol. 7, pp. 152-159, 1954.

141. Rangaswami, G., V.S. Seshadri and K.A. Lucy Channamma, (1968). A New Ercospora Leaf Spot of Cardamon. Curr. Sci., 37: 594-95.

142. Rangaswami, G., V.S. Seshadri, (1970). Fungi of South India. Univ. Agri. Sci. Banglore.

143. Ramakrishnan.T.S., (1952), Additions to Fungi of Madras-XII Proc. Indian Acad. Sci., 35b: 111-21.

144. Roy, A.J., (1974). Occurrence of *Ceratophorum heliosporum* (Sacc) Sacc. In India. Surr. Sci., 43: 59-60.

145. Rao, V.G., (1963a). Anew Alternaria blight of Celosia cristata L. Fron India. Curr. Sci., 32: 84-86.

146. Roy, A.J. (1974). Occurrence of *Ceratophorum heliiosporum* (Sacc). In India Curr.sci., 43: 378-79.

147. Rao, Y.S., (1970). Study of Plant Parasitic Nematodes Affecting Rice Production in the Vicinity of Cuttack (Orissa) India Final Technical Report (mimeo). India Council of Agricultural Research, pp. 1-115.

148. Rao, P.N. (1967). Hyperparasites on Some Ascomycetes from Hyderabad, India. Mycopath., et Mycol. Appl., 33: 161-66.

149. Rao, P.M. (1969). Foot Rot and Root Rot of Brinjal Caused by *Sclerotium rolfsii* in Vijaywadw. India Phytopatholgy, 22: 414-15.

150. Rao, P.N. (1917). Notes on South Indian Fungi. Madras Agric. Dept. Year book, 1917: 108-11.

151. Ravindran, N.; K. Nirmal Babu, K. Sivaraman, (2007). Turmeric-The Genus Curcuma, CRC Press, pp. 158-159.

152. Rojas, M.R. et.al, (1993). Plant Dis., 77; 340.

153. Rivera Angle M. Nieves, Terry A. Tattor and Ernest H. Williams Jr. (2002). Sooty Mold Plant Hopper Association on Leaves of the Black Mangrove *Avicennia germinans*(L.) Stearn in Southwestern Puerto Rico Agricultural Journal 26, 141-155.

154. Rathore, B.S. & Rathore, R.S., (1996). Downy Mildew of Isabgol in Rajasthan. PKV Res. J. 20: 107.

155. Saroj, A.; Kumar, A.; Qamar, N.; Alam, M.; Singh, H.N.; Khaliq, A., (2012). "First Report of Wet Rot of *Withania somnifera* Caused by Choanephora Cucurbitarum in India". *Plant Disease* 96 (2): 293.

156. Sahni, V.P. (1964). Some Foliacious Ectoparasites and Associated Fungi from Jabalpur, M.P. -1 Mycopath. Et. myco. Appl., 23: 328-38.

157. Shastri, K.S.M., (1969). Investigation and Control of some Important Disease of Medical Plants. Indian Physiopathology, 22: 140-42.

158. Sahni, V.P. (1952). Ustilaginales of India. Common Wealth Mycological Institute, New, Survey, England.

159. Sundaram, N.V., (1961). Notes on Some Fungi from South India. Indian Phytopathology, 14: 202-209.

160. Sathiyanarayanan Anusuya and Muthukrishnan Sathiyabama, (2014). Effect of Chitosan on Rhizome Rot Disease of Turmeric Caused by *Pythium aphanidermatum,* Biotechnology, Article ID 305349, 5 pages.

161. Sathyabrata Maiti and K.S. Shivashankara, (1998). "Betel Vine Research Highlights", J.F. Dastur, "Diseases of pan (piper betle) in the General Provinces".

162. Salem, N., D. Golino, B. Falk, and A. Rowhani, (2008). Identification and Partial Characterization of a New Lute Virus Associated with Rose Spring Dwarf Disease. Plant Disease 92: 508-512.

163. Scartezzini, P.; Speroni, E., (2000)."Review on Some Plants of Indian Traditional Medicine with Antioxidant Activity". *Journal of Ethnopharmacology* 71 (1-2): 23-43.

164. Seetha Lakshmi and K.C. Naidu, (2010). "Comparative Morphoanatomy of *Piper betel* L. Cultivars in India", Annals of Biological Research, Vol. 1, No. 2, pp. 128-134.

165. Sharma, A.;V. Singh, G. Singh and P.K. Pati, (2013). First Report of Leaf Spot Disease in Withania Coagulons Coaglans Caused by *Alternaria alternata* in India Plant Disease, Vol. 97 No. 3 p. 420.

166. Shankran, K.V., Florence, E.J.M. and Sharma, J.K., (1988). Foliar Diseases of Some Forest Trees in Kerala New Records. Indian J. Forestry 11 (2); 104.

167. Shubhi Avasthi, Ajay Kumar Gautam; Rekha Bhadauria, (2015). Occurrence of Leaf Spot Diseases on Aloe vera (L.) Burm.f. Caused by Curvularia Species from Madhya Pradesh, India BIO DIVERSIT, Vol. 16 (1) Pages: 79-83.

168. Sharma, A.; Pati, P.K., (2011). "First Report of *Withania somnifera* (L.) Dunal, as a New Host of Cowbug (*Oxyrachis tarandus*, Fab.) In Plains of Punjab, Northern India" (pdf). *World Applied Sciences Journal* 14 (9): 1344-1346. ISSN 1818-4952.

169. Sharma, N., Koul A.K. & Kaul, V., (1999). Pattern of Resource Allocation of Six Plantago Species with Different Breeding Systems. J. Plant Res. 112: 1-5.

170. Shivanna, M.B., and Rajakumar, N. (2010). Ethno-medico-botanical Knowledge of Rural Folk in Bhadravathi Taluk of Shimoga District, Karnataka. Indian J. Traditional Knowl. 9: 158-162.

171. Scot Nelson, (2005), Rust of Koolog Ula (*Abutilon menziesii*), Plant Disease PD-31.

172. Srivastava, K. (1973b). A New Leaf Diseases of *Ocimum basilicum* var *purpurescens*. Indian J. Mycol. Plant Pathol., 3: 198.

173. Sinclair, W.A., H.H. Lyon, and W.T. Johnson. 1987. Diseases of Trees and Shrubs. Cornell University Press, Ithaca, NY. 574 pp.

174. Sumia Fatima and Meenakshi Mahajan, (2014). Families of Angiosperms Vol. I, LAP Pub. Germany.

175. Stirling, A.M., (2004). The Causes of Poor Establishment of Ginger in Queensland, Australia. Australasian Plant Pathology 33, 203-210.

176. Stirling, G.R., (2008). The Impact of Farming Systems on Soil Biology and Soil Borne Diseases: Examples from the Australian Sugar and Vegetable Industries — the Case for Better Integration of Sugarcane and Vegetable Production and Implications for Future Research. Australasian Plant Pathology 37, 1-18.

177. Stone, A.G., Scheuerell, S.J., Darby, H.M., (2004). Suppression of Soil Borne Diseases in Field Agricultural Systems: Organic Matter Management, Cover Cropping, and Other Cultural Practices. In 'Soil Organic Matter in Sustainable Agriculture'. (Eds Magdoff F, Weil RR) pp. 131-178.

178. Sydow, (1912). Fungi Indiae Orientalis. Pars V.Ann. Mycol, 14.177-220.

179. Subramaniam, K.S., (1964). Studies on Sclerotial Root Rot Disease of Groundnut (*Arachis hypogea*) Caused by *Sclerotium rolfsii.* Sacc. Madras Agri J. 51: 367-68.

180. Srivastava, B.N., K.M. Srivastava and B.P. Singh, (1978.) Mosaic Disease of *Clitoria ternatia* – A New Record from India. Indian Phytopathology, 31: 248-51.

181. Shani, M.L., (1968). Deuteromycetes from Jabalpur-III Mycopath. et. Mycol. Appl, 36: 267-88.

182. Sen, B. and M. Majumdar, (1970). Fusarium Root Rot of Pea. Indian Phytopathology, 23: 727-28.

183. Shreemali J.L., (1973c). Sphaerosidean Fungi Obtainded from Indain Phylloclades, Cladodes and Phylodes. Indian Phytopathology 26: 56-62.

184. Srivastava, M.P, S. Chandra and R.N. Tandon, (1964). Post Harvest Disease of Some Fruits and Vegetables. proc. Natl. Acad. Sci, 34B: 339-42.

185. Srivastava, M.P. and R.N. Tandon, (1968). Some Storage Disease of Fruits. Curr. Sci, 37: 292.

186. Thirumalachar, M.J. and J.N. Mishra, (1953a). Contribution to the Study of Fungi of Bihar, India. Sydowia, 7: 79-83.

187. Tewari, I. (1968). on the Morphology and Taxonomy of *Elsinoe kamatii* spec.nov.on *Sygigium cuminii* from India. Nova Hedwigia, 15: 213-19.

188. Thirumalachar, M.J., (1950f). Some New or Interesting Fungi-I Sydowia, 4: 63-65.

189. Tilak, S.T. And R. Rao, (1966a). Contribution to Our Knowledge of Ascomycetes of Indian v Mmycopath et Mycol. Appl., 28: 369-72.

190. Thirumalachar, M.J. and C. Chupp, (1948). Notes on Some Cercospora of India. Mycologia, 40: 352-62.

191. Trujillo, E.E., Kadooka, C., Tanimoto, V., Bergfeld, S., Shishido, G. and Kawakami, G. (2001). Effective Biomass Reduction of the Invasive Weed Species Banana Poka by *Septoria* Leaf Spot. *Plant Disease* 85 (4), 357-361.

192. Trautwein, E.A., Carls, C.R., Erbersdobler, H.F. & Hisserich, D., (2000). Development of Types of Psyllium–enriched Bread as Part of a Cholesterol Lowering Diet. Deutsche Lebensmittel– Rundschau 96: 58-64.

193. Trujillo, E.E., Kadooka, C., Tanimoto, V., Bergfeld, S., Shishido, G. and Kawakami, G., (2001). Effective Biomass Reduction of the Invasive Weed Species Banana Poka by *Septoria* Leaf Spot. *Plant Disease* 85 (4), 357-361.

194. Tzanetakis, F.E. *et.al.*, (2010), Plant Disease, 94: 4.

195. Uppal, B.N.M.N. Kamat, M.K. Patel, (1936). A New Variety of *Oidiopsis taurica.* Indian J.Agric. Sci, 6: 110-15.

196. Uppal, B.N, M.N. Kamat, (1937). The Systematic Position of *Oidiopsis taurica* (Lev.) Salmon. Curr.Sci, 6: 103.

197. Uppal, B.N., M. N. Kamat and M. K. Patel, (1936). A new variety of *Oidiopsis caurica.* India J.Agric.Sci.6: 110-15.

198. Uchida, J.Y., (1989). Foliar Blight of *Spathiphyllum* Caused by *Phytopthora.* HITAHR Brief No. 84. CTAHR Publication, University of Hawaii. 3 pp.

199. Uppal, B.N, M.K. Patel and M.N. Kamat,(1935). The Fungi of Bombay. VIII. (Private Publication pp. 1-56.)

200. Uday Kumar, R. and Usha, R.S., (2010). Epidemiology and Nutritional Factors on Growth of *Colletotrichum gloesporioides* (Penz.) Penz. and Sacc. Ann. Pl. Protection. Sci. 18(1): 159-163.

201. Umbala, K. nad P. Ramarao, (1972). Leaf Blight of Colocasia Caused by *Phytopthora palmivora.* Indian J.Mycol. Plant. Pathol. 2: 187-88.

202. Van der Plaats-Niterink, A.J., (1981). Monograph of the Genus Pythium. Studies in Mycology 21, 1-242.

203. Verma RK, Sharma Nidhi Soni KK and Jamaluddin, (2008). Forest Fungi of Central India. Lucknow: Int. Distributing Co.

204. Vyas, K.M., S.C, Chaurasia and N. Saxena, (1978). A New Fruit not Disease of Brinjal Caused by *Rhizopus nodosus* Indian Phytopathology, 31: 363.

205. Vijayakumar, J. & S. Arumugam, (2012). "Early Detection of Powdery Mildew Disease for Betel Vine Plants Using Digital Image Analysis" International Journal of Modern Engineering Research Vol. 2, Issue. 4, pp. 2581-2583.

206. Ven Murthy, M.R.; Ranjekar, P.K.; Ramassamy, C.; Deshpande, M., (2010). "Scientific Basis for the Use of Indian Aayurvedic Medicinal Plants in the Treatment of Neurodegenerative Disorders: Ashwagandha". *Central Nervous System Agents in Medicinal Chemistry* 10 (3): 238-246.

207. Walker, H.L. and Boyette, C.D., (1985). Biocontrol of Sickle Pod (*Cassia obtusifolia*) in Soybean (*Glycine max*) with *Alternaria cassiae.* Weed Science, 33, 212-215.

208. Wehmeyer. L.E., (1963). Some Himalayan Ascomycetes of the Punjab and Kashmir Mycologia, 55: 309-36.

209. Yadav, R.K. (2013). Effect of Fungicides on the Leaf Rot of Pan Caused by var. *Phytopthora parasitica piperina* Indian J.L. Sci.3 (1): 37-39.

210. Yadav, (1963b). Additions to the Micro fungi of Bihar-I. Erysiplaceae. Indian Phytopathology, 16: 164-66.

211. Yoshimura, M.A., J.Y. Uchida, and M. Aragaki, (1985). Etiology and Control of Poinsettia Blight Caused by *Phytopthora nicotianae* var. *parasitica* and *P. drechsleri.* Plant Disease 69: 511-513.

212. Zimowska, B., (2004b). Biotic Effect of Phyllospheric Fungi on the Growth and Development of *Seimatosporium hypericinum* (Ces.) Sutton. Electron. J. Pol. Agricult. Unive., Horticult; 7(2).

Index

❑ ❑ ❑ ❑ ❑ ❑